HODGES UNIVERSITY
LIBRARY - NAPLES

P9-DGV-320

Pluralizing Plagiarism

HODGES UNIVERSITY
LIBRARY - NAPLES

Pluralizing Plagiarism

IDENTITIES, CONTEXTS, PEDAGOGIES

Edited by
Rebecca Moore Howard
and
Amy E. Robillard

Boynton/Cook Publishers
HEINEMANN
Portsmouth, NH

Boynton/Cook Publishers, Inc.
361 Hanover Street
Portsmouth, NH 03801–3912
www.boyntoncook.com

Offices and agents throughout the world

© 2008 by Boynton/Cook Publishers

All rights reserved. No part of this book may be reproduced in any form or by any electronic or mechanical means, including information storage and retrieval systems, without permission in writing from the publisher, except by a reviewer, who may quote brief passages in a review.

The editors and publisher wish to thank those who have generously given permission to reprint borrowed material:

Portions of Chapter 9, "We Never Wanted to Be Cops," by Chris Anson originally appeared as "Student Plagiarism: Are Teachers Part of the Problem or Part of the Solution?" by Chris Anson. From *Essays on Teaching Excellence* (2003–2004). Reprinted with permission of The Professional and Organizational Development Network in Higher Education.

Library of Congress Cataloging-in-Publication Data
Pluralizing plagiarism : identities, contexts, pedagogies / edited by Rebecca Moore Howard and Amy E. Robillard.
     p. cm.
  Includes bibliographical references.
  ISBN-13: 978-0-86709-595-1
  ISBN-10: 0-86709-595-4
  1. Plagiarism.   I. Howard, Rebecca Moore.   II. Robillard, Amy E.

PN167.P58 2008
808—dc22   2008008224

Editor: Charles I. Schuster
Production management: Karina Felizardo, SPi
Production coordinator: Vicki Kasabian
Cover design: Night and Day Design
Typesetter: SPi
Manufacturing: Louise Richardson

Printed in the United States of America on acid-free paper
13 12 11 10 09 VP 2 3 4 5 6

For our friend Candace Spigelman,
whose work in authorship and
whose belief in students and teaching
will continue to inspire us.

Contents

Pluralizing Plagiarism

Introduction

Plagiarisms

Amy E. Robillard *and* Rebecca Moore Howard

Plagiarism is a problem. The blogger Olvlzl (2007) expresses a widely shared sentiment: "The great crisis facing this foundation of democracy, itself, is that someone has been at the cooky jar, someone's been stealing their snickerdoodles. The great flood of plagiarism is the real danger that faces the nation, with front page stories and network news segments presenting in indepth report on the rolling crime wave." The BBC suggests that we might be facing an "epidemic" of student plagiarism (Epidemic 2004). Concern about plagiarism is so acute that the job of Roderick McDavis, the president of Ohio University, is reported to be in jeopardy (Students 2007), in part because a plagiarism scandal in the university's graduate engineering program occurred on his watch (Phillips 2006). The *Los Angeles Times* announces that instructors are reluctant to assign research papers "because the Internet offers a searchable online smorgasbord of ready-made papers" (Jones 2006). On the listserv WPA-L, William Fitzgerald (2007) reports that some of his Rutgers students are reluctant to post their papers in a place where other students might find and appropriate them. A high school in Virginia adopts the plagiarism-detecting service Turnitin.com, and some of the students file suit (Robelen 2007). Nor is the problem confined to the United States; Schmidt (2004) confirms the decline of the research paper, and *The Scotsman* reports that instructors are so overwhelmed by the task of dealing with plagiarism that they are ignoring it (Schofield 2006). Eighty percent of colleges in the United Kingdom subscribe to Turnitin.com, the plagiarism-detecting program (Conference 2006). And the call for proposals for an Amsterdam conference calls plagiarism detection an "exciting and future-oriented topic" (2nd call 2007).

People are proposing solutions to the problem. Like many other colleges, Newman University offers an online plagiarism tutorial for its students (Web-Based, n.d.). Susan McLeod (1992, 11–13) emphasizes the teaching of documentation conventions. Ann Lathrop and Kathleen Foss (2005, 164) assert the need for teachers to work with their students throughout the writing process. Rebecca Moore Howard (1993, 240–43) describes summary writing as a means of fostering critical reading practices that are essential to successful writing from sources. James Brown (2001, 169) recommends teaching source use as a "critical skill" while emphasizing the role of audience in determining what needs to be cited. The Council of Writing Program Administrators (2003) urges the design of "contexts and assignments for learning that encourage students not simply to recycle information but to investigate and analyze its sources." Alice Drum (1986, 242) advocates "a holistic approach, a recognition that plagiarism involves a student, an instructor, and the structure within which the two interact." Edward M. White (1999, 209) focuses on the need for faculty development. Donald McCabe urges institutions to foster a climate of integrity (Hansen 2007). Dierdre Mahoney (2002, 225) advocates putting a plagiarism policy in course syllabi. Richard Posner (2007, 82–83) believes in plagiarism-detecting services. Tucker Carlson (2002) endorses zero-tolerance punishments, and Gillian Silverman (2002, 12) models the instructor's eternal, unrelenting vigilance.

Yet even though the problem of plagiarism is so frequently and energetically described and decried, and even though the solutions offered are enthusiastically promoted, plagiarism continues. Even when we institute what seem to be sensible, accessible plagiarism policies; even when we institute honor codes; even when we purchase and use plagiarism-detecting software; and even when we develop plagiarism-proof assignments—the problem persists.

In one respect, we must recognize that plagiarism—excessive collaboration with other, unacknowledged texts—has long been with us (Constable 1983; Simmons 1999) and will long continue to be (Hutcheon 1986; Meltzer 1994; Stewart 1991). There is no "solution to" or "prevention of" plagiarism; there are only good measures to be taken. We must also recognize that although part of what is now characterized as an "epidemic" of plagiarism is indeed significantly attributable to writers' easy access to copious text (Atkins and Nelson 2001), it is also significantly attributable to *readers'* easy access to copious text. Like nothing ever seen before, readers and writers today have equal access to the same texts. Thus readers can detect and recognize writers' appropriations from sources like never before.

What this book argues, though, is yet another aspect of the plagiarism phenomenon: To date, the academy's depictions of the problem, and the solutions offered, are universalized. They assume that one definition and one set of solutions apply in all circumstances.

This is an astonishing fact, given how much we know about the circumstantial specificity of writing. At one time, writing instruction was based on the notion of transcendental "good writing." Composition classes conveyed the characteristics of this good writing to students, who were then expected to produce those characteristics in their writing. The days of the "ideal text" are, we hope, long gone, but the product approach to the teaching of writing seems to persist in universalized approaches and responses to plagiarism. In this universalization, plagiarism is a feature of the text that can be detected by machines; a conception of writing as social activity is denied in favor of simplistic definitions and simplistic responses.

And plagiarism is indeed a form of writing. It may be an outlawed form of writing, but writing it nevertheless is. To acknowledge this is to begin to come to terms with the extent to which composition scholars have willingly contributed to a universalized conception of plagiarism.

This book argues that plagiarism must be pluralized if we are to ethically and productively apply our nuanced knowledges about writing to this form of authorship. We know, for instance, that one size does not fit all when it comes to writing pedagogy; we know that writing instructors must take into account the spatial, temporal, and cultural contexts in which they teach as well as the populations of students in their classrooms. The same must be done in our approaches and responses to plagiarism.

In the search for solutions, scholarly publications have neglected the specificity of and variations among the many sites at which plagiarism occurs—sites such as four-year-college writing programs, community colleges, secondary schools, international classrooms, multicultural classrooms, writing-across-the-curriculum programs, writing centers, libraries, distance education, graduate education, and popular media. Instead, most scholarly publications on plagiarism mirror mass media's attempts to adduce universalized representations, definitions, preventative measures, policies, and punishments.

While the contributors to *Pluralizing Plagiarism: Identities, Contexts, Pedagogies* share in the culturewide concern about plagiarism, they recognize that it is not a unitary phenomenon that can be successfully addressed from a single perspective. Rather, plagiarism is a complex, unstable issue that must be considered from a variety of viewpoints and at a variety of sites. Clarity and stability cannot be brought to the textual field labeled "plagiarism," but teachers and the culture at large can come to understand what is at stake in plagiarism and how best to approach the topic *with* students rather than *for* or *about* students. Such work can lead to coalitions of writers and educators who can implement curricula that take students' textual work seriously and that encourage students to take writing, texts, and learning seriously.

The authors of these chapters demonstrate that our safe definitions and methods of prevention and detection do not always travel well. In "Man Bites Dog: The Public, the Press, and Plagiarism," Michele Eodice demonstrates the astonishing yet unsurprising extent to which the media shape the public's attitudes toward plagiarism. Implicating academics for their passive collusion with the media's messages, Eodice challenges writing teachers to take on the increasingly challenging task of communicating their expertise in public forums. Drawing on her own attempt to do this work, Eodice reminds us just how difficult it is to communicate nuanced views to an audience accustomed to digesting news in sound bites. Simplistic definitions of plagiarism as theft make such sound bites compelling, and it is in part for this reason that Amy E. Robillard suggests in her chapter that we work with students to categorize plagiarism as a form of authorship rather than as a type of crime. In "Situating Plagiarism as a Form of Authorship: The Politics of Writing in a First-Year Writing Course," Robillard suggests that one way teachers can avoid positioning themselves as plagiarism police is to engage students in a wider investigation into the politics of writing. Plagiarism positioned in relation to other forms of authorship, including book reviewing, political polemic, and literary forgery, becomes more than simply the lazy or criminal student's way out. Instead, plagiarism becomes but one of a number of textual practices that elicit media attention from cultural critics ever concerned with the consequences of mass literacy.

In "Time Is Not on Our Side: Plagiarism and Workload in the Community College," Kami Day outlines the ways in which community college teachers' workloads often place heavy limits on the amount of time they can devote to keeping current on plagiarism scholarship. Drawing on Basil Bernstein's distinction between the pedagogical relay (scholarship of the field) and the relayed (the ways that that scholarship is taken up pedagogically), Day demonstrates that community college teachers often focus on the relayed without enough knowledge of the relay. Citing community college teachers' tremendous influence on textbook publishers, Day encourages community college teachers to insist on more complex representations of plagiarism in some of the most popular writing textbooks.

For many years, composition scholars have adhered to a distinction between the collaborative writing of classroom-based peer groups and the collaborative learning that takes place in the writing center. In "Where There's Smoke, Is There Fire?" Tracy Hamler Carrick revisits and revises that distinction, asserting the value of tutor–tutee collaborative writing. Supervisors of peer tutors, Carrick says, must adopt a flexible approach to these concerns, helping tutors negotiate the tension between coauthoring and collaborative learning, rather than simply endorsing one and outlawing the other. In addition, Carrick calls not just for training peer tutors but also for respecting their situated decision making. Revisionism is at work in Sandra Jamieson's chapter as well, as she explains the ways in which historical developments in writing across the curriculum have led educators to overgeneralize about plagiarism. Jamieson's research into discipline-specific practices reveals that although instructors across the curriculum may endorse universal definitions of and policies for plagiarism, those universalisms may actually contradict the textual conventions and practices that are sanctioned in the disciplines.

Because "correct" textual practices are widely regarded as a basic writing "skill," instructors are especially indignant when graduate student writers transgress. Rebecca Moore Howard regards writing from sources as a matter of lifelong development; it should be explicitly taught even on the graduate level. Howard raises, too, another aspect of plagiarism with regard to graduate students: the practice of faculty mentors' appropriations of graduate students' intellectual work. An academy that takes plagiarism seriously will respect the intellectual property of graduate student writers.

Kathleen Blake Yancey brings these issues to the conceptual space of research practices in composition and rhetoric. She describes research as conversational practice, asking how our practices for acknowledging intertextuality might impede or assist the researcher. How can researchers find something that they can claim as "their" space and "their" contribution to the conversation? How can they come to understand sources as having been written by authors-in progress rather than static author-functions who can too easily become icons or straw[wo]men? How might researchers adopt a multicontextual approach rather than one dedicated to finding and filling in gaps? Yancey's conclusions are valuable not only for researchers but also for those who review research: she sketches an ethics of reviewing whose implementation would palpably advance the field of Composition Studies.

Challenging the widely held assumption that religiously affiliated colleges and universities need rely only on defining plagiarism as immoral to prevent plagiarism, T. Kenny Fountain and Lauren Fitzgerald suggest instead that these institutions' emphasis on the importance of community might be more effective in preventing plagiarism. Their chapter, "'Thou Shalt Not Plagiarize'?: Appealing to Textual Authority and Community at Religiously Affiliated and Secular Colleges," describes a pedagogy for a first-year course that draws on notions of textual authority and belonging. Fountain and Fitzgerald advocate interrogating students' socially situated conceptions of community and textual authority in an effort to help students understand that writing and citation are communitarian acts rather than individual ones.

Celia Thompson and Alastair Pennycook explore the concept of intertextuality and its relationship to the politics of knowledge and writer identity in the context of transcultural classrooms. Drawing on data collected from college students studying in Australia, they consider how multiple strands of knowledge combine to produce desired meanings across texts and readers. They highlight the value of reflexivity as a means of exploring the intertextual nature of writing as an ongoing complex process through which students create and assert different writer identities. Theories of identity that take account of socio-historically constructed sets of power relations can enable educators to gain insights into the kinds of conflicts and cultural differences that international students experience as they struggle to become authors of the academic texts that they produce. Thompson and Pennycook argue that the more instructors understand how students in general and international students in particular describe and contest their own learning experiences, especially when this may involve resistance to institutionally validated expectations and conventions, the better equipped they are to navigate through the transcultural contact zone together with their students.

The meaning of any textual event, including one potentially classified as plagiarism, is determined not by foundational categories and decontextualized procedures but by the people involved in the event, the ways in which they construct their writerly identities, and the ways in which their writerly identities are constructed by their social situation. That social situation, the context in which the textual event occurs, exerts its own defining force on the event. This does not lead us to discard institutional plagiarism policies; far from it. Institutional plagiarism policies define the textual objectives of all writers in the college, and they provide the tools with which instructors and

students navigate a textual event, determining its acceptability and consequences. Chris Anson concludes this volume, though, with a call for reflection and reflexivity on the part of those who write and implement plagiarism
policies. As the first ten essays in *Pluralizing Plagiarism* demonstrate, we
cannot assume a moral frame for every act of transgressive intertextuality.
Instead, as we work with institutional policies to interpret a potentially transgressive text, we can best understand that text when we factor in the identities
of its writers and readers and when we pay close attention to the context in
which the text was produced and circulated. *Then* we may be well positioned
to respond appropriately and productively. And *then* we can construct responsible pedagogy that engages student writers in appropriate and responsible
uses of source texts.

References

Atkins, Thomas, and Gene Nelson. 2001. "Plagiarism and the Internet: Turning the
    Tables." *English Journal* 90: 101–104.

Brown, James. 2001. "Plagiarism and Student Acculturation: Strangers in the Strange
    Lands of Our Disciplines." In *Voices from the Classroom*, 166–70. Aurora,
    Ontario: Garamond.

Carlson, Tucker. 2002. "That's Outrageous: Reading, Cheating, and 'Rrithmetic."
    Reader's Digest (July): 39–42.

"Conference to Tackle University Plagiarism Problem." 2006. *The Guardian*, October 17.
    http://education.guardian.co.uk/higher/news/story/0,,1924352,00.html.

Constable, Giles. 1983. "Forgery and Plagiarism in the Middle Ages." *Archiv fur
    Diplomatik, Schriftgeschichte, Siegel-und Wappenkunde* 29: 1–41.

Council of Writing Program Administrators. 2003. "Defining and Avoiding Plagiarism:
    WPA Statement on Best Policies." http://wpacouncil.org/node/9.

Drum, Alice. 1986. "Responding to Plagiarism." *College Composition and Communication*
    37: 241–43.

"Epidemic of Student Cheating?" 2004. *BBC*, June 30. http://news.bbc.co.uk/2/hi/
    uk_news/education/3854465.stm.

Fitzgerald, William. 2007. "Students Fearing Plagiarism if They Post Papers to
    an Online Course System." WPA-L, May 5. http://lists.asu.edu/archives/
    wpa-l.html.

Hansen, Liane. 2007. "The Honest Truth About Cheating. Interview with Donald
    McCabe." *NPR*, May 6. www.npr.org/templates/story/story.php?storyId=10033373.

Howard, Rebecca Moore. 1993. "A Plagiarism *Pentimento*." *Journal of Teaching
    Writing* 11: 233–46.

Hutcheon, Linda. 1986. "Literary Borrowing . . . and Stealing: Plagiarism, Sources,
    Influences, and Intertexts." *English Studies in Canada* 12: 229–39.

Jones, Terrill Yue. 2006. "If This Were a Term Paper, You Might Have Seen It on the
    Web." *Los Angeles Times*, June 17. www.latimes.com.

Lathrop, Ann, and Kathleen Foss, eds. 2005. *Guiding Students from Cheating and Plagiarism to Honesty and Integrity: Strategies for Change*. Westport, CT: Libraries Unlimited.

Mahoney, Deirdre. 2002. "Strategies for Discouraging Plagiarism." In *Strategies for Teaching First-Year Composition*, 224–25. Urbana, IL: National Council of Teachers of English.

McLeod, Susan H. 1992. "Responding to Plagiarism: The Role of the WPA." *WPA: Writing Program Administration* 15: 7–16.

Meltzer, Françoise. 1994. *Hot Property: The Stakes and Claims of Literary Originality*. Chicago: University of Chicago Press.

Olvlzl. 2007. "Feet of Clay Words of Steel." Weblog entry. *Echidne of the Snakes*, May 12. http://echidneofthesnakes.blogspot.com.

Phillips, Jim. 2006. "OU Sends Warning Letters About Plagiarism to Former Students." *The Athens News* (July 17).

Posner, Richard A. 2007. *The Little Book of Plagiarism*. New York: Pantheon.

Robelen, Eric. 2007. "Online Anti-Plagiarism Service Sets off Court Fight." *Education Week* 4 May. www.edweek.org/ew/index.html.

Schmidt, Sarah. 2004. "Term Papers Axed to Obliterate Plagiarism." *Canada.com,* March 31. www.canada.com.

Schofield, Kevin. 2006. "Tackling Plagiarism 'Too Much Work' for Lecturers." *Scotsman.com*, June 22. http://news.scotsman.com/education.cfm?id=911552006.

2nd call for papers: SIGIR'07 workshop PAN. Discussion group entry. 2007. *comp.ai,* May 12. http://groups.google.com/group/comp.ai/browse_thread/thread/96edeea 4cc79fa7c/bfa92d2f9e0319b6#bfa92d2f9e0319b6.

Silverman, Gillian. 2002. " 'It's a Bird, It's a Plane, It's Plagiarism Buster!' " *Newsweek* (July 15).

Simmons, Sue Carter. 1999. "Competing Notions of Authorship: A Historical Look at Students and Textbooks on Plagiarism and Cheating." In *Perspectives on Plagiarism and Intellectual Property in a Postmodern World*, 41–54. Albany: State University of New York Press.

Stewart, Susan. 1991. *Crimes of Writing: Problems in the Containment of Representation*. New York: Oxford University Press.

"Students, Faculty Are Divided Over Future of OU President." 2007. *Vindy.com,* May 13. www.vindy.com/content/national_world/340230591965792.php.

Web-Based Plagiarism Awareness Tutorial. n.d. Newman University. www.newmanu. edu/sss/writingcenter/Plagiarism/Plagiarism.html.

White, Edward M. 1999. "Student Plagiarism as an Institutional and Social Issue." In *Perspectives on Plagiarism and Intellectual Property in a Postmodern World*, 205–10. Albany: State University of New York Press.

1

Man Bites Dog

The Public, the Press, and Plagiarism

Michele Eodice
University of Oklahoma

What is being reported blandly on the front pages would elicit
ridicule and horror in a society with a genuinely free and
democratic intellectual culture.

—Noam Chomsky

While there is today a perception of increasing plagiarism—the blame laid at
the feet of impetuous technological gains of the late twentieth century, with
the unstable author its accomplice—this perception is the result of a chain of
backroom influences rather than a reflection of the empirical reality. A late-
capitalist market-driven economy counts on a corporatized media that counts
on a largely anti-intellectual consumer-oriented public to alternately distrust
and rely on the academy. Many of us in the academy, in turn, remain increasingly conflicted on the issue of plagiarism and foist the pedagogical responsibility off to other instructional realms, such as writing centers, or outsource to
plagiarism detection services, and fail to "upgrade" our understandings of how
our future students' multiple literacies will blow our traditional expectations
for student writing to bits and bytes. This chapter will examine the media's
desire to ferret out and punish[1] plagiarists, critiquing what Chomsky called
"media control" over public attitudes, and highlight the academy's role both in
reinforcing current views on plagiarism and in interrogating such views.

Shifting notions of such cultural concepts as *the public sphere, information, freemarkets*, and *literacy* have opened gaps for the mass media[2] to fill,
enabling the media to mold dispositions on issues such as intellectual property,
copyright, and especially plagiarism. Dozens of articles appearing regularly in

the press seem to satisfy a manufactured hunger for public humiliation—or printed pillory—of individuals who have transgressed a traditional and romanticized version of the author, even though, according to Judge Richard Posner, "There is no legal wrong named 'plagiarism'" (2007, 34).

A cursory look at recent articles in the popular press reveals a consistent rhetorical theme: Stories typically include hyperbolic headlines that characterize plagiarism as a "mortal sin," "heinous crime," "terrible transgression," and "enormous stigma" in an attempt to inscribe through (bad) writing itself a punishment for ("bad") writing. Deborah Tannen describes this type of journalism as less about productively challenging ideologies and more about "a show of aggression valued for its own sake," with reporters ignoring substantive public policy issues as the target of attention and aiming instead at "the vaguer notion of character in the form of personal foibles and inconsistencies" (1999, 58). Today more than half of what we read in the newspaper or view on TV includes something related to "deviance and control" (Ericson, Baranek, and Chan 1991, 24), so it should come as no surprise that the media have added the exposure of plagiarists to their repertoire of tantalizing subjects. Because of the ubiquitous influence the media have on shaping attitudes and the strong desire to punish both professional and novice writers who are accused of plagiarism, we can begin to consider the fourth estate[3] itself as a new "institution of punishment," one that can "provide us with ready-made answers" on "how much punishment is appropriate and what emotions can be expressed . . . [and] in consequence, these difficult and troublesome questions no longer arise" (Garland 1990, 3). In this way, the media work less to *mediate* than to regulate and maintain solidarity-producing effects for social stability, effectively closing off possibilities for conversation. If it is true, even as Tocqueville noted well over a century ago, that we Americans traded the *conversation* model of public discourse (one that ideally promotes associations) for the *commercial* (one that directs information), it is no wonder that in our current market-driven economy[4] we would see textual transgressions as an affront to *the community good*. Contemporary concepts of community good have been "framed" (Lakoff 2004) in ways that reject conversation—on such issues as gay marriage amendment and stem cell research guidelines, for example—and appeal primarily to morality based self-interests (Frank 2005). In *Talking Right: How Conservatives Turned Liberalism into a Tax-Raising, Latte-Drinking, Sushi-Eating, Volvo-Driving,* New York Times–*Reading, Body-Piercing, Hollywood-Loving, Left-Wing Freak Show*, Geoffrey Nunberg describes the challenge of finding "fresh language" to revive public debate, to work against our country's "apparent willingness to subordinate substantive interests to symbolic ones" (2006, 8).

Yet, it is one thing to be angry at how the press sensationalizes, how the unproductive "snarl" (as James Fallows [1999] characterizes the nastiness of the press) seems to reveal an impulse to punish, and another thing to be alert to the insidious work being done that is more in line with what Chomsky (2002) describes as "media control." In this view, instead of bringing the issue to the fore by genuinely inviting conversation and solution, the press is exercising its complicity with the overarching force of the corporate culture's machine to produce and maintain uninformed opinions. This is played out in the following ways, according to Chomsky: First, we, the "bewildered herd," primarily need distractions, or at most need to be put in positions of mere spectators, to prevent our real participation.[5] Then,

> you want to create a slogan that nobody's going to be against, and everybody's going to be for. Nobody knows what it means, because it doesn't mean anything. Its crucial value is that it diverts your attention from a question that *does* mean something. (26)

Today, the media's identity and relation to the public reflects its fidelity to a market-driven economy. Freepress, a media reform organization that supports independent news outlets, claims:

> In our commercial system, profit always trumps the public interest. There is a basic conflict of interest with running a business purely for profit that has so much influence on democratic debate, culture, and the social distribution of information. Government has historically been responsible for balancing these interests—but it has increasingly sided with business over the public, causing a serious imbalance.[6]

But according to cultural critic Mick Underwood, this wasn't always the case: The media were once "part of the public sphere of reasoned discussion." However, the media itself

> became part of the process of "re-feudalization" of the public sphere as state, industrial conglomerates and the media undergo a process of fusion. The media became the manipulators of public opinion, conditioning the public into the rôle of passive onlookers and consumers. The "fourth estate," "guardians of the public sphere," became increasingly converted into industries, wholly oriented towards the profit motive, just another business held by some conglomerate. The output of the robber barons' media no longer can be seen as contributing to rational discourse in the public sphere. Rather it serves merely to entertain and turn the potential participants in the public sphere into mere passive consumers.[7]

It is interesting to note a parallel, an example of the components that link media control, the economics of public awareness (or ignorance, if you will), and the treatment of an "issue." The economic and peer pressures that drive media constructions of plagiarism are eerily similar to the economic and peer pressures that drive media constructions of computer viruses. In "Disease'd Ventures: A Critique of Media Reportage of Viruses" George Smith (2001, 2) observes

> The majority of stories help to create a twisted image in which networked computing is always balanced at the edge of disaster. Without the technical knowledge to assess these reports critically, the public seems to face waves of

computer viruses coming at them like plagues of locusts borne upon the back of the e-mail that their daily lives now depend upon. In its insatiable and undiscriminating appetite for news, it is a system that is easily gamed.

So, as we *produce* more and more literate people, and more and more people ride the information superhighway, we also produce a particular set of consumers; like the computer users above who have invested heavily in their high-tech lifestyle, who are compelled to continually hear more about it—and who expect the worst—we create a consumer base for even the most sensational or exaggerated news about plagiarism. In the trade-off of substance for speed, any potential for developing a meaningful and sustained conversation, let alone one that might actually engage a diverse public in finding solutions, is lost. Smith also believes:

> The current method of reportage fails to discuss [computer] virus threats in a historical context, predominantly because such analyses cannot be easily shoehorned into the immediacy of crisis news. As a result, new threats are rarely, if ever, discussed in a rational, well-informed (i.e., nonhysterical) manner that compares and contrasts the expectations and realities of previous threats, and treats the current threat accordingly.

Likewise, the discourse of "gotcha" journalism also fails to present the historical contexts of authorship, heightens anxiety about a monolithic plagiarism, and requires a type of "twisting" that ignores innovation. How then can we uproot a public desire for sensationalism that compels the media to punish and replant a desire for pedagogy?

According to media sociologist Agner Fog, "various professions, like priests, lawyers, psychologists, neurologists, etc. have had monopoly on making statements about certain dangers and deviances. Thereby they gain power and influence through what has been called *issue ownership*" (2004, 5). "Big media," as Lawrence Lessig (2005) calls them, shelter the professional guild that has taken ownership of the issue of plagiarism, but academics need to take it back; we have abdicated the stump in the public square that would offer us some discursive power on the issue of plagiarism. In fact, several contemporary public intellectuals[8] believe the caricature of a head-in-sand-navel-gazing academic is drawn from life. This "retreat from public engagement on the part of many academics is increasingly lamentable," according to Henry A. Giroux (2006, 65):

> Refusing to take positions on controversial issues, such academics become models of moral indifference and examples of what it means to disconnect learning from public life. [I]ntellectuals who inhabit our nation's universities should represent the conscience of American society because they not only shape the conditions under which future generations learn about themselves and their relations to others and the outside world, but also because they engage pedagogical practices that are by their very nature moral and political rather than simply technical. (64–66)

To demonstrate the challenge of our "coming out" as public intellectuals, realize first that the four primary metaphors describing the plagiarist's actions actually stem from the canon of our own composition handbooks, according to David Leight (1999, 221). These terms become easily identified keywords the media scan for and exploit: *stealing, violating, borrowing, cheating.* Writing teachers are in the best position to unpack these metaphors with students rather than use them to label student work or behavior. As Rebecca Moore Howard (2000) [sic passim] and others have noted, we conflate all incidents of "textual transgression" with plagiarism. Instead we need to call things what they are: Purchasing a paper online is *fraud*; realizing a student misunderstands the basic reasons we cite sources (my informal poll of students showed the number one answer to "Why do we cite sources?" is "So we don't get into trouble") should signal a pedagogical move. Amy Robillard's research[9] shows that "citation practices are, at least in part, determined by affect"—based on a felt sense of how to satisfy the assignment (2006, 254). That makes sense to me: Some students are citing sources (even incorrectly) because their primary motivation is a hunch, a "feeling" that they may do something wrong; how can we enjoin students to the collective understanding that one of the primary reasons we cite is prompted by an ideal of integrity and reciprocity—the perfectly reasonable and respectful "feelings of debt and ownership"—and not simply butt covering (2006, 254).

Doggy Dog World

And interestingly, the corresponding metaphor used to describe the media— *watchdog*—is more than ever trained on itself, and the species has evolved into what Tannen calls a certain type of aggressive debater: an "attack dog." Another association with our canine friends comes from James Purdy. He found one plagiarism detection program offered

> a settable search function named "Call off the hounds when . . . " The word choice here conjures images of the classic fox hunt—mobs of hunters on horseback galloping after dogs hot on the trail of their next kill. . . . Moreover, [this] word choice also suggests an elite class chasing after lower creatures for sport. (2005, 277)

In addition, infighting among journalists and professional writers reflects a caste system, according to Susan Douglas:

> In our current hyper-commercial and anti-intellectual environment, it is the large corporations and publications that can afford to trademark, patent, and copyright everything. Prominent and profitable journalists, unless their borrowing is exact and extensive, are protected. (2)

Douglas was told she would be "tainted" if she tattled on a *New Yorker* writer who scooped her research without attribution. So even within the media machine, they are struggling to find the vocabulary and the ethical infrastructure that would reveal the complexity of the historically marked literacy practice known as plagiarism.

We need to take the next step: acknowledging complicity with the media and taking productive ownership of the issue. As Alistair Pennycook reminds us, "Many of the ways we approach supposed plagiarism are pedagogically unsound and intellectually arrogant" (1996, 227). And public outrage fueled by media reports only serves to widen the chasm between those who pay for higher education and those who are paid by it to teach those sons and daughters. As a result, rather than problematizing and theorizing plagiarism or overtly teaching students the conventions of documentation, many academics join the plagiarism police force, believe the worst about student motives, and demonize the World Wide Web; their potential as educators is lost when their energy is squandered on running student papers through expensive plagiarism detection programs. Marilyn Randall notes, "Historically, the motives ascribed to plagiarism-hunters are seldom more noble than those ascribed to 'plagiarists'; the former, usually styled as pedantic critics, are traditionally among the most reviled members of a generally reviled category of men of letters" (1999, 132). In addition, while some in the academy are motivated to identify the social factors that lead to cheating or to critique the media perspective, fewer are motivated to investigate the ways our impulse to surveil student writing and expose cheating reifies the conditions that lead to cheating in the first place. Educational and other bureaucratic institutions collude in developing a sphere of influence around the reproduction of practices—practices that foster competition and commodify intellectual contributions vis-à-vis the "earning" of grades, or grade "inflation," or the implicit "currency" of publication in exchange for academic rank[10]—that are necessary to maintain both an "institutional" and a "competitive" plagiarism (macro and micro versions respectively) that continually ties back to markets and ultimately "exploits intellectual labor" (Martin 1994, 4). Finally, we can't deny that the journalist and the academic work from the same *publish-or-perish* impulse: "One explanation for the preoccupation with competitive plagiarism is that those who write about plagiarism work in the competitive sector themselves" (Martin 1994, 5).

One example of the collusion between the media and the academy is embodied in John Lesko,[11] a professor who labels himself a "plagiarologist" (bend over and cough) and offers a .com Web resource called "Famous Plagiarists." Here is Lesko on Doris Kearns Goodwin, who, by Howard's definition of plagiarism (intentional act constituting fraud) would not be considered a plagiarist:

> Allegations of plagiarism widely circulated, significant monetary settlement paid to Lynne McTaggert, author of *Kathleen Kennedy: Her Life and Times,* from which Kearns Goodwin borrowed most extensively—although she continues to maintain that she's "absolutely not" a plagiarist. Handwritten, schmandwritten! Longhand, schmonghand! Doris Kearns Goodwin's explanation that her longhand notes were to blame for shoddy scholarship just doesn't cut it!

Not surprisingly, Lesko has developed a Plagiarism Threat Level alert. The day I visited his website, the main page showed code red: SEVERE, perhaps a result of Lesko's counterattack on Osama Bin Laden, an attack that casts aspersions on the cultural, historical, and literary practices of Muslims:

> Bin Laden was a plagiarist and *pasticheur,* following in a *noble* tradition of emulating his predecessors in word and deed, and then eulogizing himself, boasting about his accomplishments in traditional Bedu genres of poetry such as *Fakhr* (boasting), and *Madih* (praise/eulogy), and continuing all the while to insult his enemies using another established genre, namely, *hija'* or the lampoon/satire genre.

Although many of us who teach composition would disassociate ourselves from Lesko's views, we fail to educate the public from our nexus of expertise. Meanwhile, the proverbial conception of plagiarism continues to dig in its heels, reinforcing traditional and superficial understandings of how we actually make and (should) present knowledge.

Several contemporary movements, however, could possibly challenge this concept. Familiar commercial and cultural constructions (the fixed notion of what a book *is,* for example) are being dismantled through active investigation of public domain law, membership in the open-access movement, and the emergence of a digital commons. We are beginning to see how our students embody two distinct features of the future we need to openly recognize, globalization and a less constrained view of markets. Contrary to our assumptions about how they act as passive consumers, students have begun to set up new types of *relationships* with information. It is possible that even when big media and the academy work in tandem to enforce this commodification, students attempt to conceive of information in ways that bypass traditional markets. As Eodice and Pierard (2003) have learned from students who use libraries and writing centers:

> The Web environment is a familiar extension of their intellectual and social lives; most of these users see no boundary between the real time community of friends and family and the virtual communities they encounter. For this reason, it may seem plausible to students that this huge storehouse of Web resources is created for and used extensively by any and all to share, borrow, save, or purchase. (6)

And Bollier and Watts (2002) report from a major study sponsored by the Markle Foundation:

> By far, the leading metaphor for the Internet, in the public's mind, is not "a shopping mall" or "banking and investment office," but rather a "library." Despite the popular depiction of the Internet as a channel for commerce, the public mostly views it as a source of information. (9)

And in one of the best essays on the subject (written by novelist Jonathan Lethem),[12] "The Ecstasy of Influence: A Plagiarism" (2007), the alternative metaphors of *gift economy* or *public commons* offer new ways to view and understand the twenty-first century learner and her literacies. Finally, as much as some of us have resisted the implications of a more corporatized university[13] or complained about students' "commodification" of education, curricular practices remain that reinforce such notions. The first example that springs to mind is our eagerness to outsource plagiarism detection to a corporation; rather than figure out ways to guide our students in their often flawed practices with academic writing, we choose to pay for an expensive algorithm that points out their problems after the fact. This effectively tells students that learning such things as proper citation is less important than not getting caught by the external apparatus that scores them as good or bad writers. To counter this, writing center peer tutors at Indiana University of Pennsylvania and other sites are developing in-service workshops to unpack the ethical and pedagogical issues for students, faculty, and administrators. Empowered students now describe Turnitin.com as "potentially detrimental to the educational process in composition" (Brown, Fallon, Lott, Matthews, and Mintie 2007, 27). And even without the plagiarism detection program, our good intentions to head off plagiarism often send a similar message, as educator Russ Hunt (2003) describes it: "Doesn't asking students to focus first on ownership of ideas and texts instantiate a profoundly static, accumulative, building-block notion of what knowledge is, and one that supports a neo-capitalist notion of scholarship?" (3).

Preaching to the Choir

If we are in agreement, how do we take that kind of knowledge to the streets, to the press? A chronicle of my own experiences and actions might provide one illustration of possibilities. Several years ago, the provost at the University of Kansas asked me to submit a white paper on Turnitin.com. He had been asked by several faculty to provide some relief from the "rampant Internet plagiarism" they were seeing. In this paper I outlined potential ethical and legal issues and offered suggestions for reinvesting in graduate teaching assistant and faculty orientations to address how assignment design and direct instruction on citation and documentation might raise consciousness for all parties, including students. I was then obliged to consult with general counsel, and they determined that submitting papers did not violate student rights and instead fell easily under the handbook heading of "for the purposes of instruction." Unfortunately, with that shield, the administration saw no potential problems with the subscription. And despite my efforts to block the adoption of the service, I was assigned as the systems administrator of the Plagiarism Detection Service (PDS), Turnitin.com.

Since that time, a Canadian student at McGill University, Jesse Rosenfeld,[14] and others have stepped forward with resistance. In some cases the students felt cheated by a lack of direct instruction or sensed some violation of their intellectual property rights as Turnitin.com held their texts captive. But Rosenfeld was concerned about the trust that had eroded between instructors and students; he was granted an alternative to submitting his papers. The alternative? The professor read and responded to the papers himself. In Rosenfeld's words, from the *Toronto Star:*

> "... [F]rankly I'm offended that the university is violating students' rights by using a device that presumes students are guilty of plagiarism until proven innocent," said Rosenfeld. "I'm also angry because this software gives universities an excuse to keep oversized classes and not hire enough professors so they can actually interact with students ... " (Mcgill Teen 2004)

Except for several professors at Grand Valley State University,[15] I have not heard of cases of faculty actively resisting the subscription to Turnitin.com or harnessing the energy of students to argue for their rights or for more hires as a solution to the putative problem of burgeoning plagiarism.

Back at KU, I was preparing to exit as a new provost came on board. One of my last memos was a report on user issues (trends in originality reports, ratio of instructor use compared with the full faculty and student body numbers, and the like) related to Turnitin.com and to again recommend that the subscription not be renewed. Employing the ROI argument (Return on Investment), I offered better uses for the almost $25,000 the university would spend on the program. A few weeks later I learned that the new provost had indeed decided to suspend the subscription, and from my understanding this was due to concerns over cost and copyright. The local newspaper reported that a few professors had reacted negatively to the provost's decision. In language typically associated with the issue of plagiarism (evoking either war or disease metaphors), the article "Anti-plagiarism tool pulled from professors' arsenal" (2006) quoted instructors concerned that this "effective enforcement tool" would now be unavailable to them. Letters to the editor followed mainly from the public outside of the academy, criticizing the provost and fanning the flames of distrust of student work. I then decided to write my own letter to the editor.[16] I was invited to turn my letter into a column, and the paper even included my photo. I must admit that the anticipation of reaction was more terrifying than sending an article in for peer review to an academic journal.

In the column, I critiqued our increasing dependence on plagiarism services, implicitly comparing it to a crack addiction:

> The corporation that owns Turnitin.com (iParadigms) has tapped into a current obsession: schools want to catch plagiarists. But using the program can replace instruction; it becomes an addiction, a crutch. We begin to feel the program itself solves the problem. The price goes up and we just can't quit: we must continue because we are in so deep. While the report that is generated by the complex algorithm clearly shows any similarities with other texts found in its search—using a color coded scale much too similar to the terror alert chart we are now so familiar with—there is often no sign of plagiarism at all. (Take a Stand 2006)

And I offered an alternative, drawing upon my years of experience as a writing teacher and writing center director:

> I still ask myself, after 15 years of working in higher education, why we would choose punishment over pedagogy. Instead, teachers at every level should include explicit instruction on the expectations for academic integrity, providing examples of research methods, how to quote and cite materials, and how to leave a clear bibliographic trail for the reader. Outsourcing our responsibility for instruction to a corporation is not a good investment for our students. (Take a Stand 2006)

Despite my published plea, the new provost buckled to the pressure of a few vocal faculty and negotiated a two-year contract at a reduced cost—one that offered a new feature: At students' request, their papers could be removed from the database following the report. To his credit, when Turnitin.com was reinstated at the lower rate, the provost earmarked the surplus $6,000 for the writing center, which the current assistant director now euphemistically calls the "Turnitin.com Enhancement Fund." With the agreement to enable the writing center to withdraw papers from the data bank, she decided to run a test. What she learned was that it is not easy to withdraw papers, given the technological constraints of the program, and it also costs money; either the writing center or the individual student must pay ten cents a page to extract the work. We half-jokingly discussed how far that $6,000 surplus might go in retrieving student work from Turnitin.com (60,000 single pages, or about 4,000 fifteen-page papers) although realizing quickly the brilliant design in business practices that would force her to pay the "saved" money right back to the iParadigms Corporation.

Several blogs were buzzing: Here was a precedent, the first university to be awarded the ability to retrieve papers from the massive database. For a few days the university's deal with Turnitin.com and our small town newspaper articles were national news. I heard from people all over the country. Imagine the emails, RSS feeds, listservs, blogs, and networking that could, if harnessed and circulated with more intention, provide some critical mass behind a concerted effort to resist the PDS instead. Maybe next time.

After all of this drama, I recall believing that I was moving to a university that did not subscribe but soon found I was mistaken.[17] Yet I was relieved that I would no longer be the systems administrator and that an associate provost, acting as the academic integrity officer (with a J.D. and Ph.D. in philosophy), would handle Turnitin.com. Since my arrival I have been seen as an additional resource for instructors with less experience in both developing assignments to foster solid research practices and for interpreting Turnitin.com reports. I welcome opportunities to work with faculty on more proactive and pedagogical approaches to teaching academic integrity. And I continue to chip away at the gaudy veneer that says: "Look! We subscribe to Turnitin.com! We are an institution that will not tolerate cheaters!"

Beyond the kind of work I did within my former institution, through faculty development workshops and individual consultations, and beyond my stream of memos and reports on what students, faculty, and I believe about Turnitin.com, I actively sought opportunities to lend my expertise for the community good. I asked to be listed in the university speaker directory as someone to call should the issue be addressed by the media. I talked on the radio show.[18] I even wrote that "Take a Stand" column for the local newspaper. And then I called Linda Adler-Kassner.

Adler-Kassner is currently leading the Council of Writing Program Administrators' Network for Media Action.[19] This group is committed to developing media messages that can accurately portray the goals and methods of writing instruction, illustrate the crucial importance of a literate public, and bring to the foreground efforts of writing programs in providing high-quality instruction in writing. Recent efforts include the formation of message frameworks, which provide us with cogent statements on issues like plagiarism, machine scoring of writing, high-stakes testing, and the role of grammar instruction—all concerns that often become issues for the media.

I asked her if the network was growing, making inroads. Adler-Kassner believes we in composition studies are pushing against a mighty tide, and the network is employing strategies drawn in part from community organizers and media activists to reach and motivate scholars and teachers. Our field is filled with capable writers and speakers, she agrees; we also need empirical data to back our claims. Composition's detour through "cultural work," she says, has not yielded the kind of work that testifies to our knowledge and experience, especially in the area of plagiarism. Arguments being made by both academics and the media reflect similar values, yet compositionists sometimes fail to harness our professional positions to educate the public more effectively. It seems uncertain to me whether composition specialists, in particular, would rather simply speak only to each other on this issue through our journals and books because we want to remain unsullied by connection to the public forums, whether we are simply unsure of the steps that would take us beyond our own readership, or if untenured faculty find little reward in putting any energy toward educating the public. In any case, Richard Lanham (2006) has characterized our desire to steer clear of such engagement:

> Scholars often wish the world would leave them alone, so they could go about their work in library or laboratory without interruption . . . [from] all the other legitimate activities (I had first written "distractions") of university life. (2006, 185)

Henry Giroux (2006) is much more blunt in his complaint that

> [A]cademics seem unconcerned about writing for a larger public and inhabit a world populated by concepts that both remove them from public access and subject them to the dictates of a narrow theoretical fetishism. Making almost no connections to audiences outside of the academy or to the issues that bear down on their lives, such academics have become largely irrelevant. (64)

Adler-Kassner offers her thoughts on this: Perhaps it is our conflicted view that stepping into the public sphere somehow enacts our self-interests in unsavory ways that keeps us from coming forward. But to Adler-Kassner, self-interest is not a dirty word; each of us can work from self-interest in ways that align with the core values of our work. This is not selfish attention-seeking behavior—this is what being a responsible professional requires.

What We Can All Do

I am thus interested in challenging the media and offering a simultaneous challenge to my peers. When "man bites dog," it is news. But can you recall the last time you read a magazine feature on how a young scholar learned to write well? Or the last time you heard not the student bashing at the water cooler but the thoughtful description of a student's writing progress? These two sites of discourse on plagiarism—the academy and the media—both instantiate plagiarism as a practice; students, college presidents, and famous authors and journalists are accused and roughed up. To what productive end do either of these sites engage the pedagogical or contribute to an informed debate? A recent book, *Building Bridges with the Press: A Guide for Educators* (Blair 2004), attempts to replace the "deep skepticism" educators have for the press with outreach and trust, admitting that we have got to let the press in to get the truth out: "Journalists without sufficient access tend to write uninspired stories that do little to foster real debate on education" (14). However, a poll of more than 300 educators conducted by Public Agenda, a nonprofit research group, revealed:

- Ninety-one percent said there was "a lot/some truth" to the statement: Reporters cover education news according to what sells.

- Eighty-six percent said there was "a lot/some truth" to the statement: The media unfairly dwell on conflict and failure. (13)

This lack of productive media attention is effectively an erasure of how complex, contingent, and time intensive (not to mention historically and by nature highly collaborative) writing is. To energize productive attention would mean, first, to welcome an interrogation of our Western conceptions of commodity and competition associated with text production. This interrogation would require, however, a strong participation from those among our ranks. Second, the current dysfunctional, passive relationship between the academy and the media has created not dialectic but either unhealthy symbiosis or polemic. Need we further nurture the "discursive frameworks of authority and condemnation . . . the ritual procedures of imposing punishment" (Garland 1990, 17) by punishing our students as the press would humiliate a college president? Can we continue to turn our backs on this particular scholarly and pedagogical responsibility? Or trade barbs with the press, when we could develop informed statements that can represent the field? Linda Hutcheon, in her essay "Rhetoric and Competition: Academic Agonistics" (2003), proposes a move from what Tannen (1999) has characterized as a "culture of critique" to one that recognizes and engages with "counter-discourses"—leading to conversations that could resuscitate both an internal (among us academics) and external (with the public) "community of learning" rather than maintaining one of "demolition and dispute" (3).

Kathryn Valentine (2006), among other contemporary scholars theorizing plagiarism, makes a compelling case for recognizing plagiarism as a literacy practice, not rule breaking. By focusing on the potential for dishonesty and its attendant penalties ("We'll be running your papers through Turntin.com," for example), we add personal (the student's and our), moral, and ethical judgments to the already complex and strong cocktail of classroom authority. Valentine explains: ". . . [C]oncerns about plagiarism create the opportunity for professors and administrators to be concerned with and, if deemed necessary, to work to alter (through punishment) students' identities" (102). We must abandon our "common-sense view of plagiarism—that it is a textual practice that can be taught solely by working with rules of documentation on written texts" and "start with a focus on practice" (104).

We must do so by first acknowledging these conflicting notions of literacy, originality, and "performing" new discourses across cultures and languages. Doing so would be more consonant with our common goal of helping students develop and perform rhetorical strategies than donning the uniform of Deputy Dawg. Our institutions, our academic positions, our writing can and should be the locus of "new spheres of public pedagogy" (Giroux 2006, 75), spheres that foster debate about what student text production represents in our culture. While it is not requisite that academics damn the corporate influence from the rooftops, it might be requisite that we examine our practices alongside our complaints about student work and determine how our steady and informed influence can make an important public issue more of a pedagogical one, for the community good.

Notes

1. I use the terms *punishment* and *penalty* not in the more measured way David Garland does (as a legal process) but more to suggest the encompassing process of surveillance, exposure, and humiliation developed to spotlight textual transgressions committed by both the expert (a famous journalist or Stephen Ambrose) and the novice (an undergraduate). Interestingly, in Dantes' eighth circle of Hell, *Fraud* includes the *Falsifiers of Words*. See a map of this region: www.public.asu.edu/~aarios/resourcebank/maps/page8.html.

2. Mass media, as defined by Gregory Golds at Penn State University, "possesses a dominant ideology, one that represents the sum of socialized values; it exerts normative pressure to eliminate radical ideas and is based on the Puritan work ethic": www.psu.edu/dept/inart10_110/inart10/media.html

I use mass media, the press, popular press, the media, and the like interchangeably to cover a range of ways I believe Golds' description is carried out; I am not referring to individual participation by particular journalists, or even particular publications, in this essay.

3. Oscar Wilde, in *The Soul of Man*, provides one definition of the "fourth estate":
   In old days men had the rack. Now they have the press. That is an improvement certainly. But still it is very bad, and wrong, and demoralizing. Somebody—was it Burke?—called journalism the fourth estate. That was true at the time, no doubt. But at the present moment it really is the only estate. It has eaten up the other three. The Lords Temporal say nothing, the Lords Spiritual have nothing to say, and the House of Commons has nothing to say and says it. We are dominated by Journalism.

   According to a recent *New York Times* poll (Sunday, February 26, 2007 WK 15) on confidence in institutions, positive responses to "I have a great deal of confidence" in the press have dropped from 25 percent in 1973 to 10 percent in 2006.

4. As described by Agner Fog (in "Mass Media and Democracy Crisis"), who makes the connection between media motivations and a market-driven economy:
   A combination of contributions from the different disciplines shows that a fierce economic competition forces the media to produce entertaining stories that appeal to people's emotions. In countries like USA, where economic competition between news media is fierce and there is little government regulation, the sensationalist focus on button pushing crimes in the news media has created a public sentiment that many commentators have characterized as *obsession with crime* (Sasson 1995, Adler 1983) and moral panic."

   In the documentary film, *Orwell Rolls Over in His Grave, mediaocracy* is featured as a key term in a "deeply disturbing look at how mass media in the United States is controlled by only a handful of large corporations": www.turnoffyourtv.com/networks/orwellrolls/orwellrolls.html.

   Writer Danny Schechter is perhaps best known for using the term *mediaocracy* to describe the media's abdication and the political takeover of the 2000 election: www.mediachannel.org/views/dissector/mediaocracy.shtml.

5. Of course, I realize I am applying Chomsky's idea to a less urgent topic in trying to generate some discussion about the ways people think about writing. Elevating plagiarism to the same level of concern we might have for lives lost in war is not my intention. But I do believe the concepts of a *war on terrorism* or a *war on drugs* are legitimate examples of his screed, and from the volume of material produced in recent years in both academic publications and by the press, you would think there actually was a call for a *war on plagiarism* that folks just might get behind.

6. From the website for Free Press: www.freepress.net/:
   Free Press works to expand public awareness and involvement in media policymaking in the United States. We do this by reaching out to groups that are strongly affected by media but have not participated in media reform. Free Press is a collaborative organization, committed to making the whole of the media reform movement greater than the sum of its parts.

7. From the Communication, Cultural and Media Studies Infobase developed by Mick Underwood: www.cultsock.ndirect.co.uk/MUHome/cshtml/media/4estate.html and www.ccms-infobase.com.

8. See also Edward Said's "The Public Role of Writers and Intellectuals" in *The Nation* September 17, 2001: (www.thenation.com/doc/20010917/essay):

> The intellectual's role generally is to uncover and elucidate the contest, to challenge and defeat both an imposed silence and the normalized quiet of unseen power, wherever and whenever possible. For there is a social and intellectual equivalence between this mass of overbearing collective interests and the discourse used to justify, disguise or mystify its workings while at the same time preventing objections or challenges to it.

9. Amy Robillard has published on issues of student plagiarism and citation practices— their practices of citing others and our practices in citing them, the student writers:

> We cite the people we cite for a variety of reasons, and one of those reasons is that we have what Robert J. Connors calls "feelings of debt and ownership" ("Rhetoric," Part 1 7) toward the texts and the authors we cite.

See also:

Connors, Robert J. "The Rhetoric of Citation Systems, Part 1: The Development of Annotation Structures from the Renaissance to 1900." *Rhetoric Review* 17 (1998): 6–47.

———. "The Rhetoric of Citation Systems, Part 2: Competing Epistemic Values in Citation." *Rhetoric Review* 17 (1999): 219–45.

Visit the blog VITIA, www.vitia.org/wordpress/2006/04/03/cccc06-bullshit/, for a summary of her writing assignment on bullshit, designed to draw out its connections to plagiarism.

10. Linda Hutcheon (2003), former president of MLA, notes that "the current reward system values the work of the solo scholar in ways that bear the marks of capitalism (the ideas of ownership and ideas)" (3).

Also fitting here is Dennis Shirley (1986) on Bourdieu: "Bourdieu's central contribution has been the extension of the reproduction motif beyond the boundaries of epiphenomenal economic base—educational superstructure models to analyze the internal logic of an educational system which—while concealing its role—simultaneously reproduces and legitimates the capitalist social formation."

And also consider Ivan Illich (1972) on how schooling contributes to re/production of a consumer mind-set:

> As long as an individual is not explicitly conscious of the ritual character of the process through which he was initiated to the forces which shape his cosmos, he cannot break the spell and shape a new cosmos. As long as we are not aware of the ritual through which school shapes the progressive consumer—the economy's major resource—we cannot break the spell of this economy and shape a new one. (74)

And shame on us if Richard Lanham is right. In the *Economics of Attention: Style and Substance in the Age of Information* (2006), he uncovers this tension between "the idea market for attention and the stuff market for goods" when he describes how we literary types "have long viewed commerce with an aristocratic disdain . . . when four times out of five it is the marketplace that pays the salaries of the professional intellectuals who scorn it" (251).

11. From the site "Famous Plagiarists" and companion site "War on Plagiarism": www.famousplagiarists.com/. Note the use of color-coded alerts that resemble the Homeland Security threat level charts for terrorism: www.terror-alert.com/.

    Although Dr. Lesko is a professor at Saginaw Valley State University, the Famous Plagiarists Research Project represents the individual research of John P. Lesko, plagiarologist, and SVSU accepts no responsibility for the content of these pages.

    He also had the nerve to disparage two of my favorites: Johnny Cash and Coldplay.

12. For a very literary and historical exploration of the trails of influence in art, see: "The Ecstasy of Influence: A Plagiarism" by Jonathan Lethem in *Harper's*, February 2007, 59–71.

13. See the work of Richard Miller, Bill Readings, James Sosnoski, and a collection called *Beyond English Inc.* (Downing, Hurlbert, and Mathieu, editors) for more discussion of this—from critique to utopian proposals.

14. The *Toronto Star*, (Ontario, Canada), January 16, 2004: "McGill teen wins battle over online cheat check - System smears innocent scholars, student says Turnitin.com examines essays for plagiarism":

    A Toronto teen studying at McGill University has won the right to refuse to put his assignments through a popular computerized plagiarism-detector, saying it treats students like cheats until they are proven innocent. The software, designed to thwart the boom in cheating Web sites, scans a student's work for stolen passages by comparing it with a databank of research papers on the Internet. Turnitin is used by 28 of Canada's 90 universities, although its use is often voluntary.

    Full article also found on the teaching writing with technology listserv TechRhet: http://lists.southernct.edu/pipermail/writeon/2004January/000917.html.

15. *Issues Raised by Use of Turnitin Plagiarism Detection Software.* Charlie Lowe, Assistant Professor of Writing; Ellen Schendel, Associate Professor of Writing; Julie White, Affiliate Faculty, Writing Department Grand Valley State University (September 7, 2006): http://cyberdash.com/plagiarism-detection-software-issues-gvsu.

16. Eodice. "Take a Stand" *Lawrence Journal World*, October 7, 2006: www2 .ljworld.com/news/2006/oct/07/subscribe_teaching_academic_integrity_instead/.

    Includes over 20 comments responding to the events.

    Local news video clip: Lawrence, Kansas:www.6newslawrence.com/news/2006/oct/03/ku_renews_contract_effort_stop_cheating/.

17. The University of Oklahoma recently (2006) subscribed to Turnitin.com. If Rebecca Moore Howard can't make this case and block it at her home institution, I don't feel so bad. Syracuse University recently subscribed.

Simultaneous to the subscription, Syracuse adopted a new position statement based on a similar statement published by the Council of Writing Program Administrators.

August 16, 2006

Friends, I am delighted to tell you that there's now an institution (Syracuse) whose university-wide policy on plagiarism is directly influenced by the WPA Best Practices document <http://wpacouncil.org/node/9>. If you are involved in curricular activism at your own institution, this is good news for you, because of how often committees want precedents before they make policy changes. Well, now there's a precedent for an institutional policy that differentiates plagiarism and misuse of sources: <https://psdocs.syr.edu/sudocs/vpcai/finalizeddocs3.pdf>.

It doesn't go as far as the WPA document does in that differentiation. (I won't elaborate on the differences here, but they're on my blog if you're interested <http://wrthoward.syr.edu/stepaside/archives/2006/08/new_plagiarism _1.html>.)

But it's a vast improvement over most existing institutional policies. And maybe the next institution that revises its policy will decide to venture even closer to the WPA recommendations!

Becky Howard, Syracuse

WPA listserv: http://lists.asu.edu/cgibin/wa?A1=ind0608&L=wpal&F=&S=&O=A&H=0&D=1&T=1#193.

See also: "Harvard Becomes First Ivy to Use Anti-Plagiarism Tool" (Update6) By Emily Sachar online at Bloomberg.com November 3, 2006: www.bloomberg.com/apps/news?pid=newsarchive&sid=aptoNF9NdRQ8.

18. *Up to Date.* June 23, 2005, KCUR FM Kansas City: http://archive.kcur.org/kcurViewDirect.asp?PlayListID=3409

19. Linda Adler-Kassner, Associate Professor of Composition, Eastern Michigan University. Personal communication: October 24, 2006.

   WPA Network for Media Action http://wpacouncil.org/nma

   Thanks also to Joe Janangelo and Alfie Guy for talking with me about their participation in a Network for Media Action workshop at the WPA conference 2005.

References

Blair, Julie. 2004. *Building Bridges with the Press: A Guide for Educators*. Bethesda, MD.: Education Week Press.

Bollier, David, and Tim Watts. 2002. "Saving the Information Commons: A Public Interest Agenda in Digital Media." www.newamerica.net/publications/policy/saving_the_information_commons.

Boyle, James. 1996. *Shamans, Software, and Spleens: Law and the Construction of the Information Society*. Cambridge, MA.: Harvard University Press.

Brown, Renee, Brian Fallon, Jessica Lott, Elizabeth Matthews, and Elizabeth Mintie. 2007. "Taking on Turnitin: Tutors Advocating for Change." *Writing Center Journal* 27 (1): 7–28.

Chomsky, Noam. 2002. *Media Control: The Spectacular Achievements of Propaganda*. Open Media Series. New York: Seven Stories Press.

Douglas, Susan. 2006. "Plagiarists: Catch Your Own Clue." *inthesetimes.com*,www .inthesetimes.com/site/main/article/2782/.

Eodice, Michele. 2006. "Take a Stand." *Lawrence Journal World* (October 7).

Eodice, Michele, and Cynthia Pierard. 2003. "Surfing for Scholarship: Promoting More Effective Student Research." *National Teaching and Learning Forum* 11(3). http://cstl.syr.edu/CSTL3/Home/Resources/Subscriptions/NTLF/v11n3/surfing. tm.

Ericson, Richard V., Patricia M. Baranek, and Janet B. L. Chan. 1991. *Representing Order: Crime, Law, and Justice in the News Media*. Buckingham U.K.: Open University Press.

Fallows, James. 1996. *Breaking the News: How Media Undermine Democracy*. New York: Pantheon.

Fog, Agner. 2004. "The Supposed and the Real Role of Mass Media in Modern Democracy." Working Paper. www.agner.org/cultsel.

Frank, Thomas. 2005. *What's the Matter With Kansas: How Conservatives Won the Heart of America*. New York: Owl Books.

Garland, David. 1990. *Punishment in Modern Society: A Study in Social Theory*. Chicago: University of Chicago Press.

Giroux, Henry A. 2006. "Higher Education Under Siege: Implications for Public Intellectuals." *Thought and Action* 22 (Fall): 63–78.

Howard, Rebecca Moore. 2000. "Sexuality, Textuality: The Cultural Work of Plagiarism." *College English* 62: 473–491.

Hunt, Russ. 2003. "Two Cheers for Plagiarism." *Inkshed: Newsletter of the Canadian Association for the Study of Language and Learning* 20 (Fall): 10–18. www.stthomasu.ca/inkshed/nletta03/hunt.htm.

Hutcheon, Linda. 2003. "Rhetoric and Competition: Academic Agonistics." *Common Knowledge* 9 (Winter): 42–49.

Illich, Ivan. 1972. *Deschooling Society*. New York: Harper & Row.

"KU Renews Anti-Plagiarism software subscription." *Lawrence Journal World*, October 4, 2006. www2.ljworld.com/news/2006/oct/04/ku_renews_antiplagiarism _software_subscription/.

Lakoff, George. 2004. *Don't Think of an Elephant: Know Your Values and Frame the Debate*. White River Junction, VT Chelsea Green Publishing Company.

Lanham, Richard. 2006. *The Economics of Attention: Style and Substance in the Age of Information*. Chicago: University of Chicago Press.

Leight, David. 1999. "Plagiarisms as Metaphor." In *Perspectives on Plagiarism and Intellectual Property in a Postmodern World,* edited by Lise Buranen and Alice M. Roy. Albany: SUNY Press.

———. 2005. *Free Culture: How Big Media Uses Technology and the Law to Lock Down Culture and Control Creativity*. Free download. http://cyberlaw.stanford.edu/ freeculture/freeculture-pk.pdf.

Lethem, Jonathan. 2007. "The Ecstasy of Influence: A Plagiarism." *Harper's* February 59–71.

Martin, Brian. 1994. *Plagiarism: A Misplaced Emphasis*. www.uow.edu.au/arts/sts/bmartin/pubs/94jie.html.

"McGill Teen Wins Battle Over Online Cheat Check." 2004. *Toronto Star*, January 16.

Nunberg, Geofrey. 2006. *Talking Right: How Conservatives Turned Liberalism into a Tax-Raising, Latte-Drinking, Sushi-Eating, Volvo-Driving, New York Times–Reading, Body-Piercing, Hollywood-Loving, Left-Wing Freak Show*. New York: PublicAffairs Books.

Pennycook, Alastair. 1996. "Borrowing Others' Words: Text, Ownership, Memory, and Plagiarism." *TESOL Quarterly* 30 (Summer): 201–30.

Posner, Richard A. 2007. *The Little Book of Plagiarism*. New York: Pantheon Books.

Purdy, James P. 2005. "Calling off the Hounds: Technology and the Visibility of Plagiarism." *Pedagogy: Critical Approaches to Teaching Literature, Language, Composition, and Culture* 5 (2): 275–295.

Randall, Marilyn. 1999. "Imperial Plagiarism." In *Plagiarism and Intellectual Property in a Postmodern World*, edited by Lise Buranen and Alice M. Roy. Albany: SUNY Press.

Robillard, Amy E. 2006. "*Young Scholars* Affecting Composition: A Challenge to Disciplinary Citation Practices." *College English* 68 (3): 253–70.

Sairley, Dennis. 1986. "A Critical Review and Appropriation of Pierre Bourdieu's Analysis of Social and Cultural Reproduction." *Journal of Education* 168 (Summer): 96–112.

Smith, George. 2001. "Diseas'd Ventures: A Critique of Media Reportage of Viruses." www.securityfocus.com/infocus/1269.

Tannen, Deborah. 1999. *The Argument Culture: Stopping America's War of Words*. New York: Ballantine Books.

Valentine, Kathryn. 2006. "Plagiarism as Literacy Practice: Recognizing and Rethinking Ethical Binaries." *College Composition and Communication* 58 (1): 89–109.

2

Situating Plagiarism as a Form of Authorship

The Politics of Writing in a First-Year Writing Course

Amy E. Robillard
Illinois State University

I cannot tell you how many times I have been lectured about the
evils of plagiarism, but teachers spend twice as much time *lecturing*
about plagiarism than actually teaching students how to *avoid*
plagiarism. About half the teachers I have had from eighth grade
and up have told me not to plagiarize and when I asked about
correctly citing a source, their response was to "look it up."
—Allison Niesen, Plagiarism: The New Plague?

With about the same frequency that college teachers are warned that the Internet
is making plagiarism easier and more seductive for students, students are lectured in courses across the curriculum about the grave consequences of plagiarism. In his chapter in this book, for instance, Chris Anson cites a political
science instructor's syllabus warning against plagiarism: "If you plagiarize even
a single sentence from another person, *you will fail this course*." The popular
media dramatize "famous" cases of plagiarism, vilifying best-selling historians
and college students alike; college teachers take such dramatizations as warnings
about their students and become determined not to let technology get the better
of them. Lectures to students—especially to first-year students—likely become
increasingly draconian, and students likely become increasingly immune to the
warnings and threats.

I have long believed in the value of students learning from their peers; even
as a new writing instructor, I energetically embraced the practice of peer
review, often experimenting with different ways of implementing the practice.
When I taught two sections of the same course, for example, I asked students to

read and respond anonymously to papers written by students in the other section. I wanted to better understand the extent to which anonymity encouraged students to be more forthright in their feedback. More recently, I have been implementing what I call "coinvestigation"—the cooperative study of an issue of concern to all parties—in the first-year writing classroom. All parties have experience and knowledge to contribute to the study, experience and knowledge that shapes and reshapes the questions and objects of the investigation.

I have conducted a number of coinvestigations with first-year students, each focused on some aspect of authorship studies. The distinguishing feature of classroom coinvestigation in authorship studies that I want to focus on in this chapter is its ability to foster a learning environment in which all parties learn from one another; more specifically, students investigate together the politics of plagiarism in the academy, thereby minimizing the need for me to lecture to them about the immorality of this textual "crime."

It is important to differentiate coinvestigation from the pedagogical strategy known as coinquiry, a feature of critical pedagogy as it is practiced in composition studies. The salient difference is how each imagines students' gain. Whereas critical pedagogy aims to empower students with critical knowledge that the teacher already possesses, coinvestigation aims to engage students in questions to which teachers do not already know the answers. Critical pedagogues want, as Ira Shor illustrates in *When Students Have Power,* to authorize students to take control of their education. One of the most successful ways teachers have been able to do this is through democratic dialogue in the classroom, or coinquiry. This is coinquiry in the name of student empowerment, coinquiry designed to liberate students from the oppressive reigns of traditional education and to encourage students to fight for social justice. This is coinquiry with a particular goal from the outset: to uncover oppression and to fight against it. This is a kind of coinquiry where the teacher generally has a good idea of the answers she's looking for from students. As Ann George puts it, "Shor and [Paulo] Freire run into . . . difficulties trying to reconcile their notion of democratic dialogue with the fact that teachers often know more than their students" (2001, 105). To claim that the classroom is a democratic place with students taking control of their education is to attempt to minimize the teacher's authority and expertise. While principles of coinquiry do influence my pedagogy, my focus is on coinvestigation.

Coinvestigation, as I understand and practice it, does not attempt to minimize the teacher's institutional authority. I make no claims of equality in situations of coinvestigation; as the teacher involved in the course I'll describe in this chapter, I exercised an institutional form of authority, and I exercised power that was not available to the other members of the coinvestigation. Nor did I attempt to minimize that power in the classroom. I assigned reading, and I assigned writing. I asked students to respond to writing prompts that I believed would forward our investigation. And I graded their work as a writing teacher. Students, in return, shared their experiences, expectations, and responses to some of the central questions of composition studies with me but, more importantly, with one another. By describing the following course that takes up plagiarism as one of many forms of authorship my students and I coinvestigated, I want to suggest that coinvestigation into the politics of writing, generally, and the cultural work of plagiarism more specifically, can teach us a great deal about something we ought to know quite well: how to reach an audience that has heard lecture after lecture about plagiarism since the eighth grade.

Certainly I am not the first (and I likely won't be the last) to suggest that we writing teachers should engage students in the very questions we've been wrestling with ourselves. In this collection, T. Kenny Fountain and Lauren Fitzgerald offer a sequence of assignments designed to engage students at a religiously affiliated institution in concepts such as textual authority and community and the relationship of these concepts to prohibitions such as "thou shalt not steal." Margaret Price, in "Beyond 'Gotcha!': Situating Plagiarism in Policy and Pedagogy" suggests engaging students in the composition of course plagiarism policies (2002, 107) and in classroom discussions of the complexities of citation across a variety of genres (2002, 109). In "Buying In, Selling Short: A Pedagogy Against the Rhetoric of Online Paper Mills," Kelly Ritter describes a research-based assignment designed to challenge students' "personal—and culturally reinforced—notions of authorship and academic integrity" (2006, 27). Her assignment asks students to analyze the rhetoric of online paper mills, thereby addressing students' alleged disengagement "head-on" (2006, 28).

The assignments I describe in this chapter[1] aimed to situate plagiarism in a larger discussion about the politics of writing and authorship in the early twenty-first century. Students read and wrote about the practices of professional book reviewers, the history of the Book-of-the-Month club, the appeal of Oprah's book club, the controversy surrounding Ward Churchill's "'Some People Push Back': On the Justice of Roosting Chickens," Mark Hofmann's literary forgeries, and contemporary conversations—academic and journalistic—about the Internet's effect on the number of plagiarism cases. At the heart of all of these assignments was what I understood as the tension between writing as verb and writing as noun (Trimbur 2003, Robillard 2006). A conception of writing as verb manifests in a primary emphasis on *process,* on *how-to,* with discussions of plagiarism confined to *how not to* plagiarize. A conception of writing as noun—as object of study—on the other hand, renders writing itself the subject of the course, with plagiarism—its causes, but more important, its consequences—one part of a semester-long coinvestigation into the politics of writing.

What We Think We Know About Why Students Plagiarize

My motivation in designing a course in which students and I investigate together the cultural politics of writing was twofold. First, there was my desire to avoid lecturing students about plagiarism and also to foster a setting in which discussions of plagiarism do not focus on the question of *these very students* plagiarizing. In other words, I wanted to initiate discussions of plagiarism that did not elicit students' defenses (e.g., "*I* would never plagiarize, but I have friends who have") or statements about the immorality of theft, statements intended to appease me with what they thought I wanted to hear. I was not interested in understanding the reasons students plagiarize. In fact, I believe that much of the work in composition studies devoted to understanding these complex reasons suffers from an overwhelming collective desire to believe that such an understanding can prevent plagiarism. It seems to me that this work implicitly works by such reasoning as this: If students plagiarize because they are bored with our classes, let's do what we can to engage with their interests.

Devoting pedagogical attention to understanding the reasons students plagiarize is a futile undertaking. The reasons students plagiarize are as unavailable to us as are the reasons students choose to do their own work, which is to say that we can learn a great deal from students' self-reporting about their motivations in our classes, but also that such self-reporting carries with it students' desires to meet our expectations in asking the questions in the first place. The very fact that it is teachers who are asking questions of students about their motivations with regard to their academic writing shapes students' responses significantly, whether those responses are in the form of a survey (Ritter 2005) or an interview (Spigelman 2000). This is not to say that we cannot trust what students tell us; rather, we must remember that their responses are contingent and contextual. In *Distinction*, his analysis of the social functions of taste, Pierre Bourdieu acknowledges that his methodology of the survey seals off the universe of possible answers, thereby perpetuating the hierarchical relations between "the experts and the laymen" (1984, 461).

> By offering a choice among several utterances and asking for a position to be taken on the already-uttered, the survey—like political consultations—proceeds as if it had already resolved the essential problem of politics, namely, the question of the transmutation of experience into discourse, of the unformulated ethos into a constituted, constituting logos, of a class sense, which may imply a form of adaptation and resignation to the self-evidences of the social order, into a conscious, i.e., explicitly formulated, apprehension of that order. Eliminating the labour of formulation, the survey tacitly presupposes that the person questioned would have been capable of producing or even reproducing the proposition which constitutes the statement of the question, or even of spontaneously adopting the relation to language and to politics which underlies the production of such an inquiry. (1984, 460)

Surveys and interviews designed to reveal students' motivations for plagiarizing make the methodological mistake of "eliminating the labour of formulation," and of ignoring the politics of the relationship between teachers and students. *Plagiarism*, we all know, is a dirty word in the academy. The moral imperatives it carries with it are so ingrained in students' minds that any survey or interview that purports to understand students' opinions or actions with respect to plagiarism must account for students' understanding of the severity of plagiarism and their consequent desire to avoid association with it.

Another, perhaps more productive, way to express this methodological critique is to draw on James Scott's distinction between what he calls the "public transcript" and the "hidden transcript." In *Writing at the End of the World,* Richard E. Miller (2005) draws on Scott's distinction between these two modes of discourse in order to point out that "by virtue of their subordinate position within the structure of the educational system, students [. . .] have their 'hidden transcripts' where they store their reservations about what the schools are doing to them" (130). Citing Scott, Miller explains that the "public transcript" describes " 'the open interaction between subordinates and those who dominate'; it is a text that rarely fails to 'provide convincing evidence for the hegemony of dominant discourse.' " The public transcript is "always available for inspection," whereas the "hidden transcript" is a kind of behind-the-scenes discourse, and thus " 'beyond direct observation by powerholders.' " Because the hidden transcript is unavailable for analysis, it is " 'essential to any dynamic view of power relations' " (127). Miller's further explanation of Scott's work is worth quoting at length:

> Scott's contention is that subordinates are attempting to avoid any *"explicit display of insubordination,"* so they reliably collaborate in the production of a public transcript that gives the impression that they have accepted the tenets of the dominant ideology, when in fact they have neither embraced this ideology nor resigned themselves to the fate this ideology has in store for them. While the subordinates are on stage, we see them only "on their best behavior," doing what is called for in order not to put themselves in harm's way (87). Offstage, though, subordinates rehearse "the anger and reciprocal aggression denied by the presence of the domination," jointly creating "a discourse of dignity, of negation, of justice" (37–38, 114). Away from the boss, away from the classroom, away from the oppressor's gaze, we all fantasize about alternative world orders. (128)

The knowledge we've gained as a field about the reasons students plagiarize represents only the public transcript. I do not purport to explicate here in any significant way the hidden transcript; rather, I want to suggest a specific pedagogical approach that responds to a different set of questions about plagiarism, questions that do not invite students' defenses or their "best behavior." I hope to offer a new approach for discussing plagiarism in the classroom, one that focuses not on *plagiarizing* as a verb but on *plagiarism* as a noun, an object of study. In other words, we need a rhetorical approach, one that emphasizes the cultural work of plagiarism in a capitalist society that glorifies the work of the individual creator.

My approach situates plagiarism in relation to other forms of authorship rather than in relation to other types of crime. It encourages students to

investigate the cultural consequences of various forms of authorship, including
that to which *accusations* of plagiarism comprised a bulk of the mass media's
response (I'm thinking here of Ward Churchill's "'Some People Push Back'").
One of the central questions of the course, then, becomes, How does plagiarism
in its noun form function both inside and outside the classroom?

In what follows, I describe a sequence of reading and writing assignments
designed to complicate commonplace understandings of plagiarism as a textual crime undertaken by students who are lazy, or immoral, or both. I taught
this first-year required writing course in Fall 2005 at Illinois State University
to a class of 23 students whose academic interests, for the most part, lay outside English Studies. Yet all students, even and perhaps especially first-year
students, have a stake in the politics of writing both in and outside of the university. Characterized as a coinvestigation into the politics of writing in the
early twenty-first century, the following sequence of assignments situates plagiarism in relation to other forms of authorship, including book reviewing, the
creation of book clubs, literacy sponsorship, political polemic, and literary forgery. Positioned in relation to these forms of authorship, plagiarism can be
understood not simply as the lazy student's way out but as one of a number of
textual practices that elicit media attention from cultural critics ever concerned
with the consequences of mass literacy.

Book Reviewing, Book Clubs, and Oprah

I began the semester by assigning readings that described the strategies of *New
York Times* book reviewer Christopher Lehmann-Haupt (Deitch 1987), the cultural distinction between "highbrow" and "lowbrow" reading (Roberts 1990),
and the history of the Book-of-the-Month Club (Rubin 1992). Class discussions
following these readings focused on the processes by which book reviewers
choose books to review in the first place, on the cultural weight of a *New York
Times* book review, on the importance of reading "serious fiction" in public
places to develop a reputation as a highbrow reader, and on the Book-of-the-
Month Club's appeals to a collective anxiety about the self that rendered readers unconfident about choosing their own books to read. Interestingly, the
Book-of-the-Month Club owes its success to its ability to identify the average
reader's emotional weaknesses. Joan Shelley Rubin explains that the club's
early advertisements "created a persona who sets out to choose books but
instead commits a series of self-betrayals. The shortcoming to which the
copy referred most explicitly was the failure to carry out one's intentions"
(1992, 382).

Following these readings I assigned a literacy autobiography. Students
were to draw on these readings to characterize the ways that their own reading
taste had affected their identities as writers and to explore how their identities
as writers had affected their reading taste. My goal was to get students thinking about motivations for reading and writing anchored not necessarily in self-

improvement but in symbolic and cultural forms of capital. Reading and writing, we've been taught since kindergarten, are noble pursuits, an indication of a curious mind and an enlightened self. Our literacy habits say something about who we are and about who we want others to think we are. Consider, for example, Kevin Parkinson's awareness of the ways that the messages he's been hearing all his life about "success" have affected the way he approaches literacy:

> I first thought of my position at campus. I am a student, and (more specifically) a social science education major. I thought, is there any connection between my major and the types of books I read "for fun?" I thought, has society put so much pressure on me that I have been preparing for my career since the early to middle parts of my high school education? I believe I read political books because I subconsciously feel a need to practice for the future. Our school is proud of its message: "gladly we learn and teach." Perhaps I am so consumed by such a message that my reality has become preparing for class . . . five years early. (2005, 1–2)

As Parkinson does here, other students reflected on not just what they read but *why* they read, not just what they write but *why* they write. In preparation for discussion of the cultural significance of Oprah Winfrey's book club, I wanted students to begin thinking about the place of literacy practices in their definitions of themselves as students in a university. As might be expected, those students who claimed to enjoy reading lowbrow materials did so defensively, and those students who claimed to enjoy reading more highbrow materials did so rather humbly.

Following the literacy autobiography assignment, we spent a couple weeks interrogating Oprah Winfrey's position as cultural literacy sponsor, drawing mainly on R. Mark Hall's *College English* essay, "The 'Oprahfication' of Literacy: Reading 'Oprah's Book Club'" (2003). Our earlier work with the history of the Book-of-the-Month Club provided us a vocabulary for discussing the appeals on which Oprah has been able to draw as she promotes literacy as a "means of individual and cultural advancement" (Hall 2003, 646). Oprah Winfrey's book club is an instantiation of what Susan Miller has called a "cultural privileging mechanism," one that designates "some rather than others as important writers/thinkers" (1991, 187). As such, the book club offered us a particularly salient object of study from which to understand the cultural politics of authorship in the late twentieth and early twenty-first centuries. As Hall suggests, Oprah works her magic on the show by establishing intimacy with her audience, thus forging a relationship with her viewers that allows her the "authority to select the right books for her viewers" (653). What happens, though, when the living authors do not want to be sponsored by Oprah? The case of Jonathan Franzen provided for us a case study of cultural sponsorship gone wrong, raising the question of who gets to decide how to categorize a work of fiction. In his essay for the *Boston Review*, cultural critic James Campbell (2002) provides a scathing commentary on the individual and cultural work accomplished by Oprah's book club:

> But her brand of talent and intelligence has nothing in common with that of Jonathan Franzen, or any other "high-art" writer. His employment compels him to see through Oprah Winfrey, who is "natural" but not real—to understand that her naturalness is an act, and to explain why so many people are content to accept it, and are made happy by her anointing: the banal boosterism that persuades them they are involved in something big by being on television. The shallowness of the medium is expertly moulded by a "natural" like Oprah into an experience that makes people feel better while they are taking part in it. It's like a pill. (2002)

Franzen's rejection of Oprah's seal functioned, students were eager to point out, to generate more publicity for his novel, *The Corrections*, which ultimately led to more sales. I took advantage of this very public controversy to initiate discussions about Oprah's decision, not long after the Franzen debacle, to discontinue the book club. Just over a year later, Oprah announced that her book club would return, this time focusing on "the classics."

The second writing assignment of the semester asked students to speculate on some of the reasons for Oprah's decision to return to her role as literacy sponsor, this time sponsoring primarily dead authors. As Jennifer Nebel explains in her essay, "Why Change a Good Thing?" following the Franzen debacle, Oprah "had to worry about authors and publishing companies who didn't want to have the giant 'O' marked on their book. She lived in fear now that authors didn't want to be linked with Oprah's book club because they believed their book was in a higher category than the other books in the collection" (2005, 2). Further, Melissa Sullivan suggests that "books we consider classics are pre-selected for Oprah" (2005b, 2); no longer do Oprah's choices involve risk. Her book club could now safely return to its original mission of sponsoring literacy as a means for cultural advancement.

Plagiarism Accusations as Punishment

None of the twenty-three students in the course knew who Ward Churchill was or had heard about the controversy surrounding his essay " 'Some People Push Back': On the Justice of Roosting Chickens" (2001). I assigned the essay before telling them much about the circumstances under which it was written or those under which it came to the mass media's attention. I wanted students to read the essay without being influenced by the one thing that nearly all coverage of the essay picked up on: Churchill's characterization of the victims of the 9/11 World Trade Center attack as "little Eichmanns." Once we'd devoted some class time to discussing the essay on its own merits, I told students that Churchill had written the essay on September 12, 2001, and it had only come to the media's attention in early 2005 after a group of students at Hamilton College in New York found it online and pointed to it as justification for protesting Churchill's speaking engagement at Hamilton.

Churchill's essay provided opportunity to investigate a number of significant issues with respect to the cultural politics of writing. First, we talked about the ethics of representing a text with only two words ("little Eichmanns") and about the responsibility of American citizens to read in full texts that provoke such controversy. Second, we discussed the politics of the circulation of writing: Why, after all, had nobody paid any attention to this essay prior to early 2005? We talked about Churchill's responsibilities as a professor representing the University of Colorado at Boulder, and this led to discussions about academic freedom and tenure. And of course, we talked about the content of the essay, the outrage barely contained in its pages, the possible motivations behind its writing.

In an effort to engage students in close reading and to encourage them to understand the effects of the media's reduction of Churchill's argument, I assigned a short paper addressed to an audience who had not read the essay. The students' job was to shift readers' attention from the "little Eichmanns" comparison to some other aspect of the essay that they believed better represented Churchill's argument. For instance, Allison Niesen argues convincingly that the essay is about Americans' blind patriotism and unwillingness (inability?) to question the basis for that patriotism. Her essay works by repeating forms of the chorus "We are taught . . . "

> We were taught to view the September 11th attacks as a terrorist attack, an idea supported by the media. The people have the issues of the 9/11 and the current war on Iraq mixed up, to the point where they cannot tell the difference. Most people could not tell who flew the planes into the Pentagon, the World Trade Center, and Pennsylvania beyond saying "the terrorists." We have been taught to support our president in whatever he does. (2005a, 2)

Nathan Bortolini argues that the focus on "little Eichmanns" functions to allow Americans "to dismiss Churchill as a nut and an anti-American" (2005, 2).

If the media's focus on "little Eichmanns" portrayed Churchill as an unpatriotic "nut," then the ensuing accusations of plagiarism further bolstered that characterization. Once students understood the significance of both the essay and the media's representations of it, we discussed the multiple effects of the public's association of Churchill not only with Nazi Germany but with plagiarism. Plagiarism is more than just a textual crime; it is a moral stain on the author. None of the students had any difficulty understanding that the accusations of plagiarism diverted the public's attention away from the actual content of "'Some People Push Back.'" In an in-class writing assignment, Elizabeth Harrington[2] wrote that "Churchill was accused of plagiarism and making up sources as a way to discredit his essay. Since it was a highly controversial piece, mainstream media had to attack the man behind the essay." Similarly,

Melissa Sullivan noted that "it's not even a real attack against the essay—it's an attack against Churchill himself." Plagiarism accusations accomplish the cultural work of distraction, of vilification, of justifying a collective refusal to engage in a complex, if controversial, essay. The parallels between this case and so many accusations of student plagiarism were too keen to go unmentioned in our discussions. Definitions of plagiarism cannot be confined to the textual. Plagiarism stands for more than textual theft; it becomes metonymic of the immoral, callous character of the person.

The Cultural Functions of Student Plagiarism

Following our work on Churchill, we read Rebecca Moore Howard's *Chronicle of Higher Education* essay, "Forget About Policing Plagiarism. Just *Teach*" (2001). My motivation for teaching this essay lay in Howard's ethos as a director of a writing program and in her careful distinction among different *types* of plagiarism. I wanted to challenge what I assumed were students' assumptions about teachers and plagiarism: that we're all out to catch them. In her indictment of teachers who do not revise their pedagogies, Howard offers a perspective that too many students have never thought of. For instance, Howard writes,

> We expect authentic writing from our students, yet we do not write authentic assignments for them. We beg students to cheat if we assign a major paper and then have no further involvement with the project until the students turn in their work. Assigning and grading a paper leaves out a crucial middle: working and talking with students while they draft those papers. You're too busy? Then what about dividing your students into small groups that you, a teaching assistant, or a tutor can meet with, or that can respond to their members' work before the papers reach you?

Before they reach our classes, students have for years been indoctrinated to believe that plagiarism is the ultimate academic crime (the punishment for which, in another essay, Howard characterizes as "the academic death penalty" [1995]). They have been persuaded that they are always the criminals, never the innocent. They likely haven't stopped to think about the ways that teachers' pedagogies contribute to the ease with which they might plagiarize—and if they have, they likely believe that we certainly haven't.

I wanted students to get a different perspective, but I also wanted them to see how Howard's argument was taken up by media more mainstream than *The Chronicle*. For this, I assigned Tucker Carlson's debut column for *Reader's Digest* called "That's Outrageous!" (2002). He titled this particular column "Reading, Cheating, and 'Rithmetic," substituting for "writing" in this familiar threesome the attention-grabbing, anger-producing "cheating." Understanding full well that his *Reader's Digest* readership wants to see cheaters punished and plagiarism eradicated from the schools, Carlson pokes fun at the notion that teachers might have any responsibility in preventing plagiarism. Referring to Howard's *Chronicle* piece, Carlson's treatment of her nuanced argument is dripping with sarcasm:

> As the director of the writing program at Syracuse University, Howard would, you'd think, abhor plagiarism above all academic sins. Sure, she feels obliged to say it's wrong to download someone else's work in toto. But in the end, she sounds more like a skillful apologist. In her telling, students plagiarize not because they are dishonest and lazy, but because they're tired ("many of them are working long hours at outside jobs") and hen-pecked by perfectionist teachers. (40–41)

The Carlson piece prompted intense discussions about the functions of plagiarism in the mainstream media, and we were able to draw on our previous work with Churchill to work through some of the reasons conservative pundits like Carlson vilify academic talk about plagiarism that does anything other than accuse and scapegoat.

The unit on plagiarism might be characterized as a failure because my goals for it were not entirely met. In a spirit of coinquiry, I wanted students to understand that plagiarism is not monolithic and that, while we may *teach* that plagiarism is a textual issue, it is much more. These perspectives I think they did understand. But in their written assignment for this unit, I wanted them to go beyond explanations for why students plagiarize to formulating an argument about what accusations of plagiarism *accomplish*. Given the readings I'd assigned and the arc of class discussions, I shouldn't be surprised that students wanted teachers to take more responsibility for students' plagiarism. Maybe I just didn't like being indicted again, this time by students.

In her essay for the unit, Melissa Sullivan suggested that, "until recent 'plagiarism cops' such as Turnitin.com have come along, teachers would turn the other cheek to plagiarism and cheating. Not only teachers, but society as a whole has looked the other way when corporate giants have cheated. 'The widespread scandals of the past year, touching so many of our blue-chip companies, have reinforced this cynical belief that good guys will finish last' (Hanson)" (2005b, 4). Sullivan's observation, together with Elizabeth Harrington's claim that "students want instant gratification," confirms much of what we already know about why students plagiarize. Many plagiarize because they have, in Harrington's "a warped view of how to get ahead" (Harrington 2005, 2).

Had we ended our discussions of the cultural politics of plagiarism here, students would likely have walked away from the course with a distorted understanding of the role teachers play in causing plagiarism. I had wanted students to understand plagiarism in more complex ways, but I fear that the work we did might have confirmed for them that they are, indeed, victims of poor pedagogy. By situating plagiarism among other forms of authorship, however, especially literary forgery, I believe that the course ultimately provoked students to think about how plagiarism functions in a culture that is obsessed with authenticity and originality.

Literary Forgery and the Desire to Believe

Following the unit on plagiarism, I introduced the unit on literary forgery by assigning Simon Worrall's *The Poet and the Murderer: A True Story of Literary Crime and the Art of Forgery* (2002). Here is an excerpt from a November 10, 2005, class discussion of that text:

Jamie Sanders: I found Hofmann's motives interesting. At first, I thought it was just about money. He wants to be considered the artist, and he wants to be considered smarter than everyone.

Kevin Parkinson: I really liked Mark Hofmann. Even when he was going down, I wanted him to do well.

Ashley DiFilipo: I thought he was a genius, but I changed my mind when he began killing people.

Allison Niesen: He's an actor in a play, and when he begins killing people, he goes to places you don't expect him to.

Worrall's book tells the long and complicated story of Mark Hofmann's literary and religious forgeries. Beginning with a mysterious narrative about an Emily Dickinson poem that the auction house Sotheby's sold for $21,000 to a librarian from Dickinson's hometown of Amherst, Massachusetts, the book traces Hofmann's forgeries by tracking his increasingly complex motivations. Having grown up in a Mormon household, Hofmann decided early that the entire religion was bogus, and he set to work devising a plan to prove to his family and to the world that the Mormon religion was based purely on belief and that he could manipulate those beliefs at his will. As Worrall puts it, Hofmann "understood how flimsy is the wall between reality and illusion and how willing we are, in our desire to believe something, to embrace an illusion" (xv). Hofmann's motivations intensify as he becomes more and more success-ful at convincing experts—those who should know better—that the documents he has forged in the basement of his home are authentic. When his motivations begin to shift from manipulating belief to staving off debtors, Hofmann devolves to murder. Because we learn in great detail the painstaking work that went into Hofmann's forgeries, we begin to believe that forgery *is* an art form, and we find ourselves rooting for this manipulative criminal because we, too, become disgusted at how willing people are to believe in the authenticity of a document despite evidence to the contrary.

Hofmann understood that people possessed a desire to believe in stories they wanted to be true, and he understood that his forgeries did not need to be forensically perfect because, as Worrall puts it, "experience had taught Hofmann that he didn't need to try and convince people of the authenticity of his documents. They would convince themselves" (2002, 180). *The Poet and the Murderer* provoked discussions about what makes a document *seem* authentic, about why it matters to us so much, and about the importance of understanding not just what an audience *knows* but understanding *what it is they want to believe*.

Mark Hofmann is the most prolific and most famous forger of the twentieth century. He is the subject of many books and countless articles, but attention to his work generally falls into the pattern we see in the excerpted class discussion above. Once we learn he is a murderer, we condemn him as a person. We do not stop to wonder what we might learn about *writing* and *rhetoric* by attending to his work. This is what I tried to do in my first-year writing course.

The final writing assignment of the semester asked students to "explore any aspect of forgery or duplication or fraud or counterfeit in order to analyze the factors that contribute to an audience's desire to believe in the value of the inauthentic." This was an assignment about not just analyzing audience but in working to understand an audience's motivations. In this way, then, the assignment had the potential to complicate simplistic understandings of audience analysis. For me, the assignment prompted concerns about what it means to claim to understand why students plagiarize. What is it that students understand about *what teachers want to believe about students*?

Placed between Churchill and Hofmann, then, the unit on plagiarism becomes more than a unit that distinguishes among different types of plagiarism, that rehearses the importance of considering intent when accusing a student, or that points to the role that the teacher plays in causing plagiarism. Placed between a unit exploring the consequences of political polemic and a unit interrogating the ways in which literary forgery depends on a willing audience, the unit on plagiarism comes to be about belief, desire, and consequences. Students come to understand plagiarism as a form of authorship driven by particular motivations and resulting in specific effects. Plagiarism becomes newsworthy because its deceptive quality always ends up making someone look like a fool. Plagiarism comes to be about relationships rather than about stealing someone else's words and passing them off as your own. In short, plagiarism becomes rhetorical; it becomes political.

Conclusion

In response to an end-of-the-semester questionnaire about the work of the course, students synthesized some of the ideas that we'd been working through in the course, particularly the connections between literary forgery and plagiarism. Ashley DiFilipo makes an important point when she writes that "belief isn't something that is just produced, it is learned. We learn early on that the books in the bookstore and in the library are very dependable and honorable. We learn that we can trust anything in them." (2005) Similarly, Jennifer Nebel writes that "We believe what we want to believe because we don't want to see the lies and deception that are going on all around us." We want to believe that people are generally good, that they are honest. Because we want to believe this, when we learn that a student has plagiarized, we're likely to believe, as Stacey Cukla puts it, "that the student is a horrible person" (2005). Finally, Melissa Sullivan provides a different perspective on the power of belief when she writes, "After plagiarizing I think students really start to believe that they wrote the piece they just copied" (2005a).

I do not want to claim that I have found the way to get at what students are *really* thinking about plagiarism. Coinvestigation is valuable to the first-year composition classroom not because we'll finally have the answers to our most pressing questions about why students plagiarize or how we can prevent them from doing so but because it provides an opportunity to engage in disciplined discussions of the politics of writing with people who have a stake in these discussions. Investigating plagiarism *with* first-year students in a way that situates *plagiarism* as a noun rather than a verb can highlight aspects of plagiarism as a form of authorship that a study of plagiarism alone cannot. For instance, one oft-cited cause for plagiarism is a student's running out of time to complete the assignment. When placed next to the excruciatingly time-consuming practice of literary forgery, this cause for plagiarism becomes something more than a way to denigrate students who are balancing too many obligations. It becomes instead an opportunity to open up discussions of the place of what Meghan O'Rourke labels "a concern for the just distribution of labor" (2007) or discussions of writers' motivations when they are no longer connected to getting the grade. Situating plagiarism as a form of authorship rather than a kind of crime (granting, of course, that forgery is both, which only makes it all that more interesting to students) allows us, as well, to begin to interrogate our own motivations for believing—for our *desire* to believe?—that plagiarism is purely textual.

Note

1. The syllabus for this course can be found at www.english.ilstu.edu/aerobil.

2. This student's and Jamie Sanders' names have been changed per their request. All other student names have not been changed, again, per their request.

References

Bortolini, Nate. 2005. The Justice of Churchill's Claim. Unpublished manuscript, Illinois State Univ., Normal, IL.

Bourdieu, Pierre. 1984. *Distinction: A Social Critique of the Judgement of Taste*. Trans. Richard Nice. Cambridge, MA: Harvard University Press.

Campbell, James. 2002. "When Popular Culture Meets Grand Literary Ambition: The Case of Jonathan Franzen." *Boston Review*.

Carlson, Tucker. 2002. "That's Outrageous! Reading, Cheating, 'Rithmetic." *Reader's Digest* (161). 963: 39–42.

Churchill, Ward. 2003. *Some People Push Back: On the Justice of Roosting Chickens.* Oakland, CA: AK Press.

Cukla, Stacey. 2005. End of Semester Questionnaire. Unpublished manuscript, Illinois State Univ., Normal, IL.

Deitch, Joseph. 1987. "Portrait of a Book Reviewer: Christopher Lehmann-Haupt." *Wilson Library Bulletin* (December): 61–63.

DiFilipo, Ashley. 2005. End of Semester Questionnaire. Unpublished manuscript, Illinois State Univ., Normal, IL.

George, Anne. 2001. "Critical Pedagogy: Dreaming of Democracy." In *A Guide to Composition Pedagogies*, edited by Gary Tate, Amy Rupiper, and Kurt Schick, 92-112. New York: Oxford University Press.

Hall, R. Mark. 2003. The " 'Oprahfication' of Literacy: Reading 'Oprah's Book Club.' " *College English* 65: 646–667.

Harrington, Elizabeth. 2005. Cheating and Plagiarism: What Every Teacher Needs to Realize. Unpublished manuscript, Illinois State Univ., Normal, IL.

Howard, Rebecca Moore. 1996. "Plagiarisms, Authorships, and the Academic Death Penalty." *College English* 57: 787–806.

———. 2001. "Forget About Policing Plagiarism. Just *Teach*." *The Chronicle of Higher Education*, B24.

Miller, Richard E. 2005. *Writing at the End of the World*. Pittsburgh, PA: University of Pittsburgh Press.

Miller, Susan. 1991. Textual Carnivals: The Politics of Composition, Carbondale: Southern Illinois University Press.

Nebel, Jennifer. 2005. Why Change a Good Thing? Unpublished manuscript, Illinois State Univ., Normal, IL.

Niesen, Allison. 2005a. Off the Path of Freedom. Unpublished manuscript, Illinois State Univ., Normal, IL.

———. 2005b. Plagiarism: The New Plague? Unpublished manuscript, Illinois State Univ., Normal, IL.

O'Rourke, Meghan. 2007. "The Copycat Syndrome: Plagiarists at Work." *Slate*. www .slate.com/toolbar.aspx?action=print&id=2157435.

Parkinson, Kevin. 2005. Hi! My Name Is: Political Satires. Unpublished manuscript, Illinois State Univ., Normal, IL.

Price, Margaret. 2002. "Beyond 'Gotcha!': Situating Plagiarism in Policy and Pedagogy." *College Composition and Communication* 54: 88–115.

Ritter, Kelly. 2005. "The Economics of Authorship: Online Paper Mills, Student Writers, and First-Year Composition." *College Composition and Communication* 56: 601–31.

———. 2006. "Buying in, Selling Short: A Pedagogy Against the Rhetoric of Online Paper Mills." *Pedagogy* 6: 25–51.

Roberts, Thomas J. 1990. "On Low Taste." In The Press of Ideas, edited by Julie Bates Dock, 360–371. New York: Bedford/St. Martin's.

Robillard, Amy. 2006. "Young Scholars Affecting Composition: A Challenge to Disciplinary Citation Practices." *College English* 68: 253–270.

Rubin, Joan Shelley. 1992. "Why Do You Disappoint Yourself? The Early History of the Book-of-the-Month Club." In The Press of Ideas, edited by Julie Bates Dock, 377–388. New York: Bedford/St. Martin's.

Shor, Ira. 1997. *When Students Have Power.* Chicago: University of Chicago Press.

Spigelman, Candace. 2000. *Across Property Lines: Textual Ownership in Writing Groups.* Carbondale: Southern Illinois University Press.

Sullivan, Melissa. 2005a. Who's Line Is It Really Anyway? Unpublished manuscript, Illinois State Univ., Normal, IL.

———. 2005b. Why Did She Do It? Delving into America's Biggest Club. Unpublished manuscript, Illinois State Univ., Normal, IL.

Trimbur, John. 2003. "Changing the Question: Should Writing be Studied?" *Composition Studies* 31: 15–24.

Worrall, Simon. 2002. *The Poet and the Murderer: A True Story of Literary Crime and the Art of Forgery.* New York: Plume.

3

Time Is Not on Our Side

Plagiarism and Workload in the Community College

Kami Day

Johnson County Community College

I am on the English faculty of a large, well-endowed, highly reputed community college located in one of the wealthiest counties in Kansas, and all members of our English department teach composition courses. A favorite topic of conversation among us concerns the burden of grading under which we labor; but at my institution, we are fortunate in that the class load for composition instructors is four rather than five per semester.[1] In contrast, faculty at many other community colleges, including writing instructors, are expected to teach five, and sometimes more, sections per semester. A study of North Carolina Community Colleges in 1999 revealed that

- The average workload for full time faculty at those colleges is 15 credit hours per week, which usually translates to five classes (depending on the discipline).
- Full-time faculty are also expected to schedule five office hours per week on average.
- Some instructors have five different preparations per week, but the average number of preparations is three. (North Carolina Community College System 2000)

These data are consistent with most community colleges, and a conversation with any community college faculty member will confirm that nothing has changed in the last nine years. In fact, I know of at least one college at which the administration is considering requiring full-time faculty to teach seven sections of composition per week. W. Norton Grubb and Associates in *Honored but Invisible* assert that "the dark side of being a teaching institution is that

43

faculty have to teach much more—an average of sixteen classroom hours a week, 50 percent more than faculty in state colleges and more than twice that of faculty in research universities" (1999, 9). And, of course, part-time instructors often teach a course or two at each of several different institutions.

But faculty are not the only ones who do not have enough time; our students' lives are full and complex, and they often have more responsibilities outside school than do their counterparts at four-year institutions. More community college students support themselves and their families, and they often do not have enough hours in the day to study, eat well, and get enough sleep. A study published in 2002 by the Community College Survey of Student Engagement reveals that "[t]hirty-two percent of community college students work more than 30 hours per week at jobs, 80 percent do not participate in any extracurricular activities, and 21 percent have children living at home . . . [and] 56 percent [do] not receive any help from parents," according to Jamilah Evelyn in an article in the *Chronicle of Higher Education* (2002). My students' testimonials confirm these figures. In fact, I know more than 32 percent of my students work more than thirty hours per week.

Community college workload is heavy partly because we teach so many sections, but the challenge is compounded for composition faculty because one of the most important elements of the community college mission is to serve underprepared students (Grubb and Associates 1999; Kozeracki 2002; Oudenhoven 2002). And Grubb and Associates point out that "[t]he students who most need second-chance institutions are, by definition, less academically prepared than other post-secondary students, forcing instructors to find new ways to teach and requiring more . . . developmental education" (7). Because many of our students are unprepared, we English faculty start more or less from scratch teaching them to find and use outside texts, a process that involves reading several drafts of every paper and often meeting one-to-one with students. Of course, our work includes a great deal of instruction about using texts ethically, and the term *plagiarism* is typically part of that instruction at some point. At one end of the spectrum, some instructors hit it hard, focusing on detection and punishment, while at the other end, some take a more positive tack, focusing on academic honesty. Across the board, though, when community college teachers think about teaching source citation, they think often about teaching students not to plagiarize or about what the consequences should be for plagiarism, partly because they do not have much time to spend learning about and problematizing plagiarism and are not aware of its complexities and gatekeeping functions. Our students' workload is an important component of the plagiarism equation as well because they are sometimes accused of plagiarism when they did not intend to use sources unethically. In this chapter, I will explore the reasons for this state of affairs and its consequences, basing my conclusions partly on a survey I conducted of the faculty at my institution. Using Basil Bernstein's concept of the "pedagogical device" (2000, 25), which he defines as "a symbolic regulator of consciousness" (37), and his distinction between what we teach (which he calls *the relayed*) and how we teach it (which he calls the *relay*), I will propose that community college faculty have a responsibility to make themselves more aware of the complexities of the concept of plagiarism and that they must take a stronger role in promoting pedagogical approaches that help students learn ethical citation and documentation.

Pedagogizing Plagiarism

Some community college instructors might argue that their teaching load makes keeping up with the latest educational practices and theories in the field of composition impossible; they do not have time to read the work of authorship scholars who are asking faculty, students, and even the public to reexamine their cherished beliefs about plagiarism. But because we community college faculty typically spend so much more time in the classroom than our four-year institution counterparts, we should make it our business to be informed about how people learn and why we instructors do what we do. Examining our own perhaps limited definitions of plagiarism, and becoming aware of its gatekeeping role, can only enrich our knowledge of students' needs and our ability to meet those needs skillfully and compassionately. I think Bernstein's concept of the "pedagogic device" applies here. In *Pedagogy, Symbolic Control and Identity* (2000), Bernstein explains the "rules" of the pedagogic device. First, "distributive rules" have to do with "creat[ing] new knowledge" (115); they "distribute forms of consciousness through distributing different forms of knowledge" (28), and "mark and distribute who may transmit what to whom and under what conditions" (31). Those responsible for "distributive rules" are experts in "specialized fields of production (usually higher agencies of education)" (115). Second, "recontexualizing rules regulate the formation of specific pedagogic discourse" (28). Those responsible for recontextualizing are "trainers of teachers, writers of textbooks, curricular guides . . . media," and the like (114). Third, "evaluative rules regulate pedagogic practice at the classroom level, for they define the standards which must be reached." These rules "act selectively on contents, the form of transmission and their distribution to different groups of pupils in different contexts" (115). With these rules in mind, Bernstein theorizes that the discourse of the teaching of a discipline varies greatly from the discourse of that discipline; he makes a "distinction between *a relay* and *the relayed*" [italics his] (25).

For example, the discourse of history (*the relayed*) is quite different from the discourse of the teaching of history (*a relay*). A history professor has attended graduate school and earned a master's degree and perhaps a Ph.D. in history. She has absorbed knowledge created by historians, and she has added to that knowledge, so she is qualified to transmit that knowledge as an expert in Civil War history, or environmental history, or one of a number of other specialties. This expertise in history is what will be *the relayed*. She must also make decisions about how to *relay* her expertise to her students. In other words, historians create knowledge ("the distributive rules"), creating the "original discourse" that then "passes through ideological screens as it becomes its new form, pedagogic discourse" ("the recontextualizing rules"), and this discourse is constrained by the standards agreed on by whomever makes such decisions ("the evaluative rules"). If examined, pedagogic discourse reveals the results of decisions about whom we'll teach and whom we won't; what we'll transmit; cultural, institutional, and faculty values, and so on.[2] Usually, academics do not acknowledge the differences between the discourse of "the field of production," or discourse of the discipline, and "pedagogic discourse" (Bernstein 2000, 115), or discourse of teaching. If we do, we typically do not pay enough attention to the discourse of teaching. (Years ago, in a graduate literary theory course, when I asked, "So how will this apply to our teaching of literature?" the professor held up two crossed fingers to ward off the evil of sullying theory with classroom practice!)

However, in the case of plagiarism, the opposite is true—community college teachers (although I would not say *only* community college teachers) have pedagogized plagiarism, or translated the discourse of academic honesty and source citation into a discourse of teaching, without knowing very much about the subject. Interestingly, Amy E. Robillard, in her discussion about citing student work in scholarly publications, creates a parallel to this situation. She points out that we have used student work to inform our research about composition pedagogy—*the how*—without paying enough attention to the work created as a result of that pedagogy—*the what* (2006, 266). Likewise, a great deal of attention is devoted to the discourse of teaching students *how* to avoid plagiarism (*a relay*), but faculty spend minimal time—and lack of time because of a heavy workload is certainly a factor here—thinking and talking about *what* plagiarism is (*the relayed*). In fact, most us have little knowledge of the "discipline" of plagiarism—its definitions and theories—even though most of us must teach our students about it. Granted, the concept of plagiarism is not a discipline of its own, but the amount of attention we in the academy are devoting to the issues surrounding it warrants some careful thought beyond who is guilty and what we can do about the perceived problem.

A Survey of Faculty at One Community College

I encountered Bernstein's work a few years ago when I was in the process of analyzing a survey I had conducted of faculty at my institution concerning their attitudes about plagiarism.[3] Although a great deal of scholarship exists concerning academic dishonesty (of which plagiarism is a part) at four-year institutions, research on this issue in community colleges is scarce, and most of the existing studies involve only one institution each and were done before so much information was accessible to students online.[4] I believed a study of the faculty at my institution might add important data to the research; and, of course, every institution is a bit different. One of the resources that informed my work, a dissertation written by Dr. Jonathan Burke (1997), included a survey he distributed among DeKalb College (a community college) faculty. After receiving permission to adapt his survey for my study, and with the help of Institutional Research, I distributed a questionnaire to 1,202 full-time and adjunct faculty; 101 faculty returned the questionnaire.[5]

The survey results were in some ways a pleasant surprise; the faculty who responded (most of whom ask students to write from texts) did not complain about their workload but expressed the belief that they have a responsibility to instruct students in how to properly cite texts. Many, in fact, spend class time on such deliberate instruction; what they were saying indirectly was that a good number of them, in spite of a heavy workload, take time to teach students how to document correctly and then often increase their workload by allowing students who do not "get it" right away to correct and revise until they can demonstrate some expertise with this particular academic convention. The faculty did not mention workload specifically, but for several reasons I came to the conclusion that workload and time issues are significant for community college teachers. For one thing, a small percentage of the faculty returned the survey, an indication that a small percentage of community college teachers assign writing as part of their curriculum (and, perhaps, that few have time to fill out a survey!). As you might expect, a great deal of the instruction in source citation takes place in composition classrooms; teachers in other disciplines are expected to consider a long list of objectives and competencies as they plan their curricula for the five sections most of them teach each semester, so their workload precludes them from devoting class time to instruction in correct citation or making time to read several drafts of papers. Furthermore, answers to survey questions reflected an unfamiliarity with the most current scholarship on plagiarism, perhaps an indication that they lack the time to keep up with the scholarship.

Time, Intent, and the Community College Instructor

Of special interest to me were the responding faculty's definitions of plagiarism. Naturally, these definitions differed, but nearly all were a variation of "students using someone else's material without acknowledging the source." Many respondents added that plagiarism involves students using another's words as if those words were the students' own, and several specified that plagiarism involves such errors as "ineffective summary or paraphrase," "failure to place quotation marks around quoted material," or "more than a three word strand, without being quoted." In *Issues and Perspectives on Academic Integrity*, Donald Gehring and Gary Pavela (1994) take the definition further, defining plagiarism as "[i]ntentionally or knowingly representing the words of another as one's own in any academic exercise," which is consistent with Rebecca Moore Howard's admonition that we must find out "whether the writer intended to plagiarize" (1999, 163). However, many definitions of *plagiarism* say nothing about intent, and only four faculty in my study used the word "intent" or "purposefully" explicitly in their answers. The word *copy* seems to connote intent, and it appeared in many responses, such as "copying without acknowledging the source" or "copy verbatim and not using quotation marks when borrowing from another source." However, a student might copy a phrase or section of a text but not intend to plagiarize, and many of the respondents seemed to be affirming such lack of intent, although they did not make that distinction clear. If faculty are unclear about whether plagiarism involves intent or, worse, believe that students should be punished whether they intended to plagiarize, they have not taken the time to familiarize themselves with current scholarship in this area.

I cannot speak for faculty at all two-year institutions, but I believe that at my college we need to talk as much about what instances of source misuse actually are and what they mean—about what Bernstein calls *the relayed*—as we do about how to detect and deal with them—Bernstein's *relay*. The "lore" (to use Stephen North's term, 1987) among faculty that characterizes student plagiarism, and tips about what to do when faced with academic dishonesty or ignorance, is thriving. I agree with Sylvia A. Holladay that, in community colleges, "curriculum and instruction have been shaped, not by past practices or theoretical models, but by the students' needs" (1996, 31), and while I believe the students' needs should be the most powerful impetus for change, I also believe those changes should be supported by theory. True, as Howard maintains in *Standing in the Shadows of Giants*, plagiarism has undergone very little theorization in the academy. Scholars have avoided it because it is, at the very least, an unpleasant reality in academia, and, at the very worst, a threat to "not only civilization in general, but the academy in particular" (1999, 24). It is often relegated to discussions of what is wrong with students, techniques for prevention, and punishments for the guilty. However, a few scholars like Howard are theorizing plagiarism, showing that *plagiarism* is not necessarily a monolithic term and, perhaps more importantly, how discovering and punishing plagiarism, at least in the United States, is one of the guards at the gates of Western academic culture that dominates most institutions in this country.

Time, Intent, and the Community College Student

If faculty are aware of current scholarship on plagiarism, they know that consideration of the roles of time and intent is especially important at community colleges not only because of faculty workload but also because community college students commonly carry heavy workloads themselves. For one thing, they are often unprepared to deal with the rigors of academic writing; their abilities as writers occupy the spectrum from those who struggle to compose a coherent sentence to those who write fluently in several genres (and even in several languages). This range in ability is especially significant; in my classes, at least one-fourth of the students typically have never written a research paper, and one-half have not worked with MLA style (the style on which we focus in composition classes here) in the research they have written. Sometimes students are still in high school and have not yet taken a class in which they write from sources, and sometimes returning students can't remember writing from sources or remember doing such writing but can't remember using any particular style of documentation. Regardless of their experiences, most have little confidence in their ability to write from texts, and some are just plain terrified.

Because of the community college mission to provide opportunities even for underprepared students, it is more likely that incoming freshmen at four-year institutions are better positioned for rigorous academic work than are their community college counterparts. I would not go as far as Sylvia A. Holladay does when she says community college students "are locked in chaotic, crisis-driven lives [and] feel impotent when they enter the two-year college" (1996, 30), but I know that because of the demands of jobs and families (as I mentioned earlier in this essay), some students who are ordinarily honest and hardworking just run out of time and occasionally use someone else's work when they do not have time to complete their own. I am not excusing what they do, but I'll admit I was horrified to learn of Barton County Community College's policy, which attaches a grade of XF to a student's transcript if they have been "caught cheating or plagiarizing" (Burnett 2002). When I asked a Barton County Community College faculty member about this policy, she told me that assignment of the XF grade is at the instructor's discretion; no special process is outlined for assigning such a stigmatic grade. I can imagine that, in some cases, one desperate attempt to keep up resulted in a stain that will follow a student throughout her or his academic career. In January 2006, I contacted an administrator at Barton to learn what the effect of implementing the XF grade has been. In an email, she told me the policy became permanent in 2003–2004 after much discussion. In the years since, a number of XF grades have been assigned, but they are given sparingly, reflecting fraud and a rather recalcitrant student.[6] One of the respondents in my study worried that such a grade on a transcript might "mar the student for life." The respondent added, "I know I am certainly a different person now than I was at 18."

Furthermore, the increasing diversity of the student population at my institution contributes to the importance of considering time and intent. In his study of faculty perceptions of academic dishonesty, Burke notes that community college students are more "diverse than their university counterparts" (1997, 132), and I agree with him, unless the universities have open admissions policies. My students range in age from 16 to 50. Our school offers an American Sign Language interpreter program, so having a deaf student,[7] or a student with a hearing impairment, in class is common. Our accessibility and special programs are well known, so a class often includes students with disabilities. And as I said earlier, our students can be found anywhere on the spectrum in terms of preparation and ability. Furthermore, our population of English language learners (ELL) is growing as it is at most community colleges, and the question of intent may be even more important to consider where students who are learning English are concerned. Even though Kansas is not renowned for its ethnic diversity, the number of classes we offer in our English for Academic Purposes program has exploded in the last two years, and in recent semesters, my classes have included students from Azerbaijan, Somalia, Kenya, Sweden, Nigeria, Mexico, Japan, Korea, China, Iran, and Indonesia—and this is a partial list. These students have an even heavier workload than native English speakers. Many have jobs, and most are still learning English; even with a great deal of institutional support, writing a two-page essay can turn into hours of work for these students.

Several instructors who responded to my survey commented on the challenges of working with students who are learning English, and one explained that "with our diverse student population, I feel it is important to recognize that not all cultures/subgroups share our valuation of academic integrity. For some, any idea out there is open for using." My own experience confirms this concept: in a recent semester, one of my Composition I students was a woman who had been a surgeon in Russia. She was essentially beginning her education all over again so she could eventually practice medicine in the United States, and she—an excellent writer and quick learner—had a great deal of difficulty grasping the concept of attributing sources. She told me that when she wrote papers in Russia, using information from texts without acknowledging the source was acceptable. I would never have questioned the integrity of this student; such an accusation would make her a criminal, and her intentions were always honorable.

So, our definitions of plagiarism must be complicated by our awareness of our students' lives, our awareness that our students are, as Howard (1999) maintains, "not author-functions; these are human beings sitting in one's class, one's office. Their persons, therefore, must be integral to the definition of their plagiarism." This awareness is particularly important for community college teachers. Did a student download a paper from the Internet because her boss required her to close the store every night for a week? Or was a student who does not own a computer prevented from coming to the school's computer lab because of the need to stay home with a sick child? Did a student who works full time and carries a full load of courses just take too much on? Did an ELL student, after spending hours on a paper and producing only half of the required length, borrow a friend's paper out of desperation? For Howard, and for me, determining whether a student has plagiarized "*must* involve both reader and writer; and it must involve context" (1999, 164). So, I try to determine intent and context, even in cases of outright fraud, and meanwhile, with Howard, I define clumsy or incorrect paraphrasing and quoting as "patchwriting," not plagiarism. For those of us who acknowledge that intent must be considered, the word *plagiarism* connotes criminality, and we prefer not to criminalize students who are learning a discourse so unfamiliar to most of them. This faculty comment from my survey sums up the importance of considering intent:

> Some students are under-prepared to deal with certain academic rigors, such as knowing and using with confidence a writing style. Often a mistake is the best learning experience. The key is recognizing intentional and unintentional behavior. . . . instructors are on the front line for teaching the value of original work and giving credit for the work of others.

Moreover, not only does the situation vary from student to student, but an examination of scholarship in various fields reveals diverse concepts of ownership of ideas. Recently, a colleague sent me an article on plagiarism written by a sociology professor, Earl Babbie (1998). The article gives very clear examples of both plagiarized and correctly acknowledged passages, and in one of the paraphrases deemed correct by Babbie were several unique phrases from the original that he had not included in quotation marks. I would have instructed my students to quote such unique words and phrases, but when I mentioned this to my sociologist colleague, she explained to me that the words in question are common in the field of sociology and would not need to be quoted. Students who learn the conventions of source acknowledgement in one field might be accused of plagiarism if they apply those same standards to writing in another field.

It is imperative that instructors take the time to make themselves aware of the scholarship that examines the culturally created gaps between Western and non-Western concepts of academic honesty, between ideas of ownership, and even between what should be cited and what shouldn't. These gaps are what Bernstein might call "potential discursive gap[s]," spaces in which meanings (such as what academic honesty means in various cultures) "have an indirect relation to a specific material base [such as conventions about acknowledging source texts]." He sees such a gap as "a site for alternative possibilities. . . . the site for the unthinkable, the site of the impossible, and this site can clearly be both beneficial and dangerous at the same time. . . . the meeting point of order and disorder" (2000, 30). I admit to occasionally questioning students because they have not cited information in a paper, but conversations with these students often reveal their expertise about some aspects of their projects. Such scenarios challenge long-held views that, for instance, students should not include their own stories as evidence or that published scholars are the only reliable sources. These gaps force us to revise our notions of what counts as scholarship and knowledge, who owns knowledge, and what knowledge gets shared. Bernstein reminds us that those in power will work "to regulate the potential of this gap in [their] own interest" (30), but it is the space in which we can, with our students, examine the ideologies behind the Western pedagogical discourse about plagiarism.

The Role of Community Colleges in Transmitting Values

Because teaching students to avoid plagiarism ostensibly involves teaching them to be honest (rather than teaching them to avoid being caught), one section of my survey explored faculty beliefs about whether or not they teach values, and about 70 percent responded that they do have a primary role in teaching students values, a number consistent with Burke's findings (1997, 74). Burke found it significant that the attitude of the faculty at his institution was that "they have an important role to play in values education" (121), and he is supported by Frank Madden's assertion that "our [community college teachers] multi-faceted role is defined by the needs of our students and a vision of ourselves as transformative educators" (quoted in Holmsten 2002, 432). However, two of the faculty in my survey tempered their responses to the question about teaching values. One teacher acknowledged that such a question is "hard to answer" and that "we teach values when we teach content." Bernstein (2000) also maintains that there is no "distinction between . . . the transmission of skills and the transmission of values." He does, though, differentiate between "*regulative discourse*," the "moral discourse which creates order, relations, and identity," and "*instructional discourse* . . . a discourse of skills of various kinds and their relations to each other" that is dominated by "*regulative discourse*" (italics his) (31–32).

The "instructional discourse" that includes plagiarism is all about instruction in source use and citation. And the "regulative discourse" about plagiarism I have been discussing in this chapter dictates definitions of source misuse, characterizing all plagiarism as cheating and all plagiarizers as criminals and valorizing Western notions of source use and appropriation. These two discourses constitute "pedagogic discourse," which takes the discourse of authorship (*the relayed*) "from its original site of effectiveness and mov[es] it to a pedagogic site" (Bernstein 2000, 32), where it becomes *the relay*. In the process, "a gap . . . is created . . . a space in which ideology can play" (32). In accordance with the "distributive," "recontextualizing," and "evaluative rules" (114), specialists decide what knowledge will be dispensed, that knowledge passes through "ideological screens as it becomes its new form, pedagogic discourse," and "standards" are agreed on that govern classroom practice (115). In the case of source citation, ideology has often led us to be selective in how we define *plagiarism* and what we share with students. A glance at any composition textbook reveals that we do not share with students what plagiarism scholarship has taught us; we throw plagiarism at them uncritically, denying them the opportunity to problematize a concept that is often used to deny them membership in the elite academic club.

But even as we Western academicians cast a critical eye on the expectation that we support the Western regulative discourse about plagiarism, we may be able to agree that the value of honesty seems to qualify as one of Kant's categorical imperatives (although notions of what is honest and what is not certainly do vary across cultures). In keeping with their belief that teaching values is part of their responsibility, 60 percent of the faculty in my study felt they must take primary responsibility for teaching students about using sources ethically, even if giving students the opportunity to redo work means the instructor doubles or triples his or her load of paper reading. While a few of the respondents were sympathetic to the view that "students should know what plagiarism is before entering college," I believe most would nod their heads in agreement with another instructor's view: "This is a community college—it is our responsibility as instructors to teach proper documentation guidelines." In addition to providing chances for revision, over half the faculty in my survey reported that they provide direct instruction in documenting and citing sources. Admittedly, most of those were from liberal arts (which includes the English department), but 38 percent of business and technology and 26 percent of science, health care, and mathematics faculty who responded to my survey teach students how to cite and document sources. Faculty in such disciplines in universities are not typically spending time teaching these concepts and skills. Many respondents to my survey stressed that instructors are the ones who know the students, set the expectations and the "intellectual climate," and have the expertise. A journalism teacher summed it up with, "We're the teachers. We know the students. They are here to learn from us. We set the example. We set the standards in our classes."

We community college teachers are in a unique position to create an atmosphere in which honesty and trust are discussed and valued because of our small classes and the possibilities for one-to-one relationships with our students. We have the opportunity to create teaching moments when plagiarism (however we define it) occurs, possibly influencing a student enough that he or she never succumbs again to the temptation to plagiarize. And if there was no intent to cheat, creating such a teaching moment is even more important. As Sheila Trice Bell (executive director of the Washington, D.C.–based National Association of College and University Attorneys) says, academic integrity "is fundamental to the relationship between student and teacher. There's a core of trust that needs to exist there for the integrity of the educational process" (Roach 1998). Such trust is easier to establish when instructors know students as people, a relationship that is certainly possible between instructor and student at any institution but seems to be more common at community colleges. Many of my students have told me they transferred to our institution from larger state schools to increase the chances that their classes would be small and that their professors would be more accessible. McCabe and Trevino (1996) observe that "higher education has become more of a business," making "the college experience less personal for many students" and making "students more cynical about cheating." Of course, this can be true even for community colleges, especially because most such schools are commuter campuses and students scatter to their various jobs and lives as soon as class is over. But even two-year college students can feel "part of a campus

community" if teachers create a space in their classrooms where an atmosphere of trust is nurtured, where students can come to know and support each
other, and where teachers take an interest in their students as individual human
beings. In such a scenario, academic integrity is more likely to be "'socially
unacceptable'" and students are less likely to "'violate the trust' placed in
them by the faculty" (1996, 6). As Bell laments, "'[that trust] is broken when a
student turns in work that is not his or her own'" (Roach).

Furthermore, if we expect our students to be honest, chances are good
that they will be, and Dowd stresses the importance of "recogniz[ing] students as honest until proved otherwise" (1992, 13). In fact, according to
David and Kovach (cited in Dowd 1992, 5), "negative faculty expectations
could actually cause students to cheat." So perhaps the challenge is not to
spend so much time thinking about catching the thief but rather to focus on
showing students what is honest and what is not according to Western values
because they may not know when it comes to citing sources and to perhaps
spend some time interrogating those values. Donald L. McCabe and Linda
Klebe Trevino, in their 1993 study of state university students, found that
about 75 percent of the students viewed plagiarism as "serious cheating"
(1996, 5), but that means that about 25 percent did not. Furthermore, students
often "perceive cheating quite dif-ferently from their instructors." For example, some professors forbid collaboration on writing assignments, but when
professors "fail to delineate their expectations" about collaboration, most students do not think it is serious cheating, and 25 percent do not think of collaboration as "cheating at all" (5). (Note: To the students' credit, they know they
learn more by working together).

I was alarmed a few years ago when a listserv posting recommended setting aside a class period early in the semester in which the students first visual-
ize being caught plagiarizing and suffering the consequences (such as being
expelled from school) and then are read a handout that outlines the penalties of
plagiarism. It seems to me that this approach jumps right to teaching students
not to plagiarize before spending time exploring what plagiarism is; it also
assumes student dishonesty, sets up the teacher as police officer and students as
potential criminals, and uses precious time that could be more positively and
productively spent. A more gentle and integrated approach—making sure
students understand what plagiarism is and isn't and dealing with errors in documentation as they arise—makes sense in terms of establishing an atmosphere
of trust.

Even better, taking time to help students understand the value of academic
honesty does more to create an atmosphere of trust than does laying out the
punishments for crimes not yet committed. Is it possible that we instructors can
create a "regulative discourse" about plagiarism that brings to the forefront
respect, honor, and appreciation? Rather than warning students about pilfering
someone else's words, why not help them think of using another author's ideas
as collaboration with that author? Why not help them see that the purpose of

citation is not to avoid getting caught but rather, as Robillard proposes, "engender[ing] relationships among citing author(s) and cited author(s)" (2006, 266). Robillard is offering reasons that scholars should cite student work, but if we can help students imagine a respectful relationship with the authors whose work informs theirs, citing those authors might come to feel less like a tedious convention of academic writing and more like the showing of appreciation for a gift. Rather than ranting about cheating, why not speak of honoring authors whose work students are using to enrich their own? As James Rhem says in an issue of *The National Teaching and Learning Forum*, "[we] should remember that knowledge of the law aims as squarely at defining the good as at defining its opposite" (2002, 3). If we make the decision to trust our students until we have reason not to trust them, and if we approach the issue by talking about academic honesty rather than beginning with warnings about the consequences of plagiarism, we can create a community of learners in which students begin to think of themselves as scholars. It's true that many of our students in community college writing classes may never write another research paper, but they can take with them what they have learned about how other ideas and positions can enrich their own, about the importance of acknowledging the source of those ideas and positions, and about integrity in general.

Textbooks, Time, and *the Relayed*

Community college faculty have a unique opportunity to lead the call for changes in pedagogical approaches to ethical use of sources. For one thing, because community colleges buy and sell textbooks in very large numbers, we are in a unique position to effect changes in how textbooks approach writing from sources. As a case study, our department is made up of 113 full-time and adjunct faculty, and typically we offer about eighty sections of Composition I a semester, which translates to about 2,000 textbooks. We have a choice of three textbooks for Composition I, so unlike faculty at most four-year institutions, individual faculty members are constrained in their choices. Because we order texts in such large numbers, publishers are anxious to woo us as clients. If I am on a textbook selection committee, I can expect to meet a few times each with representatives from three or four publishers, and the whole department can expect to be treated to bagels or pizza by at least one or two of them. Moreover, now publishers revise textbooks at least every three years, sometimes every two, so we must "roll over" the textbook to the new edition when it comes out (or choose another text), and our students must buy new rather than used books. In addition to the textbook, most of our faculty require students to purchase a handbook—we have a choice of one—so the order for that book can be another very lucrative one for a publisher. This scenario is repeated over and over at community colleges all across the country.

Departmental adoptions of textbooks lead to a blanket approach that saturates the curriculum and influences teaching practices across the department.

Often, because of the large number of adjunct faculty, and because English faculty often bring specialties in literature rather than composition, teachers are learning composition, including information about source citation, from the textbook along with their students. This scenario can be especially insidious because most textbooks take an uncritical approach to plagiarism; we are essentially paying a great deal of money for Bernstein's "regulative discourse" (2000, 32). Ideally, of course, institutions would not be exploiting adjunct faculty, and all teachers of writing would be compositionists. The reality is that if overworked instructors with little composition background must rely on the textbooks they use to teach them about composition, that information must reflect current theory about text use and misuse, and community colleges must take a critical look at what textbooks tell us we must teach. We must pay attention to the "recontextualizing" (114) of plagiarism. We must be aware that, as Bernstein insists, "the pedagogic device become[s] a site for appropriation, conflict, and control" (42), a "symbolic ruler of consciousness" (36). In fact, he says that "any specific pedagogic practice is there for one purpose: to transmit criteria" (28). We are transmitting criteria for judging what is honest and what is not, based on Western values, but we do not often unpack, or give our students the opportunity to unpack, where those values and criteria came from and what those values and criteria mean. In our frequent conversations with textbook representatives, we could include questions about the ways plagiarism is addressed in the textbooks they are selling. In the past, our faculty have asked, for instance, for more current readings in texts, and we have seen these revisions incorporated into subsequent editions. Recently, as a member of a textbook selection committee, and disappointed to find that not one textbook under consideration encouraged students to unpack the concept of plagiarism, I took every opportunity to talk with book representatives about the gaps I saw in their texts' discussions of plagiarism. Because textbook adoptions guarantee a great deal of money for publishers, community colleges have the power to "regulate the potential of [these] gap[s] in [their] own interest, because the gaps [themselves] ha[ve] the possibility of an alternative order . . . an alternative power relation" (Bernstein, 30). We could even refuse to adopt textbooks that do not offer a fuller and more critical discussion of source use and misuse, that do not create a "regulative discourse" involving the notions of respect and appreciation for, and collaboration with, sources. If community college English departments realized their potential influence on a multimillion-dollar business that depends on mass textbook adoption, they might insist on a more informed, critical approach to plagiarism and actually get what they ask for.

Finding More Time for *the Relay*

Because of heavy workloads, one of the challenges that community college faculty face is finding the time to problematize plagiarism and create an atmosphere of trust in which students focus less on not getting caught and more on ethically acknowledging outside sources that enrich their own work. Several of my colleagues and I have conducted workshops about source citation, but they are poorly attended even though faculty have asked for them—instructors often just do not have time for one more thing in their schedule. And creating trusting relationships among students and faculty takes class time many teachers do not feel they can spare. I usually set aside the first two or three class periods as time for my students and me to learn each other's names, to get acquainted, to find commonalties among ourselves, and to begin sharing writing and practicing working together. Instructors who teach courses that involve a long list of skills or concepts students must master and then demonstrate on a test may feel the pressure to dive right into the course material rather than allowing time to build that "core of trust" that Bell insists is essential (Roach 1998).

One of the simplest solutions to the issue of *lack* of time is to give instructors *more* time by reducing their course load. I know that if I were expected to teach five composition classes a semester (as most community college instructors are), my teaching would have to change: Students would be invited to revise, but I would not assign as much writing, thereby reducing their opportunities for practice, and the time I would be able to spend in one-to-one conferencing would certainly be reduced. Furthermore, I would have much less time to do the reading and writing I believe necessary to keep abreast of scholarship in my field. As far as other disciplines are concerned, even if faculty do assign writing from sources, they do not have time to familiarize themselves with all the complexities of that task, nor do they have time to read several drafts of papers when they have a great deal of content to cover and when they teach at least five sections per semester. Students who write papers in these courses are typically given an assignment and warned about plagiarism; each paper earns a terminal grade, so opportunities to learn from their mistakes are nonexistent. If, in an ideal world, the course load were reduced for faculty in such disciplines as the sciences, for instance, those faculty would have the time necessary to invite students to revise, thereby giving them opportunity to further practice and understand the reasons for, and the conventions of, writing research in that particular discipline. As Michele Eodice and Cindy Pierard point out in *The National Teaching and Learning Forum,* "Studies have shown that students who engage in a process—starting early, developing a timeline . . . getting feedback . . . and writing drafts—will be less likely to fall into the trap of eleventh-hour copy and paste or digital plagiarism" (2002, 5). Community college students, many of whom are likely to be unfamiliar with the process of doing research, need this kind of time.

The best scenario for community colleges (or any school, for that matter) is to connect a composition course with a "content" course in a learning community. Of course, instructors in a learning community must be willing initially to carve out time to develop their course, to meet often once the course begins to assess its effectiveness, and to meet at the conclusion of the course to discuss what grades the students have earned. The coteachers must also be willing to spend, for instance, an extra three hours in class per week because both teachers are present for all class periods in the most effective learning community configuration, the coordinated learning community. Finding this time is a deterrent for many faculty members, and in too many cases faculty are not compensated for this extra time. Once the course is established, instructors need less time for these formative and summative tasks, but communication between the coteachers must be frequent, and such collaboration always takes more time than teaching alone.

However, one of the greatest gifts of learning communities involves time: *enough* time for the instructors to assign, provide some instruction in, and respond to student writing; *enough* class time for students to write and share their writing with each other. And learning communities have the potential to influence a "regulative discourse" about how instruction is delivered (*the relay*) that brings to the foreground interdisciplinary learning and collaboration and values respect, honor, and appreciation. If there is *enough* time, writing can be central and epistemological; students explore important content concepts in depth as well as being given many opportunities to practice the conventions of academic writing. In a learning community, the same group of students meets for perhaps a two-hour block three times a week, assignments are integrated, and students learn *through* writing. For example, the students in the College Algebra/Composition II course I coteach with math instructor Jeff Frost have time in class to work with their peers as they draft a paper and ample time to respond to each other's drafts as well. The students learn much of the math content through writing, but a great advantage is that we have the time I normally set aside in a composition class for students to share and respond to each other's papers, write several drafts, and revise until they (and we) are reasonably satisfied that they have achieved some level of comfort and competency with algebra and writing, including documentation. In traditional formats, even if teachers of, say, science courses believe writing to be epistemological, they cannot ask students to do much writing, much less revising, if they are teaching five classes. Nor do they have time to teach the documentation style of their discipline.

Community college faculty labor under a we-do-it-this-way-because-it's-always-been-done-this-way paradigm that involves heavy teaching workloads and long lists of competencies and outcomes. If teachers want to foster meaningful learning through writing, a paradigm shift that acknowledges how we learn meaningfully must take place, and that paradigm is at least in part about time. Andy Warhol said, "They say that time changes things, but you actually have to change them yourself." Yes, if we taught fewer classes we would be able to give our students the time they need rather than rushing them through a list of competencies or expecting universal outcomes. The "regulative discourse" of community colleges—characterized by heavy teaching loads and legions of adjunct faculty—that governs the "instructional discourse" works to maintain a kind of delivery system that privileges the efficiency of "instruction" over the efficacy of "learning" (Tagg 2003). But no one is going to give community college faculty more time, so we must explore and embrace new pedagogical models that open up time so we and our students can enjoy a fuller and more satisfying expression of our academic work.

Acknowledgments

I would like to thank Michele Eodice, Rebecca Moore Howard, Candace Spigelman, Amy Robillard, and Kirk Branch for their willingness to read drafts of this chapter and give me thoughtful, stimulating, helpful feedback. They are all, in a way, my coauthors.

Notes

1. We full-time English faculty at my institution reap the benefits of negotiations between the faculty association and the Board of Trustees about twenty years ago: Our contract stipulates a yearly course load between twenty-nine and thirty-one hours, and a composition course counts as 3.25 hours rather than the usual three hours for most courses.

2. In one of the textbooks our history department uses, *American Promise* (2001), edited by Roark, Roark, and Johnson, information about Native Americans is relegated to the prologue. What ideological screens did historical knowledge about Native Americans pass through to arrive at that position in the text?

3. I would like to thank Kirk Branch for introducing me to Bernstein's work. I encountered it in an early manuscript of Branch's *Eyes on the Ought to Be: What We Teach When We Teach About Literacy* (2007), a book I highly recommend.

4. There are, however, numerous articles written by community college faculty on preventing plagiarism (Cozin 1999; LeCroy Center 2003; Roach 1998; Whiteneck 2002). This pedagogy acknowledges the instructor's willingness to take time to read multiple drafts, hold conferences with students, and check the sources students have used.

5. My version of his survey took the form of a questionnaire that yielded both quantitative and qualitative data. Sixty percent of the respondents were from the Liberal Arts Division; nineteen percent were from the Science, Health Care, and Math Division; and seventeen percent were from the Business and Technology Division. Their assignments range from reflections to research papers and essays to PowerPoint presentations. Institutional Research created a report of the finding that included color bar graphs with accompanying narratives and all of the respondents' written comments. I coded the comments, and categories such as "intent" and "fraud" emerged. For another discussion of the results of distributing this survey, see Candace Spigelman and Kami Day's "Valuing Research at Small and Community Colleges" (2006).

6. There has been some discussion about forming a board to review cases, and although students have not taken advantage of it, they may take an ethics class in order to have the X removed from the XF. A few times, after speaking to the instructor, the dean has deleted the XF if the student has been able to articulate an understanding of his or

her offense. The administrator also included a link to Barton's policy: www.
bartoncc.edu/policiesandprocedures/learning_and_instruction/documents/Academi
cIntegrity_002.pdf.

7. My institution is well-known for its interpreter program, so my classes are likely to
include deaf students. My experience with these students is that they prefer the term
deaf to *hard of hearing* or *hearing impaired*.

References

Babbie, Earl. 1998. Plagiarism. Sciences Research and Instructional Council Teaching
Resources Depository: Other Teaching Tools. www.csubak.edu/ssric/modules/
other/plagiarism.htm (accessed August 25, 2002).

Bernstein, Basil. 2000. *Pedagogy, Symbolic Control and Identity: Theory, Research,
and Critique.* Revised ed. Lanham, MD: Rowman & Littlefield Publishers.

Branch, Kirk. 2007. *Eyes on the Ought to Be: What We Teach When We Teach About
Literacy.* Cresskill, NJ: Hampton Press.

Burke, Jonathan L. 1997. Faculty Perceptions of and Attitudes Toward Academic
Dishonesty at a Two-year College. Dissertation. University of Georgia, Athens.

Burnett, Sara. 2002. "Dishonor & Distrust: Student Plagiarism is Now as Easy as Pointing
and Clicking. What's a Professor to Do?" *Community College Week* 14 (24).
Expanded Academic ASAP. http://find.galegroup.com (accessed October 23, 2002).

Cozin, M. L. 1999. *Cheating and its Vicissitudes.* North Branch, NJ: Raritan Valley
Community College. Microfiche. ERIC no. ED 437 112.

Dowd, Steven B. 1992. *Academic Integrity—A Review and Case Study.* Birmingham:
University of Alabama School of Health Related Professions. Microfiche. ERIC
no. ED 349 050.

Eodice, Michele, and Cindy Pierard. 2002. "Surfing for Scholarship." *The National
Teaching and Learning Forum* 11(3): 5.

Evelyn, Jamilah. 2002. "Survey of Community-College Students' Academic Engagement
Aims to Provide a Benchmark." *The Chronicle of Higher Education* (10 December).
http://chronicle.com/daily/2002/12/2002120201n.htm.

Gehring, Donald, and Gary Pavela. 1994. Issues and Perspectives on Academic
Integrity. www.uri.edu/univcol/URI101/Module_VI/issues_and_perspectives.htm
(accessed February 2, 2004).

Grubb, W. Norton, and Associates. 1999. *Honored but Invisible: An Inside Look at
Teaching in Community College.* New York: Routledge.

Holladay, Sylvia A. 1996. "Order Out of Chaos: Voices from the Community College."
In *Composition in the Twenty-first Century: Crisis and Change,* edited by Lynn Z.
Bloom, Donald A. Daiker, and Edward M. White. Carbondale: Southern Illinois
University Press.

Holmsten, Victoria. 2002. "This Site Under Construction: Negotiating Space for WPA
Work in the Community College." In *The Writing Program Administrator's
Resource,* edited by Stuart C. Brown, Theresa Enos, and Catherine Chaput.
Mahwah, NJ: Lawrence Erlbaum Associates.

Howard, Rebecca Moore. 1999. *Standing in the Shadows of Giants: Plagiarists, Authors, Collaborators*. Stamford, CT: Ablex.

Kozeracki, Carol. 2002. ERIC review: Issues in Developmental Education. *Community College Review* 29 (22): 83(19). Expanded Academic ASAP. http://find.galegroup.com (accessed November 10, 2007).

LeCroy Center for Educational Telecommunications, Dallas County Community College. 2003. Critical Challenges in Distance Education: Cheating and Plagiarism Using the Internet. District Dallas TeleLearning and Dallas Teleconferences. Teleconferences@dcccd.edu.

McCabe, Donald L., and Linda Klebe Trevino. 1996. "What We Know About Cheating in College." *Change* 28 (1): 28. Expanded Academic ASAP. http://find.galegroup.com (accessed December 8, 2002).

North, Stephen. 1987. *The Making of Knowledge in Composition: Portrait of an Emerging Field*. Portsmouth, NH: Boynton/Cook.

North Carolina Community College System. 2000. Planning and Research Section. *An Analysis of Faculty Workload Policies and Practices of North Carolina Community Colleges*. Research Brief No. 2000-03. Raleigh.

Oudenhoven, Betsy. 2002. "Remediation at the Community College." *New Directions for Community Colleges*, 117. OmniFile Full Text Mega. http://vnweb.hwwilsonweb.com/ (accessed January 29, 2007).

Rhem, James. 2002. "Surfing for Scholarship." *The National Teaching and Learning Forum* 11 (3): 3.

Roach, Ronald. 1998. "High-Tech Cheating." *Black Issues in Higher Education* 15 (22): 26. Expanded Academic ASAP. http://find.galegroup.com (accessed October 23, 2002).

Roark, Al, James L. Roark, and Michael P. Johnson. 2001. *The American Promise: A History of the United States from 1865*. 2nd ed. Vol. 2. New York: Bedford Books.

Robillard, Amy E. 2006. "*Young Scholars* Affecting Composition: A Challenge to Disciplinary Citation Practices." *College English* 68 (3): 253–270.

Spigelman, Candace, and Kami Day. 2006. "Valuing Research at Small and Community Colleges." *Teaching English in the Two-Year College* 34 (2): 135–150.

Tagg, John. 2003. *The Learning Paradigm College*. Bolton, MS: Anker Press.

Whiteneck, Peggy. 2002. "What to Do with a Thought Thief." *Community College Week* 14 (3):4. Expanded Academic ASAP. http://find.galegroup.com (accessed October 23, 2002).

4

Where There's Smoke, Is There Fire?

Understanding Coauthorship in the Writing Center

Tracy Hamler Carrick

Colby College

Last fall, I invited the staff of thirty peer writing tutors at the writing center I direct to complete a brief online questionnaire. I asked them to narrate two tutoring moments: one in which they coauthored with another student and another in which they wanted to coauthor but chose not to. Secondary questions prompted them to evaluate their choices and to think about their relationships with the students they were tutoring, their perception of the students' writing abilities and other identity characteristics, and the rhetorical contexts in which the writing itself was situated. I see in their candid disclosures exciting and unexpected ways to understand the embodied, immediate, and physically proximal interactions between peer writing tutors and students that sometimes involve coauthoring.

Their commentary, which I judiciously cite throughout this chapter, ultimately brings the haunting image of plagiarism in the writing center into sharper focus, as a ghostly likeness fighting to find its material form instead as coauthorship. Clearly, not all instances of coauthorship in the writing center are the same. Some are not appropriate, are not pedagogically motivated. But as I demonstrate, because they represent the reasonable efforts of novice peer writing tutors, we should consider how honest critical dialogue about coauthoring—not plagiarism—in the writing center can usefully alter tutor training curricula. Coauthorship in these instances, I argue, should prompt pedagogical response, not punishment.

Most notably, however, are instances of coauthorship that offer sound and enriching challenges to orthodox tutoring pedagogies. The peer writing tutors with whom I shape this chapter exhibit a keen understanding of the social nature of writing, and, through their actions, join me in suggesting that, under certain circumstances, coauthoring in the writing center, what some might consider plagiarism, is pedagogy worth defending. Even fighting for.

Smoke

I would pick out words that seemed sort of strange in the context she used them, or phrases that weren't very clear, and we would both throw out suggestions of ways that they could be improved. Sometimes we agreed that something she came up with worked really well, and sometimes we would use one of my ideas. (Katherine Renwick)

Her ideas were strong and cohesive but she was having a lot of trouble putting her thoughts into words, which is what her professor had commented on. If she had been having less trouble forming coherent sentences, I would not have been as tempted to offer her suggestions. (Emily Judem)

It is true. We don't talk about it often, but peer writing tutors coauthor with students who visit the writing center. No, I am not talking about ghostwriting; peer writing tutors are not writing papers *for* others. Nor am I talking about the kind of coauthorship made visible by Andrea Lunsford and Lisa Ede, the kind of writing together that Muriel Harris describes as "a melding process by which [writers] create one text together, discovering and thinking through ideas together, talking through sections together, and writing drafts together" (Lunsford and Ede; cited in Harris 1992, 369–70), a process, finally, in which participants share both decision-making power and responsibility for the product of their collective labor (Allen et al 1987; cited in Harris). But peer writing tutors, like Renwick and Judem, do utter words, phrases, sentences, and ideas that find their ways, in whole or in part, into papers that students submit as their own. Is this plagiarism?

Certainly it is not the kind of plagiarism that collegewide faculty and staff talk most about: those papers that are written by one person (sometimes for hire) and submitted by a student who is best labeled a fraud. Writing centers should not compromise our pedagogical missions by allowing our safe(r) spaces to be invaded—by students who are not actually interested in writing or learning or by those who should rightly police them. Aside from talking about the impact that this form of plagiarism has on the culture of writing, the peer writing tutors that I work with do not spend much time spitting fuel in this fire. Nor should they.

Writing center practitioners do, however, engage in much talk about how we can reach out to students who want to avoid plagiarism but who may unintentionally plagiarize—because they do not understand the grammar and rhetoric of citation and because they need to develop sound strategies for working with source materials. Indeed, these are among the very students whom writing centers hope to attract; they are the students who have both a need ("I do not understand") and an incentive ("I will be penalized") to learn some of the things we can teach. And we join many others—composition and rhetoric teachers and scholars as well as interdisciplinary faculty and staff—as we entertain ways to address this all-too-common pitfall associated with academic writing, with plagiarism. I could talk about the many exciting ways that peer writing tutors address this educational need. But because such pedagogical work cuts across all sites of engaged composition pedagogy, I set this important conversation aside with the hope that other contributors to this volume sufficiently address it.

In some respects, for those of us who work in writing centers, these are the easy conversations to have (or not have) about plagiarism. If current scholarship accurately reflects our collective desires, writing center practitioners seem far more interested in talking about authorship, not plagiarism. But often the two become intertwined, and discussions about plagiarism in the writing center become discussions about how to negotiate boundaries between plagiarism and coauthorship (sometimes framed as appropriate and inappropriate collaboration) and the fuzzy, shifting, and contingent lines that are typically drawn between these two poles. This is not surprising. Amid the rising culture of suspicion and fear, writing center practitioners worry that our collaborative work with writers will get caught up in the dry summer forest fire that can set ablaze even the most innocuous hallway exchange about plagiarism or collaboration or coauthorship. Such worry, Linda Shamoon and Deborah H. Burns (1999) observe, has an unfortunate effect; the conversations we would have about authorship bend toward the language and discourse of suspicious outsiders. Rather than talking about authorship as a social and rhetorical event, one that, especially in academic discourse communities, always involves collaboration of some kind, we submit instead to discourse grounded in the utterly pervasive and naturalized social construction of authorship as solitary activity (see Ede and Lunsford 1990; Howard 1995). The result, Shamoon and Burns (1999) contend, is that

> much of the research produced by writing centers rationalizes and dramatizes the boundaries between helping students write and letting them write for themselves. Such boundary negotiation dominates writing center literature, explaining the nature of acceptable collaboration, tacitly or overtly stating rules under which tutor–student collaboration should occur, and restricting what tutors may and may not do. Ironically, then, writing center research promotes tutoring and, at the same time, discounts it in terms of publicly identified authorship and ownership. (185–86)

And "in leaving the concept of sole authorship in place" (Shamoon and Burns 1999, 186), coauthoring in the writing center is discounted, wholesale, as a potentially viable writing center experience. It is perceived as a violation of writing center policy. Period.

But I am uncomfortable with this assessment; I am uncomfortable dismissing tutors like Renwick and Judem and the work of their collaborative exchanges. I wonder what we set aside when we prevent tutors and students from coinhabiting the dynamic, recursive, and discursive spaces in which participants see and resee text together. Write and rewrite text together. What can they learn? What can we?

Matches

I expect that some faculty members might regard the exchange of ideas, words, and phrases like those described above by Renwick and Judem as problematic: They might consider this kind of collaborative work too excessive, and thus, would regard the work plagiaristic, the participants plagiarists. Now, very few would consider the coauthorship of a few sentences within a larger body of work to be a significant violation of academic honesty policies, but their knowledge of such activity would likely breathe a good amount of oxygen into the plagiarism fire, oxygen that might, in turn, be sucked right into the writing center—a backdraft, if you will. More specifically, such onlookers would likely entertain assumptions about how many sentences the peer writing tutor and student would revise in this way; about what other kinds of interventions the peer writing tutor might feel authorized to make; about what other suggestions the student might feel obligated to take; or about what other demands the student might place on the peer writing tutor. They might wonder: *What will stop peer writing tutors and students who visit the writing center from taking collaborative exchanges too far?*

Because a question like this could have profoundly deleterious effects, peer writing tutors spend a fair bit of time wondering, and worrying, themselves. Many of the peer writing tutors I supervise speculate about how others might construe their collaborative work with students. Some are afraid. Others, just earnest; they want to do right by the institutional community that has bestowed rewards upon them (Trimbur 1987). Consider this thoughtful comment by peer writing tutor Allyson Rudolph:

> One of my favorite techniques when working with tutees is to have them tell me, without looking at their paper, what a particular paragraph is about. I find that people tend to come up with totally brilliant intro sentences when I take the paper away and say "tell me why this paragraph is important to your paper." I write down exactly what they say, and then encourage them to use it in their paper. This collaboration actually scares me more than when tutees write down my words directly, because it *looks* more like inappropriate collaboration out of context. I would not want a teacher to be looking at a student's rough draft and see, in my handwriting, a fully formed sentence. Yet I know that the ideas and the words were entirely the tutee's. (emphasis in original)

In some ways, Rudolph's words are reassuring; they counterbalance the transgressive disclosures made by Renwick and Judem; they propose a safe and effective method for working with students who visit the writing center. Her words also evidence how deeply peer writing tutors can internalize writing center doctrine, what Irene Clark refers to "as a writing center 'bible' (Shamoon and Burns 1995), writing center 'dogma' (Clark 1990), or writing center 'mantras' (Blau)" (Clark 1999, 158). In a comprehensive overview of foundational writing center scholarship, Clark illustrates the persistence of noninterventionist tutoring policies by relating typical warnings issued to tutoring staff:

- "Do 'not write any portion of the paper—not even one phrase'" (Edwards 1983, 8; cited in Clark 1999, 158).

- "'When you improve a student's paper, you haven't been a tutor at all; you've been an editor'" (Brooks 1991, 2; cited in Clark 1999, 158).

- Do not "tell students what a particular passage means or give students a particular word to complete a thought" (Thompson 1995, 13; cited in Clark 1999, 159).

According to commands such as these, directive peer writing tutors, those who coauthor, are clearly out of bounds. They are not tutors; they might even be plagiarists. At the very least, they are willfully creating a slippery platform on which obvious forms of plagiarism could be more easily encroached. Naturally, Rudolph is concerned about appearances.

But Rudolph's concerns also feel somehow unfortunate. Amid so much other pressure to perform well, peer writing tutors believe their work to be perpetually under surveillance. It seems profoundly unreasonable to willfully support a learning environment that engenders so much anxiety, especially when our personal experiences and professional scholarship do not necessarily support the very principles and practices of nondirective pedagogies that we insist on in the writing center. In her chapter, "Writing Centers and Plagiarism," Clark suggests that when writing center practitioners enforce the strict policy of nondirective tutoring, we disingenuously withhold ways of composing that professional writers depend on. As she notes, "all of us who write and publish habitually receive commentary from colleagues and editors that frequently result in extensive changes in a text. Yet, hypocritically, our concern about plagiarism forbids us to make similar suggestions to our students" (167). But dismissing forms of coauthorship is not simply hypocritical, according to Clark. It is also pedagogically shortsighted. She recounts several case studies (Harris 1983; Neff 1994; Shamoon and Burns 1995), each illustrating the educational benefits of directive pedagogies, pedagogical approaches that involve editing, imitation, modeling, and coauthoring, to claim that a rigid commitment to nondirective tutoring prevents writing center practitioners from seeing alternative methods.

To name an act of collaboration in the writing center with the label "coauthoring" is risky, but it is equally dangerous to avoid conversation about the infinite ways that words and ideas move between actual peer writing tutors and students when they discuss papers in the writing center. It is not necessarily so easy to determine what constitutes plagiarism, or sound tutoring practice for that matter, when, as a collective body, we shut down, avoid, or redirect certain conversations. Furthermore, we cannot understand why peer writing tutors coauthor even when the stakes are so high and even when they appear to have other pedagogical options, if we rush too quickly to judge them. Before we ask if Renwick and Judem are plagiarists, we should first consider how we have positioned them and peer writing tutors like them in crimson embers and told them not to breathe.

Firefighter

To more deeply understand the precarious position peer tutors find themselves in when they accept positions in the writing center, I'd like to look back to Muriel Harris's landmark disciplinary text, "Collaboration Is Not Collaboration Is Not Collaboration: Writing Center Tutorials vs. Peer Response Groups," published in *College Composition and Communication* in 1992. This seminal article has gone a long way to assuage the suspicious among us that there is no room for coauthorship in the writing center. Furthermore, Harris provided the foundational base from which all other schemas for understanding collaboration have been built. Harris delineates two forms of collaboration: collaborative learning and collaborative writing. Her stated purpose is to examine the differences between the kinds of collaborative work sponsored in classroom settings during peer response groups and the kinds of collaborative work relegated to writing centers during writing tutorials. As the peer writing tutors cited below attest, however, the distinct lines she has drawn between these forms of collaboration may be a bit too clean for the messy work typically found in writing centers.

For Harris, collaborative writing—like the kind of coauthorship explored above—is best assigned to peer response groups. In classroom-sponsored activities, Harris contends, writers should focus on the general skills they need to meet the stated requirements of writing assignments. Peers read each others' drafts and offer specific suggestions for revision. Their comments tend to be directive—"you should put a comma here" or "your thesis needs to be narrowed, like this . . ."—and peers rarely, if at all, explain *why* a revision needs to be made. It just *does*. That is, when a revision suggestion is offered, peers tend not to explain a grammatical rule or examine larger rhetorical principles. The absence of these pedagogical moments, Harris posits, makes the peer interactions more akin to collaborative writing; without explicit attention to the question of *why,* peers are writing over or writing with each other. They are coauthors, at least of certain passages. Harris wisely sets aside any oppositional commentary—such as, *should* peers be working with each other in this way? Her purpose is not to defend coauthorship, per se; it is not to defend composition pedagogy, or the ways that some teachers design peer response groups. Her purpose is to defend the kinds of collaborative work found in the writing center; the most controversial form of collaboration is set aside and located somewhere else.

In the writing center, Harris promotes collaborative learning. Like many other writing center practitioners and scholars before and after her, Harris proposes that peer writing tutors use student texts to initiate conversation about individualized concerns, to engage the unique learning needs of one individual. When reviewing a draft, that is, peer writing tutors should look for patterns of errors and use their observations to offer opportunistic lessons. If a peer writing tutor notices that a writer regularly omits commas after introductory phrases, for instance, she might explain the standard academic English convention and then work with the writer to locate places where the comma should be inserted. Or, the peer writing tutor might consider the essay to be illogically organized. She might ask the writer to explain her organizational strategy, and in the absence of a sound response, might take occasion to review several strategies for arranging arguments in a typical compare/contrast essay.

As Harris explains, the writing tutorial is different from the peer response session because it focuses on the sole needs of a single writer, often incidental to the writing assignment at hand. It is also firmly positioned within the "questioning and explaining stage" (1992, 372) of the collaborative process. Her rationale for parceling out the work of peer writing tutors and peer responders is twofold: The first is pragmatic, self-promotional. Students who work in classroom-sponsored peer response groups should not consider a tutorial session in the writing center a redundant effort; the work engaged in the two venues is decidedly different, though certainly complementary. As Harris writes,

> tutorials and response groups, though collaborative in their approaches, also have different underlying perspectives, assumptions, and goals. Moreover, tutors, unlike peer readers, are trained to use methods that lead to results very different from the outcome of response groups. Clearly, these different forms of collaboration should not be conflated. (1992, 369)

The second justification—somewhat tacit and visible only, perhaps, because her essay has endured the test of time—is pointedly strategic. As encapsulated in the brief summary that I have shared above, Harris assures potentially doubtful onlookers that the collaborative work found in writing centers is thoroughly and completely above suspicion. In a student-dominated space that teachers rarely visit, only the safest form of collaboration—collaborative learning—is practiced. The riskiest form of collaboration—collaborative writing, a form of peer interaction that might involve the coauthorship of phrases or sentences or the collective development of an idea or kernel of thought—is more appropriately consigned to the space of a classroom where a classroom teacher is aware of and/or in control of collaborative exchanges. Harris sufficiently defends the work of writing centers by guaranteeing only the safest collaboration.

Green Wood

In work like Harris', we are given portraits of collaboration that set different varieties side by side. Although there are many possible ways to read relationships between collaborative learning and collaborative writing, one way might be to see them as developmentally correlated. Of course, I recognize the many inherent complications with developmental models—take, for instance, the troubling suggestion that one form of collaboration is subordinate to the other. But, for the sake of discussion here, I'll set my reservations aside. For in applying a developmental stage model, we are able to see the ways in which students are asked to move through writing tutor training to develop the kinds of collaborative skills expected of peer writing tutor.

Most peer writing tutors come to hold their positions after having first demonstrated competency as collaborative writers, peers who work with classmates in ways that likely do not include Harris's "questioning and explaining stage" (1992, 372). At my institution, a colleague typically refers a student for employment in the writing center because she has witnessed a student's relative comfort and skill in class-sponsored peer response sessions. In the short span of a semester, during our prerequisite training course (indeed, a luxury that many writing center practitioners do not have), peer writing tutors are expected to shift from collaborative writers to collaborative learners, to shed the learned and/or native vestiges of a form of collaboration that should not be enacted in the differently controlled spaces of the writing center. Obviously, it seems, peer writing tutors will spend at least some of their time dwelling in that space between collaborative writing and collaborative learning. We simply cannot guarantee that writing centers are "coauthor-free" spaces.

Our processes for identifying and training peer writing tutors may well force certain forms of collaboration into developmental relationships with each other. And such a practice, to be evidenced below, puts peer writing tutors in an incontrovertible bind: to honor the "no coauthorship" in the writing center guarantee, peer writing tutors must be collaborators they have not yet become, and when they ultimately demonstrate that they are not yet such collaborators, their actions and the writings they coproduce will be labeled somehow deficient or even punishable.

Arsonists

The peer writing tutors I surveyed reflect on the complex ways in which they struggle to transform their collaborative selves. They sometimes recall plainly, though not without a certain degree of remorse, the ways in which they have failed to act as collaborative learners. Most often, as the passages below reveal, it is during moments of uncertainty that peer tutors are most likely to fall back on the comfortable and familiar role of coauthor.

To become adept collaborative learners, peer writing tutors must recon-
struct their peerness. Though the writers who visit the writing center may be
the very same students with whom they sit in classes, live in dormitories, and
eat and socialize in the college commons, in the writing center, peer writing
tutors are challenged to obtain a certain distance from the writers they work
with—to slough off empathetic urges and to present a pedagogic self. But they
are not to achieve too much distance or be too unsympathetic or pedagogical.
If they do, they lose the very qualities that make their role in the academy distinguished; we value them because they are peers with whom writers feel comfortable and for whom the writing for a college course is a known and
embodied experience (see Trimbur 1987).

Peer writing tutor Judem (2006) has found herself heavily influenced by
the mental and emotional states of the writers she works with in the writing
center. As a peer she can become too involved in their personal dramas, identify too deeply with their stress levels, though she readily admits that sometimes this may not lead to the best pedagogical choices. When a student visited
the writing center after receiving an unfavorable grade, Judem worked with
her to revise the draft in response to comments from her professor that were
difficult to understand. Judem comments that

> I tried very hard not to give suggestions of words or phrases, but she asked
> several times, "what do you think?" She was very involved in the session but
> also very frustrated [. . .] Yes, I thought I was giving her too much help at
> some points [. . .] But at the same time, it was hard not to help her because
> her brain seemed to be frozen from her stress [. . .] I didn't want the session
> to make her more stressed out than she already was.

Judem is by no means alone in admitting that student frustration and stress level
affect her ability to "be more patient with [a tutee's] writing process" and to
manage a tutorial session using a collaborative learning model. Her writing
center colleague, Renwick, shares this concern and adds that she can be overly
influenced by her desire to ensure that writers are sufficiently satisfied with her
performance that they will return to the writing center for another appointment
(2006). Indeed, the honor of winning positions on the writing center staff and
the joy of receiving a paycheck for their labor is not necessarily enough. Nor
are the veiled threats that coauthorship is unacceptable. Sometimes, as Judem's
words suggest, writing center tutors are just as vulnerable as the nervous writers
who wander in to schedule appointments. And they revert, uneasily, to collaborative writing as a guiding strategy when they are not able to rise above their
own psychological reactions.

More interesting and more complicated, perhaps, are those moments
when peer writing tutors coauthor because they do not have the knowledge or
experience—not necessarily the psychological strength—to act otherwise. In a
response that is similar to many I have gathered, Rudolph (2006) apologeti-

cally explains how she can wind up writing "too" collaboratively with the writers who visit the writing center:

> It definitely reflects on my own limitations as a tutor—as someone who has always had a very easy time expressing myself through writing I have a difficult time explaining why a certain sentence is effective or ineffective. It's not easy for me to explain what makes for a strong introduction, or even to show why his incomplete sentences are incomplete. So co-authoring becomes the easy way out . . .

In this reflection, Rudolph does not simply admit that she considers coauthoring a weakness. She also states that coauthoring is the easy way; it is what she does when other options seem too difficult or are, perhaps, unimaginable. She coauthors because she has more to learn. Set beside the honest critique of her coauthoring self, however, Rudolph writes, "As long as it does not become a habit, I would not consider such collaboration inappropriate—part of being a good teacher is setting good examples, and if writing down my words helps the tutee understand what makes a sentence good, then it will happen occasionally" (2006). So while coauthoring is what she must do when she sees no other pedagogical alternatives, it is not, in the end, according to Rudolph, "inappropriate" if the act meets certain criteria.

Rocío Orantes (2006) shares a similar experience. She coauthored with a peer, a friend who needed someone to be "tough and directive." She writes: "I could see that no one had actually given her the constructive criticism that she appreciated (not her thesis advisor, not her other tutor . . . her second reader gave her some help, but she really needed someone to get dirty with her words)." Orantes illuminates another typical writing center scenario: a peer writing tutor who was compelled to come to a writer's rescue when it seemed that she had been abandoned by others, particularly others with more authority, experience, and knowledge. Like many of the peer writing tutors I have known, Orantes found herself in an awkward position—and, given her lack of experience and the limited time and resources available to her, she could devise no other way to work with the writer, except to "[overstep] some professional boundaries" and coauthor passages. In the end, Orantes defends hers and others' actions by adding that "I was a sounding board and often an active collaborator, but when the session ended, I went home and she stayed with her work."

Testimonials like these substantiate the claim that peer writing tutors can struggle to make the transition from collaborative writers to collaborative learners. Though they may exhibit proficient knowledge of the writing center value of collaborative learning, when they encounter challenging situations, they may falter as practitioners and fall back on the familiar habit of collaborative writing. That they are acutely aware of these transgressions is evidenced by their need to justify their actions. But because we cannot always preempt the moments of cognitive dissonance that can uncomfortably force a peer

writing tutor into the role of coauthor, we would do well to make coauthorship
a more explicit element of peer tutor training.

Coauthoring in the writing center does, as Rudolph acknowledges, reflect
the limitations of individual tutors. It does make visible those moments that peer
writing tutors are not yet prepared to handle, those moments during which they
lack the knowledge or experience to be the collaborative learners certain tutoring
contexts demand. We should help them negotiate their pedagogical responses,
not offer up a litany of directives. We should invite discussion of these challenging moments into our professional development activities—staff meetings,
regional and national conferences. Many writing center practitioners already do
this in some way or another. I would add only that we need to do better job to
assure each other that talking about coauthorship, typically construed as a taboo
topic, during these important pedagogical discussions is perfectly acceptable,
even necessary, if we are going to fully address the range of pedagogical pitfalls
that each of us encounter at different stages of our tutoring lives.

Firekeepers

Although the peer writing tutors cited above do exhibit a deep desire to develop
different kinds of pedagogical skills, they do not seem willing to abandon collaborative writing entirely. They do not always consider coauthorship a transgression. As the comments below suggest, peer writing tutors may be less
inclined to see their actions as indiscretions when they take into consideration
the collaboration skills of the writers with whom they are working as opposed
to their own preparedness to collaborate as colearners. That is, when they find
the writers with whom they are working to possess collaboration skills that they
deem somehow idiosyncratic, the peer writing tutors I work with are more
likely to defend coauthoring as a viable, not simply justifiable, pedagogical
strategy in the writing center. The fact that peer writing tutors take these characteristics into account as they quickly determine pedagogical approaches reflects
their deepening pedagogical acumen. It is a challenge for peer writing tutors to
design strategies for identifying, understanding, and responding to the assumptions that the writers who visit the writers center nurture about collaboration in
its myriad forms; to the collaborative traditions they bring with them from
home or from their past educational experiences; and to the collaborative skills
they may or may not have to bring to the exchange.

Because writing center discourse historically portrays the writing center as
a site for remediation, most assume that the students who seek tutorial assistance are not in control of their writing and/or are not in control of their learning. And in the limited imaginations of those who might be suspicious of
collaboration, particularly coauthorship, excessive collaboration might be construed as excessive help: Writers with whom a peer writing tutor might coauthor might be viewed as students who cannot do the work themselves and rely
too heavily on generous handouts from others. Indeed, these writers—those

who Renwick (2006) describes as people who "write down anything I [say] without first evaluating its merits in their paper"—do visit the writing center, and the peer writing tutors I surveyed are much more cautious about collaboratively writing with them. They cite work ethic, participation, and engagement as features that help them to determine how they will collaborate with others. In a typical comment, Orantes (2006) discloses that she is "often weary of directing weaker writers too much because I can see them depending on me for ideas and quick fixes rather than taking the time to improve themselves." These, Orantes and others argue, are not writers who have the sophisticated skills or authentic desire to collaborate in ways that make the experience edifying or educational.

Most often, however, the peer writing tutors I surveyed identify moments of coauthorship as moments that they proudly share with writers whom they consider thoughtful, bold, independent thinkers. As Orantes (2006) claims, "[I] knew that if she wasn't comfortable with a change she would be comfortable enough to tell me to back off." These writers are also willing to change themselves, to learn. Rudolph (2006) explains: "When I see improvement, and when I see that he is modeling his own sentences off of the sentences that I've 'written,' I feel much better about the collaboration." Most importantly, these writers come to the writing center already equipped with skills that make them desirable partners in the collaborative exchange of coauthorship. Renwick (2006) shares an experience with one such writer, a writer she describes as having confidence in her writing abilities. "This type of collaboration worked only because she felt comfortable contradicting her tutor, and was willing to actively be a part of deciding which word or phrase she herself liked best in each situation, rather than treating the first thing I said as the best possible choice." It was also the type of collaboration in which, Renwick claims, "my tutee [was able] to see her writing from a different perspective and to think critically about her selection of words and phrases." In the end, Renwick claims, "we both learned from each other." Sometimes collaborative learning and collaborative writing are not so easily disentangled.

It is too easy to review the provoking comments proffered by the peer writing tutors above and determine that those involved with writing center administration need to do a better job of training peer writing tutors and preparing them to act within the nondirective, collaborative learning models of tutoring pedagogy that Harris (1992) and others espouse. Yes, as I recognize in the previous section, we must continue working together to further develop efficient, engaging, and theoretically sound methods for preparing peer writing tutors. But, the peer writing tutors with whom I compose this chapter also ask that we listen differently when they coauthor under certain circumstances. They ask that we hear innovation, not indiscretion. And why shouldn't we entertain the possibility that coauthoring is, under certain circumstances anyway, a perfectly viable pedagogical strategy for peer writing tutors? As the four peer writing tutors cited earlier detail, it is possible to identify students for whom directive tutoring is most beneficial. Based on careful assessment, that is, peer writing tutors may determine that some students may be best served by the model of collaborative writing—because of their learning styles, their writing proficiency, their earnest desire to learn. In fact, scholars Neff (1994), Harris (1992), and Shamoon and Burns (1995) confirm this position. Coauthoring is not appropriate for all who inhabit the writing center, but it may be for some, and we should trust peer writing tutors, and indeed ourselves as the sponsors of their training, to know the difference.

Campfire

Clark (1999) argues that "Enhanced understanding of a poststructural perspective on knowledge would thus release the writing center from its absolutist adherence to a nondirective pedagogy, enabling it to recognize that for some students, a directive approach might be more effective" (166–67). When we look beyond nondirective tutoring approaches and to the ways in which poststructural theory influences perceptions of writing, coauthoring becomes a perfectly acceptable form of tutoring practice. Coauthoring enables writers to coinhabit a dynamic social space where participants negotiate meaning with their bodies, gestures, and words. It also enables them to work together to build the syntactical, rhetorical, and discursive structures that can effectively ground a text within a larger community of readers. Most significantly perhaps, when those who work in the writing center are permitted to recognize students as true peers, collaboration can yield learning opportunities for both tutor and student. The pedagogical possibilities are simply limitless.

To be sure, however, writing center practitioners must be prepared to defend coauthorship and peer writing tutors who coauthor. Not all colleagues are willing to forsake their romantic attachments to authorship as the solitary performance of an originary self. Not all will be able to relinquish nostalgic renderings of enduring pedagogical narratives that construe writing as the product of a single author. Fortunately, however, Clark (1999) reports that faculty across the disciplines may be changing their attitudes toward collaboration in the writing center. Her survey of faculty at the University of Southern California "indicates increased faculty understanding of the importance of collaboration in writing acquisition and a correspondingly decreased anxiety about the possibility of plagiarism" (156).

I suspect, though, that no matter how we respond individually or collectively to changing attitudes toward writing, peer writing tutors will likely continue to coauthor. They will continue to craft resourceful ways to feel good (and rightly so!) about the many ways they collaborate with writers despite the fact they must perform amid so many internal and external ambiguities. They will persevere despite the fact that their words may be the kindling that ignites an unwieldy bonfire in the midst of the academic quad—even if some accept peer writing tutors' organically derived rules for when, how, and why they work differently with different writers, they and the writers with whom they coauthor could wind up in the dean's office.

We should value the risks peer writing tutors take when they become co-authors—whether we agree with their choices or theory-building efforts, when peer writing tutors take this risk and *talk* about it, they demonstrate a deep desire to be a part of this ongoing conversation. So, let's throw another log on the campfire and start telling some ghost stories.

Acknowledgments

Thank you to Katherine Theriault, former Assistant Director of the Farnham Writers' Center at Colby College, with whom I had initially planned to coauthor this chapter. Our early discussions about this project have deeply informed the analysis presented here. Her voice and thoughtful reflections on writing center praxis resonate loudly in this piece and in my continuing work as a writing center practitioner.

References

Allen, Nancy, Dianne Arkinson, Meg Morgan, Teresa Moore, and Craig Snow. 1987. "What Experienced Collaborators Say About Collaborative Writing." *Journal of Business and Technical Communication* 1(2):70–90.

Blau, Susan. 1992. "Issues in Tutoring Writing: Stories from Our Center." *Writing Lab Newsletter* 19(2):1–4.

Brooks, Jeff. 1991. "Minimalist Tutoring: Making the Student Do All the Work." *Writing Lab Newsletter* 15(6):1–4.

Clark, Ilene L. 1990. "Maintaining Chaos in the Writing Center: A Critical Perspective on Writing Center Dogma." *Writing Center Journal* 11(1):81–95.

———. 1999. "Writing Centers and Plagiarism." In *Perspectives on Plagiarism and Intellectual Property in a Postmodern World*, eds. Lise Buranen and Alice M. Roy, 155–67. Albany: State University of New York Press.

Ede, Lisa and Andrea Lunsford. 1983. "Why Write . . . Together?" *Rhetoric Review*, 1:150–157.

Ede, Lisa and Andrea Lunsford. 1990. *Singular Texts/Plural Authors: Perspectives on Collaborative Writing*. Carbondale: Southern Illinois University Press.

Edwards, Suzanne. 1983. "Tutoring Your Tutors: How to Structure a Tutor-Training Workshop." *Writing Lab Newsletter* 7(10):7–9.

Harris, Muriel. 1992. "Collaboration Is Not Collaboration Is Not Collaboration: Writing Center Tutorials vs. Peer-Response Groups." *College Composition and Communication* 43(3):369–383.

———. 1983. "Modeling: A Process Method of Teaching." *College English*, 45:74–84.

Howard, Rebecca Moore. 1995. "Plagiarism, Authorships, and the Academic Death Penalty." *College English*, 57:788–806.

Judem, Emily. 2006. Interview by the author. Electronic mail. Waterville, Maine, 20 October.

Neff, Julie. 1994. "Learning Disabilities and the Writing Center." In *Intersections: Theory-Practice in the Writing Center*, edited by Joan Mullins and Ray Wallace, 81–95. Urbana, IL: National Council of Teachers of English.

Orantes, Rocío. 2006. Interview by the author. Electronic mail. Waterville, Maine, 20 October.

Renwick, Katherine. 2006. Interview by the author. Electronic mail. Waterville, Maine, 20 October.

Rudolph, Allyson. 2006. Interview by the author. Electronic mail. Waterville, Maine, 20 October.

Shamoon, Linda, and Deborah H. Burns. 1995. "A Critique of Pure Tutoring." *Writing Center Journal* 15(2):134–151.

———. 1999. "Plagiarism, Rhetorical Theory, and the Writing Center." In *Perspectives on Plagiarism and Intellectual Property in a Postmodern World*, eds. Lise Buranen and Alice M. Roy, 183–92. Albany: State University of New York Press.

Thompson, Thomas C. 1995. "'Yes Sir!' 'No Sir!' 'No Excuse Sir!' Working with an Honor Code in a Military Setting." *Writing Lab Newsletter* 19(5):13–14.

Trimbur, John. 1987. "Peer Tutoring: A Contradiction in Terms?" *Writing Center Journal* 7(2):21–29.

5

One Size Does Not Fit All

Plagiarism Across the Curriculum

Sandra Jamieson
Drew University

I first heard it when we revised our academic integrity policy a few years after I started teaching at my small liberal arts college, but I didn't comprehend its significance. I heard it again later in response to various cases brought to the Academic Integrity Committee by colleagues across the disciplines. What is interesting to me is that none of my colleagues said it directly until I sat down to talk one-on-one with them. When I did that, this is what they said: *Most of these rules about how to use and cite sources don't actually apply in my discipline*. My colleagues had worked with me through long faculty meetings in which we discussed and group-edited the new academic integrity policy, and they had brought cases of plagiarism and misuse of sources to the committee for hearing and sanction; but they did not follow those guidelines themselves, did not have any personal sense of ownership of them beyond general education, and could not afford to teach them to students who wanted to pursue graduate studies in their field. They could teach the principle that significant sources must be acknowledged, but they could not require that students in their disciplines remain within the rules of our policy in upper-level discipline-specific courses. We all agreed about paper mills and cheat sites, of course; about the paper, report, computer code, or work of art not authored by the student who submits it for a grade; and about cheating on tests. But it was impossible to generalize or universalize pretty much anything else—from what to cite to how one should indicate the work of others or even why one cites at all.

Interestingly, when I expressed my concern and desire to develop a new policy incorporating discipline-specific guidelines and conventions, to a person they defended the existing policy, arguing that in a liberal arts college we should have some universal standards and that it made sense for the English

department to set them. They added that the rules were fine for first-year seminars and introductory and general education courses and that the existence of
common rules taught in first-year composition meant that they did not have to
try to teach the rules in introductory classes and that nonmajors did not have to
learn the rules of each discipline as they fulfilled general education breadth
requirements.

I remained mystified about this response until the publication of Chris
Thaiss and Terry Myers Zawacki's fascinating study in *Engaged Writers and
Dynamic Disciplines* (2006). Thaiss and Zawacki interviewed faculty and students about the kinds of writing assigned and its adherence to convention. In
contrast to faculty in other studies (most notably Walvoord and McCarthy
1990), the faculty they interviewed did not believe the purpose of undergraduate education is to "train little psychologists, mathematicians, [or] biologists"
(117) and argued instead that "good writing is good writing and hence good
thinking, no matter what the discipline" (58). Yet Thaiss and Zawacki report
that their responses to questions and their description of practice revealed significant differences in the way "common" terms they named as being at the
heart of "good writing" (such as evidence, purpose, style, audience, and organization) are articulated in each discipline and explained to students. Even as the
faculty claimed they were simply teaching "good writing" (89), all were found
to assign and expect writing that matched the way they write (88), without noting the disciplinary embeddedness of their own writing. This matches what
Lee Ann Carroll learned from the students in her study—namely what she calls
the "gap between faculty fantasies about writing" and the struggles of their students (8). It also matches her major finding that faculty are not likely to understand the extent to which writing differs from discipline to discipline and, at
times, class to class and professor to professor. Walvoord and McCarthy (1990)
also discuss a mismatch between student and teacher expectations.

David Russell (1997) explains this gap or mismatch as the inevitable
result of disciplinary apprenticeship through which fledgling members of a
discipline "very gradually learn its written conventions as an active and integral part of their socialization in a community" (16), which makes learning to
write in that discipline seem a "transparent" process. Hare and Fitzsimmons
(1991) also observe that "literacy norms within most fields . . . remain . . .
invisible" (144). According to Russell, this is because "the community's genres and conventions appear to be unproblematic renderings of the fruits of
research" (17) rather than determining that research or interpellating its members into discipline-specific ideologies.

Aside from the intellectual implications of this lack of self-reflexivity, such
as simplistic calls to break down the walls between disciplines, Russell's analysis has some serious pedagogical repercussions. If, as Thaiss and Zawacki
(2006) put it, the faculty they interviewed "see academic writing as generic
rather than discipline-specific" (123), they will pass that belief to students who
then assume that what they learn in one class—including source-use rules—

applies to all classes. This also will lead students to perceive variation from that assumed norm as "differences in teachers' personalities rather than . . . nuanced articulations of the discipline" (132). Such a mystification of the fundamental differences between academic discourse communities can only lead to problems for students who try to write for us.

Thaiss and Zawacki's (2006) findings and Russell's (1997) analysis all seem to explain exactly what I saw on my campus and perhaps also the "cluelessness" that Gerald Graff (2003) describes. If faculty are not intending to invite undergraduates into disciplinary discourse, but undergraduates are being interpellated by the values of that discourse and feeling the need to speak its language anyway, there is clearly "cluelessness" on both sides. As faculty, we think we are teaching general skills—hence our enthusiasm for one-size-fits-all policies and plagiarism checking programs. Yet students do feel the need, and desire, to "speak our language," understanding better than us that our passion for what we do and the answers our disciplines seek to uncover are to be found in the way we speak about our research. While Thaiss and Zawacki's focus group informants revealed that "more experienced writers understand that knowing a discipline occurs gradually and involves much more than imitation of forms, templates, and styles" (129), most of the students in their study expressed the kind of anxiety and frustration that, according to the Council of Writing Program Administrators (2003), can lead to overdependence on source material in the first place. (The first thing listed under the heading "What Are the Causes of Plagiarism and the Failure to Use and Document Sources Appropriately?" is "Students may fear failure or fear taking risks in their own work.") Alienation leads to being risk averse, which in turn, ironically, leads to misuse of sources.

All of this explains why my colleagues rejected my suggestion that we develop a source-use policy reflecting disciplinary difference, arguing instead that we should spend more time teaching the ethical component of source use in the first year to reduce the incidence of plagiarism in upper-level classes. Persuaded by their emphasis on ethics, my dean drafted a "contract" that each student signs stating that they have received a copy of the academic integrity booklet and that their first-year seminar instructor has explained it to them. While we have an "administrative resolution" process for first- and second-year students who "unintentionally misuse sources," misuse at the upper level is considered a violation of academic integrity. It is true that the penalty may be mild for such "violations" when the student appears to have acted in ignorance, but charges are still required by our faculty regulations when misuse of any kind is found. Where the *WPA Statement* (Council of Writing Program Administrators 2003) uses the terms *deliberate* to indicate plagiarism and *good faith* to indicate accidental misuse of sources, Drew University (2001) uses *intentional* and *unintentional*. In each case, it is *intent* that is at the heart of this matter. And I think the issue of how and when we use source material in academic writing is a matter that should be discussed in terms of intent;

however, not in the current sense of intent to steal, defraud, mislead, or any other ethical or capitalist terms one might insert. Rather, we need to focus on what the author is intending to do by referencing sources and what established members of the discipline intend in the same situation, even if not all of them can articulate it as Thaiss and Zawacki (2006) imply. In other words, we need to focus on *use* of sources rather than *misuse* of sources. It is my contention that as long as our pedagogy, policies, textbooks, software programs, and scholarship continue to focus on the misuse of sources and ignore the larger *intention* of source use itself, we will continue to fail to address the problem of plagiarism in any discipline. Indeed, without consideration of intent, we will also continue to operate with inaccurate definitions of "correct" source use and continue to mystify the real work of the disciplines.

Discipline-specific conventions and in particular source use are the markers of membership in academic disciplines. One must learn them to be a member of a discipline, and in turn they interpellate new members into the values and expectations of that discipline through their very invisibility as ideology and classification as simply "good writing." It is the way we use the words and ideas of others that determines our relationship to them, to their ideas, and to the generation of knowledge. As is evidenced with the case of the passive voice, the speaker plays a different role in each discipline, and the discourse community signals its relationship to that speaker through the way it does or does not invoke his or her name. In some disciplines, especially the sciences, general information matters, and it is much less important to know who discovered it; in others, especially the social sciences, data matter, and the gatherer is identified to allow readers to evaluate the validity of that data (note, though, that the use of initials only in APA prevents us from knowing the gender of those cited); in still others, and especially the humanities, words and creative product are the object of study, and so it matters very much that the creator be named and given appropriate credit. These different relationships have a profound impact on both our work in a specific discipline and our relationship to that work and its dissemination.

The speakers of a discipline are, of course, its actors. They are us if we are already members of the community, and they are who we want to be if we are in the process of joining. As we master the discourse conventions of a discipline, then, we also learn how to take our place in it: how to act appropriately and how to refer to other members. We learn what is valued, and that shapes the way we do research. But we don't learn it from a book or from lectures, and the slow apprenticeship that Russell (1997) describes occurs on multiple levels. We are, in Althusser's (1971) sense of the word, interpellated into the subject-positions necessary to participate in a discipline-specific discourse community through its language and way of speaking itself. The publications of a discipline call readers into specific relationship with texts and each other; they create a community in what might be the most effective ideological apparatus imaginable. We recognize ourselves as members when we can talk the talk in the expected manner without thinking about it; when the language and our ability to communicate in it seem transparent. Indeed, the work is so successful that we are not even aware it is happening—a process that Althusser (1971, 182) describes as ideology working "all by itself." My colleagues were happy to have a general source-use policy even though it contradicted their own practices because they had not been asked to articulate the constructive force of source-use conventions, and I was able to go along with that because I had not done so either. Clearly, as Shirley Rose (1996, 34) has said, a rhetoric of citation practices is very long overdue.

Almost two decades before Rose's call for such a rhetoric, Charles Bazerman (1980, 661) observed that "if students are not taught the skills of creating new statements through evaluating, assimilating, and responding to the prior statements of the written conversation, we offer them the meager choice of being parrots of authority or raconteurs stocked with anecdotes for every occasion," and I would add, "misusers of source material." He ends that statement with "Only a fortunate few will learn to enter the community of the literate on their own." It is, of course, this sentiment that led my colleagues to urge that first-year composition continue to teach the research process, research writing, and generic source use without realizing that it also speaks to discipline-specific conversations. But if we extend Bazerman's point, and Gerald Graff's (2003, 3) arguably similar call that we save students from "cluelessnes" by teaching them that "summarizing and making arguments is the name of the game in academia," we see that by focusing on finding and penalizing those who are unable to enter general or discipline-specific discourse communities we continue to fail to create opportunity for more than "a fortunate few" to really enter disciplinary conversation and make meaning within it.

I believe that the use of universal source-use policies and generic instruction in first-year composition or the equivalent actually reduces the ability of students to join the discourse communities of the disciplines and undermines the very goals of composition (to increase communication and help students invent the university). The fact is that academic integrity policies and source-use pedagogies that originate in English departments all too often "present scholarly citation in terms limited to a view of ideas as intellectual property and of scholarly productivity as a factor in a capitalistic economy," as Shirley Rose (1996, 35) so eloquently puts it. She shows how textbooks reinforce that capitalist model of source use with their language of "ownership," "borrowing," "debt," and "intellectual property." They also reinforce an emphasis on form rather than the discursive practices inherent in and inscribed by that form. Source-use instruction has become rote learning of formulae and rules (of thumb and of law). Textbooks and handbooks reproduce lists of rules for every kind of source imaginable in MLA or Chicago style. Some also include APA, CBE, and other style sheets as if one needs only to adjust the format as one moves among disciplines. Many include discussion of how to evaluate sources and determine "appropriate" from "inappropriate" material, but that rarely goes beyond how to evaluate Websites and differentiate online publications from print publications that are available online. The emphasis is on "how to" in specific cases rather than the more difficult know-how of broad interaction with sources. To be fair, of course, textbooks cannot teach students how to act within discourse communities any more than foreign language texts can teach the exact angle to bow, the exact pressure to shake hands (which varies by community anyway), or the manner one greets with kisses. The problem is that unlike language guides and textbooks, writing textbooks suggest that the language of academic discourse does not need to be learned from within a specific context and that cultural practice does not go beyond lists and rules. Instead we penalize for misplaced commas and absent introductory phrases as if that is what counts and there is nothing more to learn.

So we say we are teaching students how to be flexible communicators, but in fact we have set up a disciplinary structure of the other kind in which students are hyperconscious of the rules and thereby less likely to be able to participate in specific discourse communities. They enter the disciplines like tourists clutching their dictionaries and phrase books, and a compulsive fear of "getting it wrong" makes them miss the whole point of "it." This is the very opposite of the goals of the Writing Across the Curriculum (WAC) movement with its emphasis on writing to learn and the discursive freedom that invites students to use writing as a way of making meaning. A major point of WAC was to create ways for students to escape the paralysis brought on by right/wrong binaries and fear of error. Freed from obsessive focus on his or her own correctness, a student can actually listen to others and speak back to them. The parallel with foreign languages may seem a stretch here, but I am going to stick with it because it helps to make apparent what the simplification of our understanding of source-use obscures. I think it is harder to enter the discourse community of an unfamiliar academic discipline than to enter that of an unfamiliar nation for precisely this reason. Those readers who are the product of Anglo-American foreign language education will recognize the fear of mispronunciation and punishment. While today the drudgery of drills has largely been replaced by a language immersion approach, the grades are still based on correct pronunciation, spelling, and grammar. And too many students are left functionally monolingual, focusing on form rather communication and pronunciation rather than engagement.

In 2000 I was in South Africa visiting schools and learning about the Government of National Unity's Curriculum 2005, the ambitious education policy "based on the principles of co-operation, critical thinking and social responsibly . . . [to] empower individuals to participate in all aspects of society" (Manganyi 1997). Part of the curriculum focuses on language, including multilingualism and knowledge of and respect for "cultural and language traditions" to "promote the development of a national identity" by promoting multilingualism to enable "learners to develop and value . . . other languages and cultures in our multi-cultural country and in international contexts"

(*Curriculum* 1997). Where possible, students were to study in their "home language" (one of the eleven official languages, which could include English and Afrikaans) or South African Sign Language and learn a "first additional language" and ideally a "second additional language." In the small, very rundown Thaba Jabula Secondary School in Soweto, I visited a ninth-grade classroom where the students were learning Afrikaans, their "second official language" after English, which they spoke fluently. I listened, impressed, and at the break I asked a student how hard it was to learn this language that she told me was actually her fourth language. I admitted that I was finding it impossible to say the name of our Afrikaaner bus driver or, indeed, Gauteng Province where we were. The German version of that *G* sound had eluded me in my middle-school German classes, and this version did so too. She looked at me with concern. "No," she said, "you're worrying about the wrong thing. You don't have to pretend to be Afrikaans. You just have to be able to communicate with them. It doesn't matter how the words sound. If we understand each other, we can work together." Her teacher confirmed this for me. "Yes, perhaps, one day we will all speak each other's languages with each other's accents, but our goal is not to make everyone the same. Each person remains who he is with his own language and accent, but everyone else also understands that language so we can communicate, and then we can also learn about each other."

This is a powerful model as we think about source use and WAC. If disciplinary conventions, including source use, are the languages of each discipline, when source-use instruction focuses on correct pronunciation (avoiding the ill-placed comma, knowing when to italicize a journal title, when to place it in quotation marks, and when to do nothing to it), it leaves us missing the point. Whether instruction is designed to create the opportunity for multilingualism and thereby "invitation into the mental positions of those who think differently from us," as Graff (2003, 13) put it, or whether it is simply advanced conversation within a discipline, if my fear of failure leads me to depend on a phrase book for my Afrikaans sentences or not speak for fear of mangling the *G*, I may never even communicate at all. I will certainly be too busy to meet the glance of my interlocutor, let alone make conversation. The student who depends too heavily on sources for phrases and sentences suffers the same inability.

Reliance on one general English department–generated policy is clearly limiting, yet it is not practical—or desirable—for all students to have to "pretend to be" members of an academic discipline to write college-level papers. A middle ground seems to be to create a sufficient awareness of basic differences and vocabulary for students to be able to communicate in the various "languages" of the disciplines and so have access to the culture and knowledge embedded within them. This, of course, also requires that, as faculty, we give up the notion that there is such a thing as generally agreed-upon "good writing" across the curriculum—give up English department prose as the colonial language—and explore ways to make the languages of our disciplines apparent to us and then to our students without expecting technical perfection or reducing difference to the generic. And this is where WAC can take on a new and more intellectually challenging role in which writing-to-learn ceases to be a general principle that does not necessarily improve writing or thinking (Russell 2001, 259) and becomes a space for demystifying context-specific writing. Russell's reviews suggest that methods for such a pedagogy would include direct instruction in the components of discourse-specific writing, thinking, and source use along with models, guidelines, "classroom talk," and a focus on discipline-specific writing processes (283–91). Our new goal, Russell concludes, should be to move beyond what we want students to *know* in any given discipline to what we want them to "*do* with the material of the course" (290) and how we want them to do that; or, as Graff (2003) might put it, to give all students the "ability to join an intellectual community that makes sense to them" (274).

If the goal of WAC that we increase communication across the curriculum (also known as CAC) and writing to learn within all parts of it is to be fully realized, we need to retrace and reconsider our history to see how what we focus on now came to dominate, and to listen to the voices that have been ignored and learn from them. Our task in this history is to understand how one discipline—English—came to have an exclusive hold over the notion of "good writing" in all other disciplines. It was WAC that led to the inaccurate definitions and generic institutional plagiarism and source-use policies discussed so far, but it is also within WAC scholarship that we can find more useful ways to think about source use across the disciplines. By retracing our steps, so to speak, we can understand where we lost our way in the shift from writing across the curriculum (WAC) to Writing in the Disciplines (WID) and also refocus our attention on plagiarism across the curriculum in new and productive ways.

The fact that WAC has survived for the last thirty years in still recognizable form is testament to what it has to offer and what it has already delivered. The goal of helping students write to learn and the related goal of reforming pedagogy to include process as well as product have largely succeeded. Writing assignments are sequenced, and students are assigned journals, freewriting, drafts, and revisions across the curriculum. Thanks to WAC, students develop general writing skills that they use to help them articulate what they learn and that, in theory, help them enter different discourse communities. But these skills and strategies were an ideological Trojan horse carrying embedded within them a set of practices that conflict with the disciplinary communities into which they were delivered, the most important being the relationship to sources and the MLA citation method that underpins universal source-use policies and plagiarism detection software.

As we became more immersed in WAC, we began to understand discipline specificity and have often been humbled by the sheer audacity of our project. Susan McLeod (2000) observes:

> when I began my first faculty seminar, I really had no appreciation of the complexity of disciplinary discourse—I assumed that as an English teacher,

> I knew what good writing was and simply needed to enlighten my colleagues across the disciplines. . . . A passionate, hour-long discussion of the use of the passive voice was one of the most memorable sessions in my own understanding of the social sciences.

I had a similar experience with a laboratory report I tried to write as I collaborated with a colleague in the chemistry department. My colleague could not understand why I was unable to produce the kind of prose she expected of first-year students and I could not believe how difficult it was to write in passive voice that did not sound ugly and disjointed. I learned that there is a world of difference between the passive voice we decry in first-year writing courses and the elegant and informative prose of the hard sciences, but my colleague had to literally rewrite my report before I could get it. For many of us, these experiences led to the move to writing in the disciplines. The question this brief history seeks to understand is why this move did not lead to a rethinking of source use.

Everything we thought we understood about our colleagues turned out to be opaque, and the most opaque of all was source use. I could ask my colleagues what role writing served in their discipline and how it helped to create and disseminate meaning. I could learn that, for some of my colleagues, writing essentially told a story about data (economics) or observation (anthropology), while for others it challenged assumptions (chemistry) or interpretations (history), and for still others it offered interpretation (art history) or connected ideas (sociology). I could also learn that not everyone in those disciplines articulated the role of writing in the same manner, just as my colleagues in English disagree about the role (and importance of) literary analysis. The disciplines in parentheses above could be mixed and matched depending on one's subfield, theoretical or methodological framework, or specific research. At times there seemed to be greater similarity among disciplines than within them. But I never thought to ask about citations and their relationship to source material and the ideas of others. And no one thought to tell me.

While those of us involved in WAC programs (Thaiss and Zawacki's 2006 findings notwithstanding) can talk at great length about the content and purpose of writing, the routine conventions of source use and citation seem like an afterthought. They are often taught at the editing stage of the writing process, and several software programs will even change papers from one format to another as if the issue were really just where to put the punctuation as composition handbooks and software suggest. This afterthought model leads faculty across the country to support a source-use policy that is applicable only to literary studies, because it further obscures the overall discipline-specific differences. Perhaps this model also explains the fact that while there are a few excellent articles on the subject, a very small proportion of the thousands of articles and studies on WAC, WID, CAC, and all their derivatives focus on source use or the discursive nature of research writing within the disciplines.

As with the passive voice, perhaps, we think we know what we will find. Or perhaps we do not know how to ask the question and/or our colleagues don't know how to answer it.

Anne Herrington (2000) reminds us that for many, a mission of WAC was "aiming to foster the success of all students, particularly those who for reasons of class, race, or other factors are less likely to succeed." Although we may indeed have largely forgotten this mission, as she suggests, it is never more urgent than in source use where one-size-fits-all policies exclude and discipline some, while somehow permitting others with more advanced and flexible writing skills (what Thaiss and Zawacki call third-stage writers) to enter the discourse of specific disciplines. With the increasing dependence on electronic plagiarism detection, sustained research on source-use practices is long overdue. When we focus not on *how* sources are cited within specific disciplinary discourse communities but on *why* they are cited, we will be in a better position to develop policies and pedagogies that invite students into the discourse of the disciplines rather than disciplining those who do not make it.

Interestingly, if we go back to Bazerman's (1980) article on the relationship between reading and writing, we see the beginning of a thread that could have led to very different source-use policies, and this is where the historical exploration is so important. After summarizing the work of James Britton and his coauthors (1975) in *The Development of Writing Abilities (11–18)* and his comment "source-book material may be used in various ways involving different levels of activity by the writer," Bazerman (1980, 657) observes those "various ways" and "different levels of activity" can be understood as part of an "on-going, written conversation." The fact that he takes great pains to acknowledge the differences between spoken and written conversation indicates what a novel idea this was a quarter of a century ago. By 1996 Shirley Rose could describe the same thing as a "courtship ritual" with no need of justification, but before we move to the recent past we need to really engage with this idea of conversation as Bazerman (1980) approached it. He observes that "conversation requires absorption of what prior speakers have said, consideration of how earlier comments relate to the responder's thoughts, and a response framed to the situation and the reader's purposes" (657). By that definition, my invocation of Russell (1997, 2001), Thaiss and Zawacki (2006), Graff (2003), McLeod (2000), Britton (1975), Bazerman 1980, and Rose (1996) seems to clearly mark this article as a conversation, and we are so used to this idea that it seems somewhat banal even to make the observation.

What makes the observation important is what marks this as a conversation *in the discipline of composition*. That discipline-specific context is marked by much more than my absorbing, considering, and responding to the sources listed above; it is revealed in the way I introduce and cite those sources and the way you will find them presented in the references list (along with the fact that in an early draft of this chapter I called it a "works cited list"). The fact that I wrote this essay using MLA and was then asked to "translate" it to Chicago for this volume also indicates something about the discipline of composition—our emergent but still partial identity *as* a discipline separate from English. But the fact that I assume my readers will understand the irony of this request indicates the same "insider knowledge" as I reveal in my assumption that readers will know what WAC, CAC, WID, and WPA stand for. Bazerman 1980 alerted us to this distinction back in 1980 when he wrote:

> The model of conversation even transforms the technical skills of reference and citation. The variety of uses to be made of quotation, the options for referring to others' ideas and information (e.g., quotation, paraphrase, summary, name only), and the techniques of introducing and discussing source materials are the tools which allow the accurate but pointed connection of one's argument to earlier statements. The mechanics of documentation, more than being an exercise in intellectual etiquette, become the means of indicating the full range of comments to which the new essay is responding. (661)

Although still steeped in the language of afterthought ("*technical* skills of reference and citation" and "*mechanics* of documentation"), Bazerman 1980 was clearly challenging us to look more deeply. Had we done so, our conception of Writing in the Disciplines would have been much more tightly focused on the specific relationship to source material in each discourse community, and our understanding of unintentional plagiarism would be focused on source use rather than *mis*-use.

We had another chance to pick up this thread a decade ago when Shirley Rose (1996) drew on another work of Bazerman (1988) to lead into a Burkean analysis of the conversation within discipline-specific source-use decisions as courtship ritual. She places her analysis in the context of Bazerman's work, observing that Bazerman's "exploration of writers' motives is necessarily limited" and asserting that "a complete rhetoric of citations must be able to address writer's motives and purposes, for these cannot be taken for granted without risk of reducing them to simplistic terms" (38). Through the Burkean lens, Rose sees scholarly citation as "a microcosm of the academic discipline understood as both scene and outcome or cooperative action, the act of citing—collaboration between the author and other authors and between author and reader—serves as a representative anecdote of all written discourse as collaboration" (40). Further, "the scholarly writer's rhetoric builds her identification with both her readers and the other writers she cites in her text as she negotiates for a place in a relatively small and well-defined community" (41).

I'd like to engage in a little analysis of the structure of the last few paragraphs of this paper to help us think more about disciplinary difference. I have quoted heavily from two articles that I consider very significant to this conversation about the history of plagiarism across the curriculum. I have done so with the purpose of demonstrating their relationship and setting a ground for further analysis. If I were to run these paragraphs though some magical software program that would track the percentage of original prose

contained therein I'd be done for. I have broken the oft-repeated general rule
of thumb that quotation does not make up more than 10 percent of a written
paper (at least for the last few paragraphs). And in not citing examples of
sources who "oft repeat" advice, I have broken a rule of citation often
invoked in composition classes at least. To my credit, I have block-indented a
quotation that is over four lines, and I have indicated a source quoted by
another source, introduced "borrowed" material so no one is in any doubt as
to who is "speaking" at any given time, and not ended a paragraph with a quotation. However, if these paragraphs were part of a psychology paper I would
still have breached etiquette because according to APA I should not have
quoted at all. I should have summarized or paraphrased. I should also not
have included first names, which might focus attention on gender and the
impact of the person observing rather than on the observations themselves.
For some teachers of mathematics I did not need to cite any sources; I could
have simply summarized the general history of the discipline and moved on
to my point (ideally several pages ago). But for *this* conversation in *this* discipline I feel that I need to quote for exactly the reasons Rose (1996) argues we
use sources at all.

First, she says, we include familiar "words, ideas, and conclusions" of
others to remind our readers of our shared knowledge. To quote early WAC
scholars is both to give them what my students call "their props" and in so
doing, also, to show that I know who is who in the field—or not. Readers who
are inclined to respect those "founders" will be more likely to pay attention to
my point and to think that I have done my homework. If I did it right, my readers will identify with me and feel that *we* are having a conversation that is
important. Indeed, by explaining this I am simply reminding you of what you
already know. But I am also, as Rose (1996) further points out, providing you
with "a narrative of the process by which [I] arrived at [the] ideas" I discuss in
this article. If I am successful, the rhetorical move is as follows: "this is what
we already have believed, this is how I propose to challenge or further develop
our belief, and you, dear reader, will believe this new way too" (Rose 1996,
41). On the other hand, the fact that I have failed to cite many other scholars in
the history of the field could lead some to dismiss me as an upstart rather than
a member of the discipline; a follower of footnotes, or what Bazerman (1981)
calls "a parrot of authority" (661) rather than a member of this scholarly community to which I presume to speak. "Thus," as Rose puts it, "the citation
choices meant to foster identification have the potential for creating division"
(41) or outright rejection. If I had cited many sources, you might have assumed
I did not know enough to make wise decisions about whom *not* to cite.
Conversely, you might have assumed that I am widely read in the field. If
I were to cite a source with which you are unfamiliar, Rose's Burkean analysis
suggests that I offer you a gift: You can strengthen your relationship to the discourse community and "achieve closer identification with the author" by locat-
ing and reading that work (41).

Now let us turn our attention back from one discourse community (ours) to the world of our students. If they include only recent sources, as Rose (1996) observes, we may find them refreshingly up-to-date or depressingly unprepared for the purpose because of their unfamiliarity with historical context. And vice versa. If a student were to explain that Charles Bazerman has written many important books and articles in the field of composition or that David Russell writes about WAC, we would know that she has just learned that fact and does not understand the field sufficiently to know that it is discipline-specific common knowledge. And so on. These rules do not easily lend themselves to handbooks or handouts. They are learned by interacting with a discourse community; by reading as Bazerman (1980) observes and Thaiss and Zawacki (2006) emphasize, but also by trial and error and the comments of others on our work—whether they are the teacher-to-student comments valued by the students in Thaiss and Zawacki's study and in so many others, or the editorial comments and feedback from our colleagues that makes all writing, indeed, a collaboration. Russell's (2001) detailed analysis of naturalistic studies in WAC/WID highlights what many other surveys have reported and what Thaiss and Zawacki found in their study of students; however, those same studies do not all present faculty attitudes to student disciplinary membership in the same way (Russell 2001, 259–98), and this is what indicates that we need more study, especially with regard to the role of source material.

Rose (1996) observes that all too often the sources used by "inexperienced academic writers," and I would add more pressingly novices of a disciplinary discourse, are not "integrated into their texts" to the degree that the students are not integrated into the academic community (43). They may use too many quotations, not enough, or not the right ones; but they also may not introduce those quotations, indicate where paraphrases begin, or provide full citations. They may assume that what they know is common knowledge, or they may assume that what they just learned is not common knowledge. As I did earlier, they may adopt informal prose or inaccurate terminology. But there is a distinction to be made in this list. All mark the writer as an outsider, but only some will result in charges of misuse of sources.

We can focus as much as we like on ethics. Asserting as the WPA statement does that "Ethical writers make every effort to acknowledge sources fully and appropriately in accordance with the contexts and genres of their writing" (Council of Writing Program Administrators 2003), even if we do not classify those who fail as "unethical." To reduce discipline-specific or generic source-use conventions to good and evil, ethical and immoral, is to miss an important pedagogical moment, as many have observed before me. I believe that what we must do instead is remember that South African student learning Afrikaans, and early WAC calls for us to develop strategies to make disciplinary discourse apparent and the connection between discourse conventions and content clear. And then we need to teach those languages. Students may learn general "good writing" in the safe(r) official home language of first-year composition or other first-year and introductory courses, even the first two stages of the research paper as described by Brian Sutton (1997) ("generalized academic writing concerned with stating claims, offering evidence, respecting others' opinions, and learning how to write with authority"[48]); Graff's (2003) summary and argument; and Bazerman's (1981) evaluating, assimilating, and responding to prior arguments. In contrast, in majors, minors, and specializations they must also learn a "first additional language" and a "second additional language" sufficiently that they can enter the culture and knowledge base of a discipline rather than simply learning its facts and remaining "clueless" about the larger issues, concerns, or motives of members of those disciplines. In other words, they need to be taught to really write-to-learn and communicate across the curriculum and in the disciplines. While we should not stop teaching "good writing," we must determine exactly what that is and how a useful form of it may be taught in first-year writing and WAC classes. But those courses must also begin the process of explaining how and why writing is context specific and the importance of understanding any culture or discipline through its language. It is not the accent that matters, what matters is that we are able to communicate sufficiently for us to learn about ideas. We need to teach students to use sources in dialogue rather than to fear the penalty of misuse in isolation.

References

Althusser, Louis. 1971. "Ideology and Ideological State Apparatuses (Notes Towards an Investigation)." In *Lenin and Philosophy and Other Essays*. Trans. Ben Brewster. New York: Monthly Review.

Bazerman, Charles. 1980. "A Relationship Between Reading and Writing: The Conversation Model." *College English* 41 (6): 656–61.

Bazerman, Charles. 1988. *Shaping Written Knowledge: The Genre and Activity of the Experimental Article in Science*. Madison: University of Wisconsin Press.

Britton, James N., et al. 1975. *The Development of Writing Abilities, 11–18*. London: Macmillan.

Carroll, Lee Ann. 2003. *Rehearsing New Roles: How College Students Develop as Writers*. Carbondale: Southern Illinois University Press.

Council of Writing Program Administrators. 2003. "Defining and Avoiding Plagiarism: WPA Statement on Best Policies." http://wpacouncil.org/node/9.

Curriculum 2005: Lifelong Learning for the 21st Century. A User's Guide. 1997. www.polity.org.za/html/govdocs/misc/curr2005.html#foreward.

Drew University. 2001. "College of Liberal Arts Standards of Academic Integrity." www.depts.drew.edu/composition/Academic_Honesty.htm.

Graff, Gerald. 2003. *Clueless in Academe: How Schooling Obscures the Life of the Mind*. New Haven, CT: Yale University Press.

Hare, Victoria Chou, and Denise A. Fitzsimmons. 1991. "The Influence of Interpretive Communities on the Use of Content and Procedural Knowledge." *Written Communication* 8 (3): 348–78.

Herrington, Anne. 2000. "Principles That Should Guide WAC/CAC Program Development in the Coming Decade." *Academic Writing: Interdisciplinary Perspectives on Communication Across the Curriculum.* http://wac.colostate.edu/aw/forums/winter2000/index_expand.htm.

Manganyi, Chabani. 1997. Foreward. *Curriculum 2005: Lifelong Learning for the 21st Century. A User's Guide.* www.polity.org.za/html/govdocs/misc/curr2005.html# foreward.

McLeod, Susan. 2000. "Principles That Should Guide WAC/CAC Program Development in the Coming Decade." *Academic.Writing: Interdisciplinary Perspectives on Communication Across the Curriculum.* http://wac.colostate.edu/aw/forums/winter2000/index_expand.htm.

Rose, Shirley K. 1996. "What's Love Got to Do With It? Scholarly Citation Practices as Courtship Ritual." *Language and Learning Across the Disciplines* 1 (3): 34–48.

Russell, David. 1997. "Rethinking Genre in School and Society: An Activity Theory Analysis." *Written Communication* 14 (4): 504–54.

Russell, David. 2001. "Where Do Naturalistic Studies of WAC/WID Point?" In *WAC for the New Millennium: Strategies for Continuing Writing-Across-the-Curriculum,* edited by Susan H. McLeod, Eric Miraglia, Margot Soven, and Christopher Thais. Urbana, IL: National Council of Teachers of English, 259–98.

Sutton, Brian. 1997. "Writing in the Disciplines, First-Year Composition, and the Research Paper." *Language and Learning Across the Disciplines* 2 (1): 46–57.

Thaiss, Chris, and Terry Myers Zawacki. 2006. *Engaged Writers and Dynamic Disciplines: Research on the Academic Writing Life.* Portsmouth, NH: Heinemann/Boynton Cook.

Walvoord, Barbara E., and Lucille P. McCarthy. 1990. *Thinking and Writing in College: A Naturalistic Study of Students in Four Disciplines.* Urbana, IL: National Council of Teachers of English.

6

Plagiarizing (from) Graduate Students

Rebecca Moore Howard
Syracuse University

The phrase *plagiarizing graduate students* calls up an image of dishonest students. That image has been made familiar through such relentless media coverage as the headline from a Charleston, South Carolina, television station: "Cheating College of Charleston Students Get New Grade" (McKenzie 2006).

Cheating College of Charleston students? The filthy swine! How dare they! Viewers and readers are scripted to experience righteous wrath and then satisfaction as they learn that these filthy swine will receive the punitive grade of "X-F." Serves 'em right. As the audience participates in this familiar script, they are called upon to experience a sequence of emotions very much like those of the viewers of TV westerns: indignation at the perfidy of the bad guys and then happiness as the bad guys get what's coming to them.

If cheating students are the bad guys of the academy, cheating graduate students are the baddest of the bad. In the banking model of education, in which factual knowledge is transmitted seamlessly from teacher to student and in which the student then flawlessly applies that knowledge, graduate students should know better. Because they are "advanced," they should have long ago learned the rules. In this model of education, therefore, their transgressions seem even worse than those of the cheating undergraduates.

That logical analysis does not, however, even scratch the surface of faculty emotions on the topic. The specter of cheating graduate students takes on intensified force because it edges so close to the audience, the professors themselves. Faculty may feel a comfortable distance between themselves and the undergraduates whom they teach, but graduate students are another matter entirely. Graduate students are the soon-to-be colleagues of the faculty, a mirror of what the faculty themselves were, only moments ago. Graduate students are collaborators and coauthors with the faculty. The successes of the graduate students are the successes of their mentors.

And their failures are our failures. Every time I speak with a colleague and mention the Ohio University case, I am met with stricken faces. Faculty and administrators everywhere know of the fifty masters' theses in engineering that were charged with plagiarism. Faculty themselves have been called to account for the case (Lederman 2006). Faculty are being demoted ("Professor's Term" 2006), theses invalidated (Phillips 2006), degrees revoked (Gray 2007). The situation recalls Neil Hertz's (1982) hypothesis, offered back in 1982, that faculty are so exercised about student plagiarism because they are so insecure about their own textual practices. Whereas the image of cheating undergraduates incites faculty indignation, the image of cheating graduate students incites fear. If graduate students cheat, the faculty are themselves *responsible*.

It is in this environment of fear that we professors work with our graduate students, and it is the emotion of fear that we must control if we are to work with them constructively. We must, I believe, differentiate graduate students' (and all students', for that matter) misuse of sources from their plagiarism. We must acknowledge the ways in which graduate students are not yet finished scholars, and we must recognize the textual practices of which they do not yet have full command. We must, in other words, look at issues of graduate students' handling of texts as developmental issues. Successful writing from sources does not come from observing rules but from repeated, mentored practice. It's not something that all students, even the best students, can fully know how to do when they come to graduate school. So it is part of our responsibility as we work with students through their graduate programs.

There is another piece, one from which we must not avert our eyes: Our responsibilities toward our graduate students include our not exploiting them as unacknowledged workers, ghostwriters, for our own research. Before I take up that issue, though, I'd like to look carefully at the mentoring our graduate students need as they work with texts.

Graduate Students as Plagiarists

Much of the literature on plagiarism assumes that plagiarists are either unethical thieves or hapless folk who haven't learned how to cite sources. These are "neat" problems: One enjoins students to be ethical and punishes them when they are not. One transmits correct information about citation of sources and penalizes students when they do not follow these rules. In the first scenario, the instructor is a model of ethical behavior; in the second, the transmitter of procedural information. In both cases, the instructor is gatekeeper who determines and adjudicates students' adherence to ethical standards and textual procedures.

Less often do practitioners engage more difficult issues of writing from sources. Several researchers have reported on the difficulties that students have with two key components of successful writing from sources, summarizing and paraphrasing. These practices of academic writing are much less straightforward. They do not call on students to adhere to a clear behavioral standard, nor are they rule bound. Paraphrasing and summarizing are practices enacted with each text encountered, and their challenges are experienced anew with each text that a writer engages. Every writer is challenged every time she undertakes to paraphrase or summarize a text, and not every writer succeeds in accomplishing the task without too-close copying from the source.

Plagiarism? Technically, yes. In fact, it is the form of plagiarism most acknowledged by students answering a 2004 survey conducted at Syracuse University. To categorize patchwriting—too-close copying from sources—as plagiarism is to miss the point, though. The point is that it is hard to write from sources. Faculty in graduate programs can too easily believe that summarizing and paraphrasing are elementary skills. Frey, Fisher, and Hernandez (2003) demonstrate that summary writing is taught in middle schools. Why, then, would it be a concern for graduate students?

Diane Pecorari (2003) offers one answer: because even graduate students don't always succeed in paraphrasing and summarizing. Pecorari conducted a synchronic study of seventeen international graduate students working in a wide range of disciplines in three British universities (321), students who indicated enthusiasm for and investment in their work (326). Pecorari studied preliminary and final drafts of their dissertations, comparing text to sources (321–22). Sixteen of the students "had one or more passages in their writing samples in which 50% or more of the words came from their sources without being indicated as quotation." Of those, all but two had multiple passages in this category (325). "Ten had passage(s) at or above the 85% level, and six had at least one passage with 100% of the language taken from its source but not signaled as quotation" (326). "[E]ach of the 17 writers failed to use sources transparently, and did so in a way which could be labeled plagiarism" (331). None tried to "cover their tracks" (335).

The students in Pecorari's (2003) study were L2 students, speakers of international rather than British or U.S. English. We cannot, however, bracket their writing practices as those of a linguistic or cultural Other. Though scholars such as Sapp (2003) and Sowden (2005) have established the cultural multiplicity of textual standards today, L2 graduate students' difficulties in writing from texts are not simply a reflection of home cultures with standards different from those of the United States or United Kingdom. They are as much—if not more—a reflection of the difficulty of writing from sources, a difficulty that is exponentially multiplied when one is not writing in one's home language, about texts that were not written in one's home language. Studying the work of 165 undergraduate students, Keck (2006) concludes that although L2 writers are less successful in their attempts at summary and paraphrase, both L1 and L2 writers were challenged. Applying Keck's findings to Pecorari's research enables this reasonable hypothesis: Although L1 graduate students in British universities would probably have fared better than did the L2 students whom Pecorari studied, they would still not have worked from sources without textual transgression. My own reflection on these difficulties urges me, as a graduate faculty member, to work with all my graduate students, in an ongoing way, on their practices of writing from sources.

Graduate Students as Victims of Plagiarism

I feel equally compelled to mentor my graduate students in protecting themselves from faculty who would appropriate their work. The Ohio University story is perhaps the best-known graduate-student-plagiarism-story circulating at this moment. What capture much less attention—in part, I would speculate, because they are so much more disturbing—are the stories of faculty plagiarizing from graduate students. As I draft this chapter, a story comes to me over *CNet,* an online Canadian news source:

> The Carleton Graduate Students' Association is spearheading an initiative to educate some 3,300 grad students on how to safeguard their intellectual property while ensuring they're being properly recognized for their work. (LaRose 2007)

The story hastens to assure readers that there are no known problems with the appropriation of graduate students' work but then continues ambiguously in this vein:

> "A lot of the time, this stuff does happen to students but they have no real way of being able to cite it or try to figure out how to go about bringing the issue to light." . . . Examples include a student not receiving authorship on written work, or having a professor take credit for their work. (LaRose 2007)

What the *CNet* story does not reference are all the previously published accounts of faculty exploitation of graduate students. The following samples provide a sense of the problem:

- In 1971, James O. Morris accused labor historian Philip Foner of having plagiarized from Morris' master's thesis. Professor Melvyn Dubofsky also found that portions of his doctoral dissertation had been appropriated by Foner (McLemee 2003).

- In 1991, a Stanford engineering professor apologized for not acknowledging that two pages of his new book were written by a graduate student (Leatherman 1991).

- In 1994, says Antonia Demas, her professor at Cornell University "took credit for her dissertation, used it to obtain a grant from the U.S. Agriculture Department, claimed awards she won for her work, and changed some of her research results" (Reynolds 1998, A16).

- In 2002, Cornell University was ruled not liable for David A. Levitsky's alleged appropriation of Demas' dissertation. Levitskey went on to assume the presidency of the University of Chicago (Bartlett 2002).

- In 2003, Dwayne D. Kirk, a graduate student in plant biology at Arizona State, discovered that large portions of his first published article had been copied and pasted into a book chapter subsequently published by his mentor. Charles J. Arntzen justified the appropriation on the basis that Kirk had been "a member of his research team" (Bartlett and Smallwood 2004a, A14).

- When Chris Radziminiski complained that his professors at the University of Toronto had appropriated his drinking water research, the university threatened legal action against him. In 2006 his charges were confirmed, and he received formal apologies (LaRose 2007).

Lest it appear that these incidents are pretty much confined to the sciences, I can testify to my own experience when I was a new faculty member at my current institution. I found myself at dinner with five other new members of the humanities faculty. My host was an established member of a humanities department. When the conversation turned to how one decides the best means for acknowledging the contributions of a graduate student to one's publication, the scorecard was five to two in favor of no acknowledgment whatsoever—"a footnote, if the contribution is really substantial."

Noting that "[e]xploitation is one of the seamier sides of academia, something which is seldom discussed or even acknowledged," Brian Martin (1986) recounts even more cases that have been described to him. In both Martin's (1986) article and in parts of Chris Woolston's (2002), the victim graduate students are given pseudonyms. For them to go public under their own names is to risk even further injury: the disapprobation of their scholarly community.

Martin (1986) observes, too, that no statistics are available for assessing how often exploitation occurs. While the U.S. Center for Academic Integrity has energetically surveyed college students about their textual practices, no one has undertaken a comparable survey of faculty appropriations of their students' texts:

> Why is academic exploitation so little studied? One reason is that it is not in the interests of the exploiters to expose the phenomenon, and the exploiters are usually in positions of power and able to prevent exposure by the implicit or sometimes explicit threat of bad recommendations or defamation suits. Second, exploitation contradicts the genteel, professional image of academia which is promoted for public consumption; even academics who oppose exploitation are hesitant to disrupt the smooth running of the system. Third, studying exploitation does not nicely fit in any academic discipline or specialisation: no one sees it as their professional duty to investigate it. Finally, some forms of academic exploitation are so common that even the exploited accept them as part of the natural order of things. (Martin 1986)

How, one might wonder, can this possibly happen? The answer is no doubt complex. One probable component is the absence of uniform ethics codes for faculty:

> How investigations are conducted and how faculty are disciplined are deter-
> mined by each institution and vary from school to school. And since plagia-
> rism is not illegal, only unethical, there are no laws to guide colleges and no
> statute of limitation on how long a individual can be held accountable for an
> act of plagiarism. (Leach 2005)

Students at many institutions have become aware of the difference between the textual ethics expected of them and those not stipulated for their professors. From the University of Alabama (Dawkins 2005) to Harvard (Rimer 2004), students' objections are becoming a familiar refrain: "Weighing in on the matter, Harvard's student newspaper, *The Harvard Crimson*, said the university appeared to have one set of rules for its famous professors and another for its students" (Rimer 2004).

A second probable factor in the appropriation of student work is faculty's sense of increasing pressure to publish. Shapiro (2007) traces the phrase "publish or perish" back to 1934, but faculty today feel that they are reinventing its oppressive power.

Equally important, perhaps, is the vulnerability of graduate students. In addition to Martin (1986), Bartlett and Smallwood's articles (2004a, 2004b) argue that graduate students who protest their exploitation face a hard path through their disciplines. Many choose to submit silently and wait for a time when they have the power to maintain authority over their own texts. Robillard (2006) has eloquently described the ambiguous status of the student author. That ambiguity does not end with a bachelor's degree. It continues through graduate school, and the texts produced by graduate students are of greater potential value to faculty who do not respect those students as authors, who regard students' texts as fair game, and who feel pressured to produce publications.

Recommendations

Questions of graduate student plagiarism raise a variety of issues for faculty who work with these students. By way of concluding this chapter, I'd like to make a few suggestions.

First, when it comes to graduate students' own textual practices, faculty should not regard these as already "finished" but should seek out ways to engage textual practices productively. The goal should be to help make transparent the ways in which knowledge in the discipline is built from source texts and the ways in which those texts are cited in that discipline. From their entry into graduate programs to their receipt of the Ph.D., graduate students need to be mentored in their textual practices.

Second, Carleton University has offered a model that all graduate programs might usefully adopt: graduate student orientation that includes an overview of students' intellectual property rights (LaRose 2007). Nor should this orientation be theoretical or decontextualized; on the contrary, graduate students need to know about the possibility of faculty appropriation of graduate students' work.

The orientation should describe ways in which students might protect themselves from such appropriations. For example, although all texts in the United States are automatically copyrighted, with no registration necessary, placing the copyright symbol and the year of composition in front of one's name on a paper places the reader on notice: The writer considers the text to be her own property. This will not stop all faculty plagiarists, but it may deter some.

Third, faculty should be taking up the question of the authority of students' texts. The conversation that I found myself in as a new faculty member was an important one that compelled all of us to consider difficult issues. Such conversations can be structured in new faculty orientation and also in institutionally sponsored meetings, workshops, and symposia that include student voices.

Finally, faculty should receive institutional rewards for collaborating with their graduate students and for assigning coauthorship to the graduate students' contributions. Angela Garcia (2006) describes a sociology graduate seminar that was deliberately structured to produce a collaboratively authored review of the literature on the seminar topic. In a similar vein, Carrick (2006) explains how a graduate seminar in composition and rhetoric was structured to produce an edited collection of essays. Institutions can value such arrangements when faculty are considered for rehiring, tenure, and promotion, and that reward system will encourage faculty to consider their graduate students as novice colleagues rather than as their personal property.

References

Bartlett, Thomas. 2002. "New York Court Rules That Cornell U. Is Not Liable for Professor's Alleged Misdeeds." *Chronicle of Higher Education* (18 February). http://chronicle.com/free/2002/02/2002021805n.htm.

Bartlett, Thomas, and Scott Smallwood. 2004a. "Mentor vs. Protege." *Chronicle of Higher Education* (17 December): 14–15.

Bartlett, Thomas, and Scott Smallwood. 2004b. "Professor Copycat." *Chronicle of Higher Education* (17 December): A8–12.

Carrick, Tracy Hamler. 2006. "Spot Keeps Turning Up: Equality in Authorship(s) and Pedagogy." In *Authorship in Composition Studies*, edited by Tracy Hamler Carrick and Rebecca Moore Howard. New York: Wadsworth.

Dawkins, Stephen. 2005. "No Formal Policy for Copycat Profs." *Crimson White* [University of Alabama] (19 January): www.cw.ua.edu/vnews/display.v/ART/2005/01/19/41ee0c05c597c.

Frey, Nancy, Douglas Fisher, and Ted Hernandez. 2003. "'What's the Gist?' Summary Writing for Struggling Adolescent Writers." *Voices from the Middle* 11 (2): 44–50.

Garcia, Angela. 2006. "Combining Professional Development with Academic Learning in Graduate Seminars." *Radical Pedagogy* 8 (2): http://radicalpedagogy. icaap.org/content/issue8_2/garcia.html.

Gray, Kathy Lynn. 2007. "Ohio U. Revokes Degree of Student Accused of Plagiarism." *Columbus Dispatch* (28 March). www.columbusdispatch.com/dispatch/content/ local_news/stories/2007/03/28/revoke.html.

Hertz, Neil. 1982. "Two Extravagant Teachings." *Yale French Studies* 63: 59–71.

Keck, Casey. 2006. "The Use of Paraphrase in Summary Writing: A Comparison of L1 and L2 Writers." *Journal of Second Language Writing* 15 (4): 261–78.

LaRose, Lauren. 2007. "Students Protecting Intellectual Work." *CNews* [Canada] (8 April). http://cnews.canoe.ca/CNEWS/Canada/2007/04/08/3953293-cp.html.

Leach, Susan Llewelyn. 2005. "Profs Who Plagiarize: How Often?" *Christian Science Monitor* (27 April). www.csmonitor.com/2005/0427/p15s01-legn.html.

Leatherman, Courtney. 1991. "Faculty Notes." *Chronicle of Higher Education* (14 August): A5.

Lederman, Doug. 2006. "Student Plagiarism, Faculty Responsibility." *Inside Higher Ed* (1 June). http://insidehighered.com/news/2006/06/01/plagiarism.

Martin, Brian. 1986. "Academic Exploitation." In *Intellectual Suppression: Australian Case Histories, Analysis and Responses*, edited by Brian Martin, C. M. Ann Baker, Clyde Manwell, and Cedric Pugh. Sydney: Angus & Robertson, 59–62. Accessed online: www.uow.edu.au/arts/sts/bmartin/pubs/86is/exploitation.html.

McKenzie, Gia. 2006. "Cheating College of Charleston Students Get New Grade." *ABC News 4 Charleston* [SC] (8 August). www.abcnews4.com/news/stories/ 0806/351171.html.

McLemee, Scott. 2003. "Philip Foner Influenced a Generation of Young Labor Historians, but Critics Call Him a Plagiarist Who Helped Himself to Their Research." *Chronicle of Higher Education* (27 June): A11.

Pecorari, Diane. 2003. "Good and Original: Plagiarism and Patchwriting in Academic Second-Language Writing." *Journal of Second Language Writing* 12 (4): 317–45.

Phillips, Jim. 2006. "OU Sends Warning Letter About Plagiarism to Former Students." *Athens News* (17 July). www.athensnews.com/issue/article.php3?story_id=25446.

"Professor's Term as Department Head Ends Amid Plagiarism Probe." 2006. *Akron Beacon Journal* (29 June). www.ohio.com/mld/beaconjournal/14926595.htm.

Reynolds, Jason M. 1998. "Cornell Ph.D. Charges Her Professor With Copying From Her Dissertation." *Chronicle of Higher Education* (13 March): A16.

Rimer, Sara. 2004. "At Harvard, Lapses by Scholars Put Focus on Plagiarism Policy." *Chicago Tribune* (26 November). www.chicagotribune.com/news/nationworld/ chi0411260242nov26,1,6901939.story?coll=chi-newsnationworld-hed.

Robillard, Amy E. 2006. "Students and Authors in Composition Scholarship." In *Authorship in Composition Studies*, edited by Tracy Hamler Carrick and Rebecca Moore Howard. New York: Wadsworth.

Sapp, David. 2003. "Towards an International and Intercultural Understanding of Plagiarism and Academic Dishonesty in Composition: Reflections from the People's Republic of China." *Issues in Writing* 13 (1): 58–79.

Shapiro, Fred R. 2007. "'Boola Boola'—and Other Words of College Wisdom." *Chronicle of Higher Education* (30 March). http://chronicle.com/temp/reprint.php?id=mrzc6xfb9p62bhjq0r58yn3cxfxw9ybx.

Sowden, Colin. 2005. "Plagiarism and the Culture of Multilingual Students in Higher Education Abroad." *ELT Journal* 59 (3): 226–33.

Woolston, Chris. 2002. "When a Mentor Becomes a Thief." *Chronicle of Higher Education* (1 April). http://chronicle.com/jobs/2002/04/2002040101c.htm.

7

"Thou Shalt Not Plagiarize"?

Appeals to Textual Authority and Community at Religiously Affiliated and Secular Colleges

T. Kenny Fountain
University of Minnesota

Lauren Fitzgerald
Yeshiva University

Teachers at secular institutions might well assume that those of us at religiously affiliated colleges and universities (or at secular schools largely populated by students of faith) would not have to deal with plagiarism at all or that we would have an easier time doing so because of the belief system that underwrites these contexts. In *The Plagiarism Handbook: Strategies for Preventing, Detecting, and Dealing with Plagiarism*, for example, Robert A. Harris advises faculty at religiously affiliated institutions to show students "why plagiarism is wrong" by appealing "to Biblical principles": Plagiarism is "a violation of the eighth commandment (You shall not steal) and the ninth commandment (You shall not bear false witness), since it involves stealing someone's words or ideas and then lying about it" (2001, 30–31). Though Harris recognizes the need to avoid such moralistic absolutes and urges teachers, instead, to remind students of "how plagiarism affects society"—referring to the "Golden Rule" ("Do unto others as you would have others do unto you")—his injunction to religious moral codes emphasizes the way plagiarism discourse is often overdetermined by religious discourse (34, 35). After all, many in academic cultures still operate under the assumption that plagiarism is what Margaret Price calls a "pure moral absolute ('Thou shalt not plagiarize')" (2002, 90).

Yet rather than granting teachers the ability to appeal persuasively to absolute concepts of right and wrong, religious arguments against plagiarism complicate matters of textual authority, attribution, and interaction—what we will term *text-usage*. Even if teachers can find support for a conflation of good moral action with proper attribution, they may not have the authority to make this connection meaningful for students. If a teacher is not a member of her students' religious community, then her wish to deploy a religious or moral metaphor may have little effect. Moreover, applying "thou-shalt-not" to the avoidance of improper textual citation often does not reflect the long historical traditions of religious writing, which do not follow the same notions of authorship and originality that we expect from our students. For instance, Judeo-Christian discourse traditions such as sermons and especially the Bible make use of sources in ways that would in current academic circles be considered plagiarism (Hope 2003; Howard 1999, 120–24; Love 2003).

Regardless of the context, these appeals to moral injunctions, though ironically presupposing a relationship to some religious or moral textual authority, do nothing to teach students how to use texts in the sophisticated and authoritative ways that academic disciplines require of them. In fact, moral and religious renunciations of cheating that rely on the adaptation of religious laws to academic contexts run the risk of being naively inappropriate. Typically speaking, most teachers value, if not hold sacred, the separation of church and state in the academy and the distinction between religious education and secular pedagogy. Even those comfortable and open with their faith and who teach students of similar backgrounds will usually create classroom environments that, while honoring religion, do not seek to teach it directly. Yet the deployment of religious and moral sanctions against plagiarism insincerely uses religion as a means to an end—and can be, in other words, an act of bad faith. The practice of avoiding all serious religious discussion in the writing classroom renders disingenuous the subsequent use of religious or moral pronouncements to shame students into good behavior. Such moral citations to avoid plagiarism, in other words, function solely as a means of policing behavior. Students need for us instead to attend to matters of textual authority and community, strategies that are useful in secular contexts as well.

This moralistic and religious view of plagiarism is one that we, in this chapter, wish to argue against. Though the strategies we suggest grow out of our work at a religiously affiliated institution—Yeshiva College (YC), the undergraduate college for men at Yeshiva University, the first and largest American institution of higher education under Orthodox Jewish auspices—they are applicable to any context because of the ways in which they draw on appeals not to religious mandates but instead to textual authority and communitarian notions of belonging, which are foundational to any understanding of academic discourse and disciplinarity. We believe that what we learned about plagiarism pedagogy at YC applies to secular contexts as well. After all, the religious and secular are not easily separated, in the world at large nor in the academy, and not just because people of faith attend and teach in secular institutions. The religious and the secular also overlap in discussions of academic writing because our dominant discourses of plagiarism are still unfortunately moralistic and religiously infused. And this religious and moral prohibition against plagiarism is deployed in secular colleges at least as often as it is at religiously affiliated institutions.

The academy, in general, and composition courses, in particular, require students to "use" texts (the words and ideas communicated through source material) to construct an authoritative academic subject position, one that consequently marks their membership into one particular discourse community or another. We suggest one way of doing this is by helping students better understand and interrogate the concepts of textual authority and community that prohibitions such as "thou shall not steal" fail to address. This chapter puts these ideas of community and textual authority, both religious and academic, in dialogue to explore possible roles they can play in the teaching of writing, particularly sophisticated text-usage. We do so by focusing on one composition classroom and the particular in-class activities and formal assignments that made possible a discursive space in which to better understand the intersection among plagiarism, textual authority, and community. But rather than "convert" the writing classroom into a religious course focused on theological discussions, we have found that writing teachers, in religiously affiliated and secular colleges alike, can develop pedagogies that are *informed by* both or either their religious and academic contexts and the language that inhabits and constructs these contexts. Rhetoric, community, and textual authority, unlike morals and religion, can be taught and learned, in good faith, in the writing classroom. We acknowledge that the institutional context we describe is unique, but we believe too that its unfamiliarity usefully makes visible issues that might otherwise remain hidden from view.

Textual Authority and Community in Academic Discourse

At the same time that teaching at a religiously affiliated institution helped us to see the shortcomings of moral arguments against plagiarism, this context also provided us with a useful alternative, another area in which the religious and secular overlap: textual authority and community. One advantage of teaching students at religiously affiliated institutions, not to mention religious students at any institution, about plagiarism is that they often bring with them complicated, intimate relationships with texts, relationships constituted by their membership in religious and philosophical communities. The three major Western religions, Judaism, Christianity, and Islam, are text based and comprised of complex constructions of textual knowledge, textual authority, and even authorship. Depending on your belief, the Bible, for instance, is, among others things, a collaborative text, compiled by multiple authors at different historical moments, or a divinely inspired and authored work with no or insignificant human agency. Of course, one cannot assume that students at religiously affiliated institutions or religious students at secular institutions are fully aware of or even comfortable with their relationships to the authority of, say, the Torah or the Qur'an. These unique relationships are at once personal and communal, founded on an intimate scholarship that incorporates individuals into a larger body of believers; one's subject position as a religious follower is marked by one's faith in, use of, and interaction with religious texts. And part of being a member of Judaism, Christianity, or Islam is the devotion, often the surrender, to an authority (God) who is usually mediated through the reading and interpretation of these texts.

Still, this formation of textual authority can be a useful bridge to the understanding of textual appropriation in academic contexts. To become an authentic, contributing member of any academic community, one must use texts as various as classical poetry and laboratory-generated data. Far more than simply demonstrating knowledge of the rights and wrongs of citation, successful academic writing involves creating an authoritative academic position through the incorporation of others' words, ideas, and data and in relation to the larger academic community. Successful academic writing, then, does not simply require having something original to say but instead is intimately linked to issues of textual control and interaction. More is being constructed through the use of source material than just a clear and persuasive argument. Ken Hyland, among others, views the research essay as "a rhetorically sophisticated artifact that displays a careful balance of information and social interaction" (1999, 341). In a similar vein, Mike Baynham's concept of the model research paper relies on a Bakhtinian "double-voiced" quality that both "articulates the argument which structures the essay" as well as "brings in the voices of authoritative others in support of the argument" (1999, 494). Stuart Greene even goes so far as to distinguish between the writer and the author, the latter characterized by "critical thinking skills" used to contribute to a field of knowledge and compose a central argument that may not actually derive from the source material itself (1995, 187). Ron Scollon confirms that facts are "established through [and inseparable from] authority [or the way the information is presented]" (1994, 38):

> [A]uthorial presence depends on appearing to have a clear stance in relation to the facts. What is crucial is not the status of the facts as such, but rather making it clear what one's own position is in relation to those facts. (41)

In other words, academic authority is textually generated and mediated through the ability to understand and reproduce what Ken Hyland has termed the "sanctioned social behaviors" of the academic disciplines (2). Academic discourse and the formation of academic authority, then, are social processes involving a writer's ability to interact with the textually mediated ideas of others (8). As such, the academy and all academic disciplines are, inevitably, constructed through texts that instantiate both certain ways of knowing the world and the social processes involved in reproducing those ways of knowing (5, 11). Recently, Kathryn Valentine has argued that plagiarism and the avoidance of plagiarism are "literacy practices" or "complicated ways of making meaning" that involve both the negotiation of texts as well as the negotiation of identity (2006, 89, 105).

Thus, the research paper, or what Ilona Leki and Joan Carson term "text-responsible prose" (in which "writers are responsible for demonstrating understanding of a source text"), is the representation of the writer's relationship with/to source material as well as the means by which this relationship is developed (1997, 41). What is at stake, then, in academic writing is authority, specifically the student writer's skill at enacting an authoritative stance, or an academic subject position, through the incorporation of other sources. From this perspective, academic writing and the avoidance of plagiarism always involve issues of textual authority and ethos. As a result, any pedagogy that seeks to discourage plagiarism primarily through moral arguments ignores the complexity inherent in text-usage. The sophisticated use of texts, from the skillful paraphrase to the competent citation (to the evaluation of dubious sources or experiments), is necessary not simply to pass a course. Competence with texts bears witness to one's ability to and success at becoming recognized as a good student or scholar. Whether or not we agree with this assumption and whether or not we are actively engaged in convincing our colleagues otherwise, the construction of academic authority through textual interaction and attribution—text-usage—stands as the initiation rite through which our students become members of one academic community or another. Amy Robillard has made plain the "affective relationships" performed by citation that not only track who said what and when but also constitute "personal allegiances" between those doing the citing and those who are cited (2006, 261). Academic writing, then, is a means of subjectivity formation, as writers learn to use the ideas and sources of others to represent their position in a certain community.

Related to this idea of community is the perhaps troubling responsibility one has to the other members of the group. The shared worldview of a community not only marks purposive action toward some goal but also demands ethical relations among members. Of course, the concept and even the myth of community should not be viewed as benign. By implication, community suggests an inside and an outside, the rewards of membership and validation for those included in the group and the punishments of unacceptance and unacknowledgment for those excluded from it. In his infamous critique of community models of discourse in composition studies, Joseph Harris posits two troubling aspects of community, namely the "sweeping and vague" assumption of an ahistorical transcendence and the "seductive and powerful" appeal of the supposed "shared purpose and effort" that community entails (1989, 12, 14, 13). Concerned more with its totalizing effects, Bernadette Longo has written about the tensions inherent in the concept of community, particularly the tendency to construct grand narratives that Jean-Francios Lyotard understands as instruments for the deployment of power (2003, 302–06). A community's need to recognize its members inevitably involves the simultaneous need to police its borders, thus constituting said community through the act of recognizing it.

Though we agree with Harris' and Longo's critiques, we also find the problematic idea of community to be one worth exploring, primarily because of the way the inescapable metaphor continues to surface in the academy, particularly in relation to plagiarism, academic discourse, and proper text-usage. Whether one understands academic discourse as Bruffee's "conversation of mankind," as a discourse community, or as Hyland's social interaction, academic authority is often understood in communitarian terms of "insider" and "outsider" (Bruffee 1983, 207–09; Hyland 2004; Swales 1990, 21–32). In fact, the current legacy of plagiarism anxiety is implicated in the wish to foster the acceptable community of intellectual, academic, and textual practice. Such appeals to wholeness and cohesion, in fact, are often made by the same well-meaning instructors who, in seeking to avoid moralistic, religious, or criminal tropes, have defined plagiarism as an issue of academic integrity. Kathryn Valentine persuasively argues that likening plagiarism to academic dishonesty forces a binary logic (honest/dishonest) that inevitably moralizes through an "ethical discourse," thus failing to account for intentionality and the ways in which writers negotiate identity through textual practices (2006, 90, 93). The same can be said for the notion of "academic integrity," which, as it is often deployed, implies both honest action and communitarian wholeness. To conflate avoiding plagiarism with academic "honesty" and academic "integrity" is a way of separating, so to speak, the wheat from the chaff, by marking some students as having integrity and others as lacking it. More than merely a word used to describe a particular student's character or ethos, the "integrity" of academic integrity has both troubling and potentially productive resonances with communitarian values, resonances we (in this chapter and in the pedagogical case it describes) try to salvage by both using and problematizing the notion of community. Of course, we do not suggest that these discursive spaces of religious and academic belonging can and should be expected to operate in precisely the same ways; after all, a student's responsibility to her classmates or a graduate teaching assistant's to her graduate colleagues is not the same as one follower's connection to another. Nevertheless, academic discourses, and their textual instantiations, are constituted by notions of community and authority that can be usefully and constructively (and not merely punitively) deployed.

The Appeal to Community and the Yeshiva College Context

Despite these complications of community, we, Fountain and Fitzgerald, found it to be a particularly useful concept in part because at YC and in Judaism, more generally, it is central. Judaism is marked by what Jacob Neusner has famously called "fellowship," that is, "a relationship among individuals characterized by both reciprocity and profound concern for one another and dedication to a goal held in common" (as quoted in Heilman 1983, 203). This emphasis on community is especially apparent in Jewish religious education, which often takes place in groups and pairs. (Even the Talmud, the sacred text usually studied in such groups, reveals this emphasis on community, being polyvocal, and representing, on each page, not only the primary text but years of commentary on that text as well as commentary on the commentary [Goldenberg 1984, 139].) This group study traditionally takes place in Talmudic academies known as yeshivas, and YC prides itself on offering students a way to combine this religious study with the secular liberal arts curriculum. Generally speaking, this background seems to make many students open to collaborative learning even in their secular studies. To take one very relevant example, undergraduate peer tutors at the YC Writing Center usually come to their jobs with a great deal of experience in and sensitivity to the dynamics of group work (see Fitzgerald 2008). Of course, communitarian values of belonging and collaboration are not unique to Judaism but instead are equally important to other religious traditions, from Christianity to Neo-Pagan movements, as well as to secular and ecumenical philosophical groups.

Issues of plagiarism and text-usage intersect with YC's religious environment in fascinating and even contradictory ways. Sometimes, the importance of community can come into conflict with the Western enlightenment preferences of the academy, particularly the focus (in the humanities, in any case) on individual production and singly authored texts. When working in pairs or groups is a celebrated—and institutionalized—method of learning, some students can find it hard to understand why the secular curriculum requires them to do their work in isolation. In other instances, religious premises are used to further the ends of the secular curriculum. YC's policy statement, *Upholding Academic Integrity: Definitions of—and Consequences for—Cheating and Plagiarism* begins with an appeal to the combined religious and secular principles of the institution: "Committed to the highest values of both Judaism and Western civilization, Yeshiva College strives to ensure that each student will maintain the highest moral, ethical, and academic standards" (2).

We first got involved with plagiarism pedagogy at YC when deans, faculty, rabbis, and students became concerned that the institution was not living up to these standards. As administrators of the YC Writing Center, we offered to organize a day-long faculty development workshop on "Supporting Academic Integrity." Our goals were to raise awareness about YC's policies and the complexity of plagiarism as a set of textual practices, as well as to conduct WAC-related faculty outreach that would help colleagues across the curriculum address text-usage in their courses. Organized around an interactive presentation by an outside speaker (Sandra Jamieson), the event also incorporated presentations by YC faculty from various disciplines who discussed how highlighting academic integrity across the curriculum can involve more than simply plagiarism prevention but also such issues as informed consent in human subject research.

At the same time that the secular side of the college was seeking to address these issues, several rabbis were spearheading an academic integrity campaign among the religious faculty. Along with rallying his colleagues, Rabbi Jeremy Wieder delivered a lecture to students (later reprinted in the student newspaper) that addressed cheating and plagiarism according to the Judaic legal code. Rabbi Wieder's speech proved incredibly influential that year, in ways that we go on to discuss below, so it is worth pausing here to sum up his key points. Central to Wieder's lecture was the concept of *gneivas da'as*, which he defined as "attempting, through creating a false impression, to ingratiate one's self with someone else, presumably in the hope of gaining some favor or some future benefit" (Wieder 2002). "Cheating and plagiarism," he went on to explain, "are very obvious forms of *gneivas da'as* because they too aim at deception." With plagiarism, "The person is submitting work as if it's his own, as if he deserves a certain grade, as if he deserves certain credit." As a result, said Wieder (using the masculine pronoun because of YC's all-male student body), "he's not entitled to that credit, he's not entitled to that impression of what a wonderful student he is, he's not entitled to that grade." As with the more commonplace academic discussions of plagiarism, *gneivas da'as* also draws on theft and stealing (the term literally means "stealing the mind," and "*gneiva*" refers to "theft"). Significantly, however, the "stealing" of *gneivas da'as* does not refer to a student's illegitimate appropriation of words or ideas from an original author's "mind," for example, but rather from the mind of the person who has been deceived, such as a teacher. In other words, this form of "stealing" emphasizes the effect the plagiarist has on those who are deceived, not on the actual act of deception. More important, *gneivas da'as* should at all costs be avoided, Rabbi Wieder pointed out, because it can involve much more than a simple act of deceiving one person or group; it can have a negative effect on the larger community, in this case, of Orthodox Jewry. Rabbi Wieder warned students that such acts tarnish the "reputation" of both Yeshiva University and religious Jews as a whole. Most powerfully, he requested that any student who commits this violation remove all visible symbols of his religious identity (including his yarmulke) so that outsiders will not confuse his actions for those typical of the larger group. In this way, plagiarism as an act of *gneivas da'as* becomes the more serious offense of *chilul Hashem*, the desecration of God's name, because it can make outsiders doubt the piety of His chosen people.

Classroom Activities and Assignments

Drawing on this rich context, and bringing to bear his own interest in plagiarism and textual authority, Fountain developed the following series of assignments for his first-semester composition course and worked with Fitzgerald, as the composition director, to distribute these assignments to colleagues in the YC Composition Program: (1) a case-study exercise, (2) a reading activity,

(3) a commentary essay assignment, and (4) a rhetorical analysis. Each of these four assignments made explicit use of the local, institutional texts that addressed plagiarism and cheating that year as well as a number of national publications, engaging students in this conversation at both levels. Though these assignments, described below, were originally designed to form a sequence, they can be used individually and adapted to suit a number of composition contexts. In fact, we include these assignments not merely to retell the story of Fountain's classroom experiences or to support our argument. Rather, we share these lessons because they instantiate pedagogical suggestions, involving text-based writing, communitarian values, and textual authority, that we hope might be useful at other institutions, religiously affiliated, secular, or both. If the material practices of proper citation and academic discourse are shot through with notions of community integrity or disintegration, with textual authority or textual fraudulence, it follows that students must learn not only to understand but to work with these concepts. Though far from perfect, these assignment suggestions should be understood as one possible way of addressing plagiarism prevention without resorting to empty moral or religious imperatives.

A Case-Study Exercise

Using YC's official statement of policy on *Upholding Academic Integrity,* Fountain created an in-class discussion activity aimed at helping students better understand the institution's plagiarism and academic dishonesty policies as well as the ideas behind them. He created six hypothetical scenarios based on what the handbook specifically prohibited and what might possibly be discouraged as "bad practices." Students in his class were placed in small groups and were asked not merely to read the cases and decide what was and was not a violation but also, using a heuristic-based worksheet, to suggest what could or should be done by the student writers, the teachers, and any other parties involved to remedy the situation. The goal was not only for students to know what not to do but to know how to avoid being placed in academically questionable or compromising situations. For example,

> Ira is at home with his parents for the weekend, where he is putting the finishing touches on his history paper. Because his father is a good writer and editor, Ira asks his dad to take a look at the paper. His dad reads the paper carefully, likes what Ira has done, and suggests only minor sentence-level changes. His dad suggests words, phrases, and sentences that Ira can use to make the paper sound clearer and more professional.

Though this ubiquitous case of "too much help" is nothing new to teachers who assign major writing projects, the students who had to deliberate on this case were shocked to know that this was, according to the YC policy, a breach of academic integrity and constituted plagiarism. After all, they protested, aren't parents supposed to help educate their children? Returning to the idea of deception, or *gneivas da'as*, and specifically that the teacher grading this essay would not be able to detect the extent of the assistance provided by the parent, students understood that this help might inadvertently mislead the teacher into believing that this writing represented only the student's intellectual labor (when it arguably did not). One student pointed out an element of self-deception in that the "offending" student has no way of being sure that he (in our all-male context) has since learned how to do this type of work independently.

The educational exercise, however, did not end at this point because the students then had to offer suggestions for each party involved in the case. Eventually the group charged with this example decided that perhaps it was the student writer's responsibility to discuss the YC policy with his parents and other relatives who offer to help him with his homework. If students can make parents understand the fuzzy line between "good help" (according to the statement, modeling ways to revise similar sentences) and "bad help" (rewriting the sentences), parents can continue to be involved in ways that are academically appropriate. They suggested too that such discussions would act as a consciousness-raising (though not their term) activity for parents, who probably have not given much thought about the complexities of text-usage in academic environments.

To both explicate and problematize the "do and don't" nature of the policy statement, some cases called for a bit more interpretation:

> Akiva has been assigned an essay in his YC English Composition I course, an essay that closely resembles one that he wrote last year in high school. While he is supposed to be writing the paper, he also has to study for two mid-term exams. Because he received a good grade on the essay he wrote earlier, for a previous high school class, Akiva decides to retype the essay, make some minor changes, and turn it in to his YC English professor, in order to fulfill this teacher's assignment.

Though the policy specifically forbids submitting identical work for two different college courses without the consent of both faculty members, it makes no explicit mention of recycling work produced at other institutions. Again, through a discussion of the learning objectives of writing assignments—to expressly practice the educational goals and skills of that particular course—many of the students in class argued that such recycling was dishonest because the teacher would not know about it. Interestingly enough, not all students were ultimately convinced by this argument; they suggested that it was the faculty's responsibility to make the policy more explicit and the administration's responsibility to revise and expand the document so that ambiguities like this one could be more thoroughly explained, if not completely resolved.

The success of the case study exercise was not simply describing the good, the bad, and the ugly of plagiarism in a more student-directed light but instead presenting, first, the situational complexity of the issue that often calls for ongoing decision making; second, the communal responsibility inherent in academic integrity; and, third, the situated nature of academic integrity and plagiarism as socially constructed realities. Because student writers have to make continual, context-specific choices about appropriate text-usage, avoiding plagiarism can be understood as a form of "situated cognition," a type of knowledge production and text-usage that is concomitant with a specific rhetorical situation; in other words, "the activity in which knowledge is developed and deployed" cannot be separated from the task of learning or the deployment of that knowledge (Brown, Collins, and Duguid 1989, 32). Proper attribution and intricate guidelines for text-usage are, thus, forms of genre-knowledge, or cognitive, cultural, and social knowledge needed to understand and reproduce disciplinary and other generic texts (Berkenkotter and Huckin 1995, 3–41). For example, in APA style, preference is given to last names, dates of publication, and the use of paraphrase (as opposed to quotations). Only by using this style (genre convention) can a student come to fully understand and deploy the knowledge (genre-knowledge) needed to do so. Because genre-knowledge is both dynamic and situated, students can never fully build and activate the type of knowledge needed to use texts appropriately without being placed in academic writing environments (Berkenkotter and Huckin 1995). But as Fountain's students suggested, this knowledge—of the ins and outs of avoiding plagiarism as well as the ambiguity and confusion surrounding "best practices"—is the responsibility of more than teachers and students. It must be disseminated through the larger community as well. Parents and administrators need to be informed (by student writers and teachers, respectively) about not only the severity of the issue (which most of them already know) but more importantly the principles behind plagiarism prevention pedagogy, namely that work in the academy is understood as a product and even representation of the particular academic subject position of the person who produced it.

A Reading Activity Based on Local Texts

Early in the semester, Fountain gave his class a packet of journalistic and op-ed pieces on plagiarism, cheating, academic integrity, and academic dishonesty taken from national newspapers and magazines, such as *The New York Times* and *Newsweek*, as well as the campus paper, *The Commentator*. These texts represented a variety of viewpoints and purposes, for instance (1) a news article reporting the rise of cheating and the use of honor codes as a way of dealing with the problem, (2) an opinion piece from a college teacher disheartened by her role as plagiarism police, (3) another from a writer who is flattered to discover that her own work has been inadvertently "taken" by someone else, (4) an open letter to the YC student body from the student government leaders "reiterating the responsibility of students to maintain a high standard of academic integrity ("Letter Regarding Finals" 2002), and lastly (5) Rabbi Jeremy Wieder's speech (Wieder 2002), which was reprinted in *The Commentator*.

Much more than the other readings, it was the last two texts, representing the concerns of the local and religious community, that provoked the most genuine and thoughtful responses from Fountain's students. The brief, open letter from the student leaders was used for an in-class activity, to help students prepare for an informal, text-based writing assignment. Students were asked to pay careful attention to the wording of the following selection (taken from the letter) for clues about the overall purpose of the text as well as the ethos of those who created it:

> Our community strives to build a moral, *halachic* [legal, according to Jewish law] society built upon integrity and honesty; all forms of cheating and plagiarism strike at the root of this endeavor. If you participate in these destructive acts, you not only separate yourself from your fellow students, you also threaten to damage our reputation within the Jewish community as well as the world beyond our walls, and you corrode the environment befitting the University. ("Letter Regarding Finals" 2002)

A text as rhetorically rich as this practically begs for in-depth study of its use of argument and persuasion. This text does, in fact, use religious and even blatantly moral arguments to discourage academic dishonesty but, interestingly, not through the metaphor familiar to most academics, that of theft. Instead the dominant rhetorical figure employed in the letter is that of community. For these writers, acts of cheating and plagiarism are contrary to the express goals of the community, thus inflicting damage to the group and subsequently removing the individual from that group. For them, to be in the community is to participate with and within the community; acting contrary to the community's wishes is to be outside of it. Students in Fountain's class pointed out the particular strengths of the references made to "corrosion" and the "walls" of the community, the first highlighting the weakening or removing of strength from metals, and the second the traditional parameters set up to demarcate the appropriate geography of the community. When Fountain discussed with the students the normativity of communitarian values, namely that communities often involve policing that seeks to silence or dismiss viewpoints deemed dangerously contrary to the goals and values of the group, one student (in a free-writing task) argued that in voluntary communities (such as academic ones), this regulating force though unfortunate is one that members consent to in return for the privileges of membership.

For the next class meeting, students were asked to read another local text on the issue, the transcription of Rabbi Wieder's speech, and to write an analysis of its use of argument and persuasion. This task inevitably made transparent the idea of academic writing as the creation of an authoritative position.

The assignment was originally designed as a semiformal essay to offer, first, students the chance to practice writing from/with texts and, second, Fountain the chance to monitor how well they were learning the skills of quotation, summary, and paraphrase as well as balancing their own ideas with those of another text.

Purpose:
Though this assignment is informal, it is, nonetheless, important, giving you an opportunity to practice the skills involved in analyzing both a written argument and a rhetorical situation.

Form
This informal essay, which should include an introduction, well-organized paragraphs, and a logical conclusion, must include the following information:
- What is the context surrounding this rhetorical event?
- Who are the participants?
- What is Rabbi Wieder's primary purpose?
- What is the larger issue of his discussion?
- What is his major claim?
- What type of claim is it?
- What rhetorical appeals do you see happening in his argument?
- What evidence does he provide to support his major claim/overall purpose?

Keep In Mind: This assignment DOES NOT ask you to evaluate or critique Rabbi Wieder's address but instead to analyze it as a rhetorical event.

Because answers to the first two questions were stated explicitly in either the text of the speech or the introduction to the article itself, students were left with six questions that called for close reading and critical thinking. The "Keep in Mind" statement was included to allay potential fears that they were being asked to "criticize" this religious leader or the content of his speech (a message that Fountain found he had to carefully reiterate in class; after all, as one student asked, what gave them the *authority* to criticize Rabbi Wieder?). Given early in the semester and meant to develop rather than test skills, this assignment asked students to carefully explore the idea of authority: What gives Rabbi Wieder the authority to make these statements? How is this authority made visible in his argument? What effect does his authoritative position vis-à-vis his argument/his claims have on the audience? In a sense, the goal was for students to understand the power and authority (appeals to ethos) of this speech about academic integrity and how this power was deployed.

Overwhelmingly for the students, the most powerful section of the speech was the one in which Wieder offered an analogy based on advice from the Talmud. When faced with sinful inclinations that cannot be controlled, the Talmud recommends that one "should go to a place where people don't recognize him . . . do what he needs to do, and thus avoid desecrating [God's]

name publicly" (Wieder 2002). This is not, Wieder pointed out, an excuse for
wrongdoing. At this point, Wieder returned to the issue of academic dishonesty with his own advice that he delivered "*blev kaved* [with a heavy heart]":

> if you have to [violate policies of academic integrity], please take off your
> yarmulke . . . and then do what [your] heart desires . . . on that day that some
> people do get dragged in front of the Academic Standards Committee . . .
> please walk in there without your yarmulke, so no one should think that it's
> the yarmulke . . . that gave you the *rshus* (permission) to cheat. (Wieder 2002)

The significance of these images is staggering. Not only do they seem to conflate academic dishonesty with "*aveira* [sin]" and "*yetzer harah* [evil inclina-
tion]," but they also seem as moralistic as Robert Harris' advice to teachers that
we cite above: Plagiarism is bad, and moral shame can be used to prevent it.

But in speaking with his students, and particularly about their reaction to
this passage, Fountain was afforded another understanding. Delivered in the
main study hall, where much of the religious education of the institution
occurs, this speech, like others delivered there, necessarily deals with subjects
and concerns unique to YC's academic environment, which combines (if
sometimes uneasily) both secular and sacred education. Because of the context
of the situation, the speech genre required by the location of the utterance, and
the subject positions of the speaker and the addressees, Rabbi Wieder's oration
was a sermonic one and not simply a lecture about academic policy. All of
these factors created a unique, even kairotic, moment in which the intermin-
gling of the discourses of religious teaching and academic warnings were not
only unavoidable but necessary.

For the students, the issue was not whether plagiarism was or was not a sin
but that willfully committing it violated the standards of two communities, both
religious and secular. By removing the yarmulke, Wieder's hypothetical student
would not only uncover his head before God, he would also remove from his
body the most immediate and outward sign of his Judaism. Wieder's argument
makes strong appeals to religious and moral authority, again not through references to theft but instead to deception and damaging the reputation, even the
very integrity, of the community. Academic dishonesty, in this sense, represents
a symbolic act of *gneivas da'as* and deception and not merely by pretending
that one is *academically* what one is not. Such students also mislead others as to
their *religious* identity. If removal of the yarmulke can be seen as differentiating
oneself from the community, the next logical step is a very persuasive one: The
deed that would warrant the removal of the yarmulke, namely academic dishonesty in the guise of plagiarism, instantiates that separation.

In awe of Wieder's skill as a rhetor, the class was surprised by the convic-
tion of the somewhat radical connection he makes between the Talmud and academic practice. For them the point was irrefutable; if academic dishonesty were
against Jewish law, then a student's willfully plagiarizing or cheating might

encourage other students to do so as well. Students have to hold themselves accountable to one another, they told Fountain, and purposeful deception undermines that mutual accountability. Academic honesty was what they owed not only to themselves and their teachers but also to other students.

Because the task asked students to analyze the argument and specifically what made the text so persuasive, many of them discussed Wieder's authority, his ethos, articulated both in his subject position as a respected rabbi and teacher and in his use of other texts. Although the exigency of the occasion required the use of religious texts, the speech itself carefully rooted its claims in (religious) texts with which the students felt the audience would be familiar. By using these texts to construct his own argument, one that was in no way located in the original texts, Wieder relied on text-usage to mediate authority. His work was only as "good" as his use of source texts. Though the speaker and location of this speech clearly added to its authority, as the class recognized, Wieder also created, through text-usage, an authoritative subject position for himself.

A Commentary Essay Assignment on Plagiarism in the Local Context

Using the conventions set out in John Trimbur's *The Call to Write*, the students wrote commentary essays on the troubling concept of "academic integrity" on college campuses, giving attention to YC and/or the Orthodox community in general (Trimbur 2004). A slightly abbreviated version of the prompt follows:

> You should *describe/define* the issue(s) of academic integrity/honesty, cheating, and/or plagiarism.
>
> - What is/are the major issue(s) at stake? Who is affected and how?
> - Maybe also think about why the issues exist in the first place.
>
> You should also *offer some sustained, analytical comment* on the issue, a comment that is driven by some point you are trying to make about the issue.
>
> - How should we interpret/understand the issue(s)? What is your evaluation of the issue?
>
> - Maybe also think about whether or not it should be an issue, or what could be done to end the issue.
>
> **The Sources:**
> Other Texts: The six (6) readings that I have provided will be the basis for your commentary, because you are commenting on those issues. You must use at least two (2) of the sources directly through quoting, paraphrasing, and/or summarizing. If the words you use in your essay are not your own words, cite them. If the ideas you use in your essay are not your own ideas, cite them. Obviously, I want you to be careful how you use the text. I don't want to see plagiarism in a commentary that discusses academic integrity.

Your Own Ideas: You should also use your own careful analysis of the issues you are discussing. In fact, giving your own analysis/interpretation is the purpose of commentary writing. This analysis will be based on what you have read, what we have discussed, and what YOU believe/know to be true.

The Purpose:
This assignment is designed to help you in the following ways:
- Improve academic writing skills by writing a commentary that describes/defines an issue and offers an interpretation/way of understanding the issue.
- Practice using various outside sources to inform/strengthen your position on a subject/issue.
- Critically/analytically approach (in essay form) the subject of academic integrity.

The Audience:
You should write this commentary as if it will be published in *The Commentator*. This does NOT mean that you should write this commentary like a journalistic piece. This DOES mean, however, that you should imagine that you are writing to the YC community (mainly students and faculty).

This essay required that students (1) incorporate what they had learned and decided about plagiarism and academic dishonesty and then (2) apply that knowledge to their own local context. In a sense, their task was similar to that of Rabbi Wieder—to speak with authority, to take a position, to help an audience understand the greater significance, and to do all of this through the use of other sources. Most students referenced the news-based articles only to establish the problem, choosing to make more productive use of the local texts in the bulk of their essays. And though the assignment did not expressly request it, many of the students made policy recommendations for both students and faculty. Students, they argued, should be required to read these Yeshiva-produced texts so as to better understand the larger significance of a personal decision often made in haste. Going even further, upperclassmen had a responsibility not to enforce compliance but to make compliance the only reasonable option. One student felt that if older students spoke out against academic dishonesty and refused to engage in it themselves, then younger students might follow their lead.

Echoing some of the best research in plagiarism pedagogy, students' advice to faculty was clear: Don't merely teach students *how* to cite a text; also teach them *why* they should cite it. If students cannot see their own investment in text-usage, if they do not understand how the personal and the communal intersect on this issue, these connections will not matter to them. Faculty entrusted with the task of initiating students into these various academic communities should do more than stand as gatekeepers. One student, undisturbed by this metaphor, likened the situation to one in which someone climbs over the gate, rather than properly going through it, and is then tossed back out. If one doesn't understand how to walk through the gate, conceive of the importance, and possess the skills to do so, then he or she will not care how he or she gets in, making the gatekeeper's task all the more difficult.

A Rhetorical Analysis of the College's Academic Integrity Policy

The final assignment asked students to write an analysis of both (1) the rhetorical situation in which YC's *Upholding Academic Integrity* document was created and (2) the argument/persuasion of the document itself, making meaningful use of at least one other academic integrity related text students read that semester.

The Task
Review Trimbur's chapter on "Public Documents: Codifying Beliefs and Practices" on pages 183–209.

1) The rhetorical analysis section should contain the following:
• Publication information
• Brief summary of the YC document
• The creators of the document and their authority to "speak" on this issue
• The writers' purpose(s)—How will this document be used? What types of beliefs and practices are being codified by this document?
• The various (primary and secondary) readers
• The writers' relationship to the various readers
• The writers' use of language and persuasion
• Tone and style

2) The analysis of the document's argument and use of persuasion should contain the following:
• The context surrounding this rhetorical event/document
• The larger issue this document is addressing
• The major point/argument of this document—What types of beliefs and practices are being codified by this document?
• The ways this YC document uses issues of substantiation, issues of evaluation, and issues of policy (if at all)
• The ways this document uses the rhetorical appeals of ethos, logos, and pathos (if at all)
• The evidence or examples or elaborations this document uses to support the major claims/purposes

The Sources
You must use and cite Yeshiva College's policy statement *Upholding Academic Integrity*.

You must also make some meaningful use of at least one other essay in "The Ethics of Writing" packet. DO NOT use any other sources. DO NOT surf the net.

NOTE: The rhetorical analysis section and the argument analysis section may be combined or integrated to make the essay more readable, engaging, authentic. DO NOT think of this essay as merely answering items on a checklist.

This assignment, challenging for students with no previous academic exposure to genres of professional/technical writing, went the farthest perhaps in allowing each student to speak as an authority, one able to understand, analyze, critique, and often revise the document. And the idea of community to which many of them returned was not the religious one but the academic one. Primarily the students felt that the policy statement did not go far enough in explicating "good practices" and that not enough space was devoted to debatable cases. If the handbook sought to make clear that plagiarism itself was sometimes unclear, then the document needed to provide a range of examples, from obviously wrong to doubtfully so. And if the policy statement was to represent the entire college, the document had to broaden the discussion to be more inclusive of the sciences, particularly what constituted plagiarism in such genres as laboratory reports. Finally, the students felt the document had to be taught, had to be referenced in class, and had to become an unavoidable component of their college education. If sophisticated text-usage mediated academic authority, thus creating one's academic subject position, and if the creation of that subjectivity initiated one into the academic community, then the point was not to discourage or even detect plagiarism but to teach students how to write.

Conclusion: Revisiting Community

Though the focus of this chapter has been on one particular class at one specific religiously affiliated institution, we believe that the assignments discussed here are not limited to this context—nor are the insights of Fountain's students limited to their beliefs and the worldviews of their religious backgrounds. If learning to write is about joining a community, and if successful writing involves the creation of an authoritative position through the use of texts, then plagiarism, whether deliberate or inadvertent, is always already a matter of community and authority. No matter how problematic this might be, part of learning to write is understanding the complexity of texts. Shame and fear might teach students what practices to avoid, but they cannot and will not teach them what practices to strive for.

Throughout this chapter, we have both made use of and critiqued the notion of community and communitarian values in plagiarism pedagogy. Undeniably the appeal to community can be dangerous if it reifies the totalizing, ahistorical, and normative aspects that proffer a myth of wholeness and integrity that is not only impossible but often undesirable. Yet throughout our interactions with faculty, administrators, and students both at YC and at other academic institutions and settings, we have found appeals to community a productive way of addressing plagiarism not as a policing issue but as a pedagogical one. In fact, we find communitarian models for plagiarism, though not untroubling, to be more productive than the criminal metaphor of theft, the moralistic one of lying, and the ethical discourse of honesty. To conclude, we wish to make plain the ways in which plagiarism can be understood from a communitarian model.

1. Plagiarism definitions maintain community boundaries yet represent an attempt to join community: Moralistic definitions of plagiarism have a gatekeeping function that exclude from the ideals of authorship writers who engage in certain textual practices. Yet the ironic counterpart of the first premise is that inappropriate text-usage is often interpreted as an attempt to make it through the gates. In deconstructing the kinds of textual activities usually considered plagiarism, Rebecca Moore Howard argues that what she has famously called "patchwriting"—"the mixing of one's language with the source text" (Howard 1999, 139)—is often an attempt to mimic the discursive and generic conventions of the discipline in which he or she writes. Writers mix the words of the source text with their own to approximate what she calls "the language of the target community" (7). Understanding plagiarism as fortifying while simultaneously perhaps offering (illegitimate) access to community affiliation brings into focus citational practices and text-usage as instantiations of community values, conventions, and epistemologies that most academics who have already spent years negotiating their own academic subject position take for granted.[1]

The dual components of our first proposition operate in opposition to each other and are, to a certain extent, mutually constitutive: One group defines as prohibited the very strategy that the other group uses to try to join the first. The tension and the potential for escalation (that is, the more the second group tries to join, the more the first will outlaw its membership strategies) help to account for some of the panic around plagiarism, why faculty and administrators feel we are in a "crisis" (Howard 2000, 484). What must add to this feeling of crisis are the contradictions inherent in definitions of plagiarism: Many people take for granted that how plagiarism is defined and what constitutes a "plagiaristic" activity are—or should be—transhistorical and transcultural. In fact, as we can learn from our international students and our colleagues in other fields, what is considered to be plagiarism varies from context to context. In investigating this quality, scholars of plagiarism like Howard and Price have answered Joseph Harris' call for a "more specific and material view" of community (Harris 1989, 20). This leads to the second connection between plagiarism and community.

2. Plagiarism is community specific: As Price says, "what we call plagiarism is located in a specific setting: *this* historical time, *this* academic community" (Price 2002, 90). As evidence of this, Price points to the irony that teachers are not usually expected to cite pedagogical sources and, especially, that institutional plagiarism policies often borrow heavily, and without acknowledgment, from policies elsewhere, as per the convention of corporate documents (Price 2002, 101–02). If the gates are not, in the end, stable or secure, and if, as Joseph Harris

says, the community borders are "hazily marked and often traveled," maybe we should not work so hard to maintain them (Harris 1989, 17). Price calls on us to "acknowledge to students and ourselves that plagiarism is part of an ongoing, evolving academic conversation" and once we do so, to "invite students to add their own voices to that conversation" (Price 2002, 90).

3. Plagiarism prevention and plagiarism pedagogy can build on community: The idea of "plagiarism prevention" makes many of us (Fountain and Fitzgerald included) uneasy, in that the term implies plagiarism to be a unified, coherent entity, like a virus, that we must avoid, perhaps by carefully washing our intellectual hands *after* touching each other's words and *before* returning to our own. Instead, plagiarism is a set of textual practices involving a certain relationship to, interaction with, and use of source material, the guidelines for which are determined with some variation by a number of different communities of practice. Plagiarism pedagogy, then, must seek to encourage communally appropriate text-usage in particular communal contexts and must do so with the help of as many community members as possible. The Council of Writing Program Administrators, in their document "Defining and Avoiding Plagiarism," proposes that we *all* have "Shared Responsibilities," urging "instructors, administrators, and students [to] work together" (3, 1). In Fountain's course, the issues of plagiarism and text-usage not only developed out of a discussion of community but also, in a sense, were enlivened by the students' understanding of community and communal ties, particularly those ties that could be understood as both religious and academic.

If the issue of plagiarism involves the entire academic community, then the solution must as well. Perhaps the true success of Fountain's assignments had nothing to do with the directions and guidance they offered and everything to do with the texts and documents they engaged. In organizing the daylong faculty development workshop on "Supporting Academic Integrity," we originally sought to raise awareness about plagiarism policies and the complexity of plagiarism as a set of textual practices. We also hoped that the workshop would double as WAC-related faculty outreach, helping colleagues across the curriculum address text-responsible writing. This workshop led to some rich discussion among our colleagues, but what we didn't anticipate—and couldn't have planned for—were the ways this discussion would inform what students were talking and writing about on campus. The letters and documents published in the student newspaper along with the ongoing efforts by student leaders represented a genuine investment in the resolution of a problem facing the entire community. Having such texts to read and refer to in class obviated the need for students becoming involved because they already were. If we want students to take ownership of policies and guidelines and to join our various academic communities, we not only have to admonish them or teach them, but we must also work with them. As faculty, we are dismayed by top-down implementations of broad-based policy, preferring—often demanding—

agency in such change. Yet we rarely adopt such a model when in comes to student acculturation to the academy (Price 2002, 107).

Perhaps the goal of plagiarism pedagogy should not be simply to usher our students through the intellectual, discursive, and textual gates of our community but instead to forge with them a sense of community, a sense of shared values and epistemologies. In this essay, we have sought to explain our own ways of fostering such discussions and relationships, tactics very much stemming from and appropriate to our administrative, pedagogical, and student contexts. Though we have made suggestions that individual teachers can use in their own classrooms, we believe that these and similar assignments work best when the larger institution—students, faculty, and administration—are simultaneously engaged in a discussion about plagiarism as well. In other words, for them to be meaningful, plagiarism discussions and the important work students need to do to understand them cannot be limited only to the composition classroom. These initiatives need to be integrated into the larger campus culture, so students can see that it really does matter to everyone. After all, if the process of text-usage—the learned practices of textual authority, attribution, and interaction—is how one constructs an academic subject position, then all faculty who assign writing must help students negotiate this complex process of formation. One way to do this is to make use of, call into question, and perhaps even transform our existing notions of community and textual authority to understand them both as socially situated rhetorical and discursive processes, not fixed, stable concepts that one either "gets" or doesn't. To be successful in the academy, students must learn to take plagiarism and text-usage seriously. At the same time, to truly teach academic writing, faculty (and administrators) must take seriously the textual, contextual, and communitarian nature of plagiarism. Allowing students to write seriously and openly about issues of plagiarism, community, and authority might be one place to begin.

Note

1. A useful analogy is second-language learning. Avoiding patchwriting—that is, accurately paraphrasing in "one's own words"—is something of a catch-22 for nonnative speakers of English or native speakers outside of North America and the United Kingdom because they are learning both the language of English and the academic discourse conventions of a particular field or number of fields. There is a wealth of research on text-usage and nonnative speakers, and the following offer an excellent place to begin: Pennycook, 1996; Currie 1998; and Bouman 2004.

References

Baynham, Mike. 1999. "Double-Voicing and the Scholarly 'I': On Incorporating the Words of Others in Academic Discourse." *Text* 19 (4): 485–504.

Berkenkotter, Carol, and Thomas N. Huckin. 1995. *Genre Knowledge in Disciplinary Communication: Cognition/Culture/Power*. Hillsdale, NJ: Lawrence Erlbaum Associates.

Bouman, Kurt. 2004. "Raising Questions About Plagiarism." In *ESL Writers: A Guide for Writing Center Tutors*, edited by Shanti Bruce and Ben Rafoth, 105–16. Portsmouth, NH: Boynton/Cook Heinemann.

Brown, John Seely, Allan Collins, and Paul Duguid. 1989. "Situated Cognitions and the Culture of Learning." *Educational Researcher* (18): 32–42.

Bruffee, Kenneth. 2001. "Peer Tutoring and the 'Conversation of Mankind.'" In *The Allyn and Bacon Guide to Writing Center Theory and Practice*, edited by Robert W. Barnett and Jacob S. Blumner, 206–18. Boston: Allyn and Bacon, 2001. Originally published in Gary A. Olson, ed., *Writing Center Theory and Administration* (Urbana, IL: NCTE, 1983).

Council of Writing Program Administrators. "Defining and Avoiding Plagiarism: The WPA Statement on Best Practices." Council of Writing Program Administrators. www.wpacouncil.org.

Currie, Pat. 1998. "Staying Out of Trouble: Apparent Plagiarism and Academic Survival." *Journal of Second Language Writing* 7: 1–18.

Fitzgerald, Lauren. 2008. "'Torah Is Not Learned but in a Group': Talmud Study and Collaborative Learning." In *Judaic Perspectives in Rhetoric and Composition*, edited by Andrea Greenbaum and Deborah H. Holdstein. Cresskill, NJ: Hampton Press.

Goldenberg, Robert. 1984. "Talmud." In *Back to the Sources: Reading the Classic Jewish Texts*, edited by Barry W. Holtz, 129–75. New York: Summit Books.

Greene, Stuart. 1995. "Making Sense of My Own Ideas: The Problems of Authorship in a Beginning Writing Classroom." *Written Communication* 12 (1): 186–218.

Harris, Joseph. 1989. "The Idea of Community in the Study of Writing." *College Composition and Communication* 40 (1): 11–22.

Harris, Robert A. 2001. *The Plagiarism Handbook: Strategies for Preventing, Detecting, and Dealing with Plagiarism*. Los Angeles: Pyrczak Publishing.

Heilman, Samuel C. 1983. *The People of the Book: Drama, Fellowship, and Religion*. Chicago: University of Chicago Press.

Hope, Andrew. 2003. "Plagiarising the Word of God: Tyndale Between More and Joye." In *Plagiarism in Early Modern England*, edited by Paulina Kewes, 93–105. New York: Palgrave Macmillan.

Howard, Rebecca Moore. 1999. *Standing in the Shadow of Giants: Plagiarists, Authors, Collaborators*. Stamford, CT: Ablex.

Howard, Rebecca Moore. 2000. "Sexuality, Textuality: The Cultural Work of Plagiarism." *College English* 62: 473–91.

Hyland, Ken. 1999. "Academic Attribution: Citation and the Construction of Disciplinary Knowledge." *Applied Linguistics* 20.3: 341–67.

Hyland, Ken. 2004. *Disciplinary Discourses: Social Interactions in Academic Writing*. Ann Arbor: University of Michigan Press.

Leki, Ilona, and Joan Carson. 1997. "'Completely Different Worlds': EAP and the Writing Experiences of ESL Students in University Courses." *TESOL Quarterly* 31 (1): 39–69.

Letter Regarding Finals. 2002. *Yeshiva University Commentator* 67, 7 (Dec. 31). http://media.www.yucommentator.com/media/storage/paper652/news/2002/12/31/EditorialsopEd/A.Letter.Regarding.Finals-655196.shtml (accessed December 31 2002).

Longo, Bernadette. 2003. "Tensions in the Community: Myth, Strategy, Totalitarianism, Terror." *JAC* 23 (2): 291–317.

Love, Harold. 2003. "Originality and the Puritan Sermon." In *Plagiarism in Early Modern England,* edited by Paulina Kewes, 149–65. New York: Palgrave Macmillan.

Pennycook, Alistair. 1996. "Borrowing Others' Words: Text, Ownership, Memory, and Plagiarism. *TESOL Quarterly* 30: 201–30.

Price, Margaret. 2002. "Beyond 'Gotcha!': Situating Plagiarism in Policy and Pedagogy." *College Composition and Communication* 54: 88–115.

Robillard, Amy E. 2006. "*Young Scholars* Affecting Composition: A Challenge to Disciplinary Citation Practices." *College English* 68 (3): 253–70.

Scollon, Ron. 1994. "As a Matter of Facts: The Changing Ideology of Authorship and Responsibility in Discourse." *World Englishes* 13 (1): 33–46.

Swales, John M. 1990. *Genre Analysis: English in Academic and Research Settings.* Cambridge, U.K.: Cambridge University Press.

Trimbur, John. 2004. *The Call to Write.* Brief 3rd ed. New York: Longman.

Valentine, Kathryn. 2006. "Plagiarism as Literacy Practice: Recognizing and Rethinking Ethical Binaries." *College Composition and Communication* 58 (1): 89–109.

Wieder, Jeremy. 2002. "A Rosh Yeshiva's Response to Cheating." *Yeshiva University Commentator* 67 (Nov. 10). http://media.www.yucommentator.com/media/storage/paper652/news/2002/11/10/EditorialsopEd/A.Rosh.Yeshivas.Response.To.Cheating-664196.shtml (accessed November 2007).

Yeshiva College. *Upholding Academic Integrity: Definitions of—and Consequences for—Cheating and Plagiarism.* n.d.

8

Intertextuality in the Transcultural Contact Zone

Celia Thompson
University of Melbourne

Alastair Pennycook
University of Technology, Sydney

"We're So Afraid to Come Up with Our Own Ideas"

Frieda, who was a second-year international undergraduate arts student at the time of her interview,[1] commented that in university in Indonesia she was not required to undertake any research for her essays because it was sufficient to write "merely your opinion." There were no computer-based catalogs, so bookshelves had to be searched manually. Support material was not required, compared with Australia where "It's hard to write something based on just what you know." Frieda's first experience of referencing the work of others and using an electronic catalog was in her first semester of university study in Australia. It was also at this time that she first encountered the term *plagiarism*. Frieda recounts one of her lecturers telling her:

> Don't think that you can write the way you read in books, because all of these books are good books and the writers are really professional. You can find some books don't have many references because they're professor, and until you are a professor in that field, you can't write without referencing.[2]

As Frieda explains, "She doesn't mind that we reference every sentence because that's a process to write a really good essays." So here we have the seemingly paradoxical situation where to produce acceptable texts/knowledge, students are being encouraged to reproduce sentences that derive wholly from the writing of others, at least according to Frieda. Although she says that she is willing to comply with these demands for referencing, she experiences a crisis in confidence about the value and status of her "own" thoughts. Frieda describes how she reached the point with one of her lecturers where she felt it became impossible to present her ideas as her "own" because the lecturer would not have believed that they were hers. Frieda was convinced that the lecturer would have thought that they belonged to an author whom she (Frieda) had failed to acknowledge, so she decided to attribute them to a particular author anyway, to avoid being challenged by the lecturer. This resulted in Frieda's feeling alienated from the writing she had produced:

> The problem is that I end up with an essay full of references. There's rarely a sentence, which doesn't have any references, And I think that's awful . . . *I feel this is not my type of essay.* It's really the way that she (the lecturer) likes it. She thinks it's right. Some lecturer gave more freedom and more flexible in writing essays but this one, she clearly has her own idea already (about) what is a good essay. It's better to follow that.

While Frieda is clearly dissatisfied with her own writing, exclaiming "I don't know what I write!," she nevertheless felt obliged to produce texts/knowledge that complied with the demands of Western academic cultural tradition as exhorted by her lecturer. As the following extract shows, the only sentence that does not contain an in-text reference is the first, which serves as an introduction to and synthesis of the exemplifying sentences that follow. The extract is taken from the assignment Frieda submitted for this research entitled "Images of Japanese feminism in Mizoguchi films":

> The dominant image of women in Japan is as mothers and wives. Generally, being a woman ideally means primarily getting married and having children (Yoshizumi 1995, 184; Kawashima 1995, 289). As Creighton (1996, 205) points out: "Most Japanese women have been raised to consider the domestic realm their foremost responsibility, marriage and motherhood their primary goal" and Morley (1999, 40) confirms: "Marriage has always been the cultural norm expected of women in Japan." In a larger scope, women are the pillar of society as they are in charge for upbringing the better future generations (Ohinata 1995, 200) and preserving the integrity of family and society (Hauser 1991, 297–8; Iwao 1993, 4).

Frieda reiterates her frustration with this style of writing, stating:

> I don't like it because it limits me to say only the things that I can find in books. I feel like, it's like gathering information and report them . . . We're so afraid to come up with our own ideas. If I were given more. Freedom to do it on [*sic*] my own way . . . I would come up with more of my own ideas, rather than just supporting and finding more and more authors—other people's ideas.

It seems then for Frieda that compliance with the referencing requirements and the worldview imposed by her lecturer is epistemologically restrictive ("It limits me to say only the things that I can find in books"). In addition, she is fearful of thinking independently ("We're so afraid to come up with our own ideas") and feels she is little more than a conduit for the ideas of others. Frieda is presented here with a homogenizing approach to difference in the classroom, and although she can see and articulate some of the ways in which this view of writing is both problematic and hypocritical, she is unable to find the cultural resources or writing practices that might enable her to do more than acquiesce.

Intertextuality in the Transcultural Contact Zone

Frieda's struggles here, of course, need to be seen in the context of the near-obsessive fear in the academy of plagiarism. We want to begin by arguing that the term *plagiarism,* while possibly useful as a means of identifying certain base acts of presenting the work of others as one's own, by and large obfuscates more than it clarifies because it is too laden with negative and moral connotations (Briggs, 2003). Moreover, if all texts are filled with the ideas and words of innumerable others (Bakhtin, 1986), the quest for genealogy and authorship needs to be recognized as a highly complex and problematic undertaking. Frieda's struggles also point to the ways that students from different cultural backgrounds may feel their voices are being drowned out by the insistence on particular textual conventions. Different textual assumptions are integral to our understanding of the political nature of text/knowledge production, intertextuality, writer identity, and textual ownership. This is particularly so where students come from diverse cultural backgrounds with widely different educultural[3] experiences.

There have always been far greater dimensions of difference in our classrooms than have been typically acknowledged, both in terms of a basic, often class-based, cultural divide between educational culture and home culture for many students, and in terms of the diversity of languages and cultures that students in a country such as Australia bring to classrooms: Sixteen percent of the Australian population speak a language other than English in the home (Australian Bureau of Statistics, 2007). Nevertheless, diversity in tertiary classrooms has been greatly enhanced by the increased internationalization of education and particularly in relation to education through the currently desired cultural capital of English. In Australia, for example, overseas students (who are usually full-fee paying) comprised almost one quarter (23 percent) of all university students in the first half of 2006 (DEST 2007). Such students bring with them not only dollars and diversity but a range of attitudes to education from the pragmatic to the resistant, some taking the line that they will simply do whatever it takes to get their required degrees, others insistent that the education they are buying—using their own local dollars to acquire global linguistic and cultural capital—is a product to be negotiated. It is in this complex transcultural contact zone that divergent attitudes toward texts are projected, refuted, appropriated, reinscribed.

In recent times, the need to recognize and work constructively with cultural difference in Western university classrooms has been highlighted in the literature (Canagarajah, 2002; Carroll and Ryan, 2005; Lin et al., 2005). This growing body of research has also led to studies into the relationship between cultural difference and questions of authorship and textual ownership (see Hayes and Introna, 2003; Liu, 2005; Sowden, 2005; Marshall and Garry, 2006). According to Singh and Doherty (2004), university teachers "need to critically engage with assumptions about teacher, student and cultural identities. Communicative relations in such contact zones need to be renegotiated, reworked, and remade in new and contingent ways" (10). Similarly, we have chosen here to look at such classrooms in terms of "transcultural contact zones," where forms of difference are produced, challenged, and negotiated in the doing of writing pedagogy.

In a recent study (Chandrasoma, Thompson, and Pennycook, 2004) we reframe the notion of plagiarism in terms of transgressive and nontransgressive intertextuality, which has allowed us to focus primarily on textual relations and secondarily on whether particular intertextualities transgress institutional conventions. We also draw attention to the growing body of work that has started to shed light on the complexities and issues that underlie textual borrowing. For instance, research that has focused more closely on student writing, motivation, and development has shown that textual borrowing is more of an issue of academic literacy than academic dishonesty and is therefore best viewed primarily as a developmental problem (Angélil-Carter, 2000); indeed, it has been argued that "apparent plagiarism" may be a successful developmental process (Currie, 1998).

In a similar vein, other work has pointed to the potential advantages of exploiting positive aspects of textual borrowing (Pennycook, 1996; Price, 2002). And graders' perceptions of emergent student authorship—and thus the extent to which a text is seen as original or borrowed—have been shown to depend largely on writers' unequal access to discursive resources within a larger sociopolitical context (Starfield, 2002). These studies point to the role of cultural, social, and political forces in influencing the ways in which textual borrowing may be interpreted. The view that teachers and students are implicated in relationships of power that are sociohistorically and intertextually constructed has been well established in the literature on second language education (e.g., Pennycook, 2001; Phan Le Ha and Viete, 2002; Starfield, 2002) and also has profound implications for the ways in which we discuss the concept of textual ownership.

For the purposes of our research, we have started with the notion of "text" as a form of situated political practice (Luke, 1997) that acknowledges the "political/discursive (subtextual), social/historical (pretextual), and local/contingent (contextual) ways in which texts and readers produce (intertextual) meanings in relation across texts" (Pennycook, 2001, 112). The fact that texts are populated with other texts is crucial for our understanding of the concept of intertextuality and even more so in the transcultural contact zones of our contemporary classrooms. Our research has emphasized the importance of avoiding the creation of decontextualized rules to identify acts of transgressive intertextuality; rather we emphasize the importance of considering a range of contextually contingent factors relating to student development, writing strategies, emergent authorship, common knowledge, interdiscursivity, and interdisciplinarity before deciding whether a particular text is transgressive. We have concluded, therefore, that textual borrowing cannot be adequately dealt with either in terms only of detection and prevention or of simply teaching the correct citation practices but can be best understood as one aspect of textual construction that is deeply embedded in a wide variety of cultural, textual, and academic practices that are centrally concerned with questions of language, education, knowledge, and identity.

"We Aren't Really Trying to Make It Appear That It's Our Own"

Georgia was born in the United Kingdom and lived there for three years before moving to Hong Kong. She spoke Cantonese at home and attended secondary school in Hong Kong, where the medium of instruction was English,[4] until she was 16 years old. She then moved to Australia to complete her final two years of secondary education before enrolling as an international student at an Australian university in an arts degree. She was a first-year undergraduate in her late teens or early twenties at the time of data collection for this study. Before coming to university, Georgia stated that she had never been concerned about or required to document source materials. She commented that the notion of textual ownership in Australia was conceived of in very different terms compared with Hong Kong:

> It seems like to me that Australia emphasise much more on this, whereas in Hong Kong . . . no-one really asked us to do it. (For) all projects, everyone just follow books, just copying, even diagrams, just copying the diagram and stick it there. You don't have to acknowledge it. We probably assume it's just like a textbook and we're just doing an exercise and we're free to just use it. It's not like we are stealing it. We never thought of stealing the ideas at all. We aren't really trying to make it appear that it's our own. It's that obvious it's not our work. We're just showing that we understand.

Writing, then for Georgia prior to coming to Australia, involved copying and recycling the work of others to demonstrate to her teachers that she had understood what they had covered in class. The notion of inappropriate use or of stealing material from source texts would not have been considered because students would not claim ownership of the ideas they had used. There would be no intention to deceive the reader about questions of authorship. For the teachers reading the students' writing, it would be obvious that the students had copied ideas from their sources and that this was a means of demonstrating that learning had occurred. When Georgia was asked how she felt about using other people's language, she replied:

> I used to love it. When I was in Hong Kong I remember when we were really young, they taught us, they give you a passage, for example, "Mary likes going to school. She, I don't know, she learns this and this." Then, we're supposed to write another one just changing the name and write exactly the same thing. That's how you learn how to write (laughs) . . . I feel that I'm not copying. I'm actually changing the words, but using the same expression and I feel that expression is just grammar and it's just that someone is better at it, so I feel that I'm allowed to do that.

A number of points emerge from Georgia's description of her own learning. Firstly, Georgia clearly used to derive considerable pleasure from learning to write using a "parallel structuring" approach. Secondly, writing is learned not only by attempting to imitate the structure of a particular written genre, but also by copying the expression produced by a writer who is better at generating grammar: The student-as-learner is permitted (and expected) to imitate and seek close guidance from the "expert" who acts as the mediator through whom the student's learning occurs. Georgia seemed to equate *expression* with *grammar* and went on to say, "Everyone's free to use language in a particular way . . . no-one has the claim to say, 'this belongs to me,' because the words are there." For Georgia, language seemed autonomous and available for anyone to use however they chose, yet was owned by nobody. There is a clash here between a communal and democratic sense of language and an individualistic and possessive view. Thus, because the concept of individual ownership of language and ideas was outside her experience of learning and writing prior to coming to Australia, she was potentially vulnerable to charges of transgressive intertextuality by her lecturers.

Georgia's assignment on *Tone Languages* that she submitted for this research, however, suggests that despite holding a radically different set of expectations regarding the nature of writing and textual ownership prior to arriving in Australia, she had nevertheless been able to satisfy her Australian university assessors by producing an essay they considered worthy of an H2A (this translates to a percentage grade between 75 and 79), a mark that is well above average for a first-year arts faculty essay. Georgia's opening paragraph contains two attributed direct quotations; in contrast, the concluding paragraph of her essay contained no in-text references. When she was asked why this was the case, she responded that she had presented the ideas of other people in the rest of her essay, so the conclusion was the point at which she could express her "own" thoughts and ideas:

> After all, the knowledge is shared by people . . . after I gain all this knowledge, then I decide on my position which may be the same as some of the authors, but it is mine. So now I present it in my own way. So from that point onwards, people if they want to use my (work) they have to reference it to me, maybe.

Georgia felt that by the time she had managed to write the conclusion to her essay, she had "paid her dues" to the authors of her source texts by referring to them throughout the rest of her essay; she had worked out what she thought about the texts she had read (her "position"), so that even if her position turned out to be the same as some of the writers she had read, it would nevertheless be one that she felt she had earned the right to "own" ("it is mine"). Furthermore, Georgia wanted to believe that her efforts at performing as an academic writer would result in subsequent readers referencing her writing; she would be rewarded for her endeavors by having the same status conferred on her as that of the authors of her source texts: She would have earned her place alongside them as a legitimate member of the disciplinary community she had been engaging with. Georgia's choice of the qualifying word *maybe*, however, suggested that she was not totally convinced that her struggle to write herself into her assignment had been successful.

Georgia's case not only highlights the difficulty she feels in establishing a sense of ownership over her writing but also suggests a sense of frustration at the inability of the academy to tolerate alternative approaches to the construction of texts and knowledge from student writers: It is only "really famous poets," not students, she claimed, who can produce texts that are "actually wrong" but "they are still considered right." It is precisely at such points of tension that we as Western educators can begin to reflect on how to work constructively with the kinds of differences our international students bring to our university classrooms.

Writer Identity, Development, and the Struggle for Textual Ownership

Georgia's writing also needs to be seen in terms of development and identity. There has been much debate on how students' multiple identities contribute to the ways in which they engage with academic discourse communities (e.g., Angélil-Carter, 1997; Canagarajah, 1997; Clark and Ivanic, 1997). Canagarajah (1997) provides evidence of how ethnically and racially marginalized students develop their resistance to new academic conventions into which they are being acculturated (186–87) and suggests that a sustainable methodology within similar contexts should be an integral part of the writing pedagogy. Critiquing certain aspects of resistance theory, Welsh (2001) suggests that students learn through developing resistance and that their "legitimate opposition to subordination" (554) should form an essential part of the process of gaining new cultural capital.

It is here that Kristeva's work (1986, 1996) is also significant because she provides the crucial theoretical links between textuality and subjectivity, thus heralding Pennycook's claim that "engagement in discourse is part of the continuing construction of identity" (2001, 149). Kristeva's intertextual subjects (or "personalities") in process (and) on trial are analogous to the students-as-emergent-authors in this study who are awaiting assessment and confirmation from their lecturers as legitimate academic writers; they are agentive subjects involved in a heterogeneous ongoing process of (trans)formation and becoming (Kristeva 1986, 30). For Kristeva, both producers and readers of texts experience what she terms "the same putting-into-process of . . . identities" that engage with one another to produce meanings; these meanings, however, are not fixed but are in a constant state of flux and may change over time (Kristeva 1996, 190–91).

Kristeva's concept of intertextual identity as projecting into future planes and contexts is commensurate with Bakhtin's approach to the creation of textual meanings and ownership that he articulated through his theory of dialogism and the dialogic-self (1981, 427; 1984, 213). Bakhtin suggests that dialogue occurs not only between different individuals ("external" dialogue), which create intertextual encounters between writers, readers, and source texts, but that dialogue also occurs within the individual in what he terms "interior" or "internal" dialogue (1981, 427): a "dialogue with the self" (1984, 213). In these exchanges that take place within all individuals, the words that are used are "double-voiced." Within each of these double-voicings, Bakhtin believes a tension between voices occurs as each strives to communicate with the other: "These voices are not self-enclosed or deaf to one another. They hear each other constantly, call back and forth to each other, and are reflected in one another" (1984, 74–75).

Such a fragmented and conflicting view of the self is common in poststructuralist thinking whereby identity (or "subjectivity") is conceived as constructed by language and produced through different social, political, and economic discursive practices, "the meanings of which are a constant site of struggle over power" (Weedon 1997, 21). It is this sense of tension (the dialogic-self), struggle and fragility in conjunction with a notion of subjectivity as evolving under the scrutiny of others ("on-trial"), that so appositely describes the processes of identity formation experienced by the students in our research as they have battled for authorship and ownership of the assignments they produced for assessment by their lecturers. From her interview, it was clear that Georgia not only struggled to understand how learning and the construction of her "own" knowledge took place: "If someone has said it, then I have to reference it, then I think that all my piece will be, has to be, sourced because all the ideas I've learnt"; she also indicated a sense of frustration that textual ownership, while desirable, seemed always to be out of reach for her as long as she remained a student: "How nice to say that it's *my* idea." Georgia seemed to feel that she was nothing more than a repository and mouthpiece for the ideas of others:

> I never really think, "Ah, this is what I know," because, you know, with, "what I know," I've probably (been) taught, so I can't really exactly say, "Ah, this is my insight and is a new idea." And, in fact, I think there's nothing new

under the sun (laughs), sometimes. I feel that way. Everything people say, it's just gathering information from all different sources.

These emergent and conflictual selves also need to be set in the context of student development, that is, the changing linguistic, academic, and authorial abilities of the student. The practice of text/knowledge construction known as "patchwriting"—"copying from a source text and then deleting some words, altering grammatical structures, or plugging in one-for-one synonym-substitutes" (Howard 1992, 233)—constitutes an example of one such aspect of emerging developmental strategies. Howard's work (e.g., 1992, 1995, 1999) effectively highlights the problem of ownership and authorship of texts by exploring questions about exactly how writers write, claiming that all writers pass through a series of developmental stages. Patchwriting, or more extensive examples of copying in student academic writing she suggests, may be indicative of the need to use the writing of others in order to create our "own" texts. The writing practices of Natalie, the third of our research participants, exemplify this approach to text/knowledge construction.

"Why am I wasting my life . . . just . . . summarize other people ideas?"

Natalie is a third-year international undergraduate arts student in her late teens or early twenties studying in Melbourne. Her first language is Thai, and she has been studying English for fifteen years. She submitted the assignment discussed later in her first year of university study and was given a *B* grade. On several occasions in her interview, Natalie emphasized the importance she placed on developing and using her own ideas for assignments. She specifically asked, "Why am I wasting my life . . . just . . . summarize other people ideas?" and admitted that, in her first year at the university, she tried to avoid subjects with a research orientation and favored what she saw as practical or vocationally oriented subjects such as languages.

It is interesting to see here how Natalie resisted what she perceived as the time-wasting exercise of reproducing the ideas of others, in favor of practical, vocationally oriented subjects. As she explains, "I don't care whether the lecturer think I'm intelligent or not, I just want to get quite good mark . . . I just want to pass this subject; just go and look for a job." Natalie certainly seems to operate in a very different cultural space than her lecturers and successfully resists the homogenizing imperative to reproduce the ideas of others. Nevertheless, she hopes to obtain future employment benefits from the education system she eschews and uses "patchwriting" as a means of coping with the demands of academic text production.

The assignment Natalie submitted for this study was set as part of the assessment for the subject "Spanish, politics, and history" and required students to focus on Spanish politics after the death of Franco in the mid-1970s.

Students were asked to address the question: Was Spain's political transition also an economic one? Natalie commented that she knew nothing about Spain when she started working on the task and that she completed the assignment in 48 hours. She described the essay as a "summary of my reading, rather than something with my ideas." As can be seen from the following extracts, Natalie blends her ideas and language with those of the Carr and Fusi text (1981) she lists in her bibliography and to which she refers with an incomplete in-text reference. The italicized sections indicate a word-for-word correlation with Carr and Fusi:

> Up to then [the late 1950s] the Spanish economy was predominantly Agricultural *with industrial appendages concentrated in the Basque provinces and Catalonia.* It was an autarchy, *a self-sufficient, self-capitalising economy protected from outside competition by tariffs. Administrative controls were created and regulated by state intervention. The Institute of Industry (INI), a state holding company, was set up to direct the establishment of basic industries and supplement investment. Prices and wages were controlled; foreign trade and exchanged rates were closely regulated.* As Carr and Fusi argue, . . .

The Carr and Fusi version (1981, 49–78) is as follows (the italicized sections are worded the same as in Natalie's text):

> In 1939 Spain *was* different; it was an agricultural economy *with industrial Appendages concentrated in the Basque provinces and Catalonia.* (49, paragraph 1)
>
> The two key concepts were autarky and interventionism. *A self-sufficient, self-capitalizing economy protected from outside competition by tariffs* and *administrative controls* would be *created and regulated by state intervention.* (50, paragraph 2)
>
> *Prices and wages were controlled; foreign trade and exchange rates were closely regulated;* the National Wheat Service fixed the production of wheat and marketed it; *the Institute of Industry (INI), a state holding company,* based on an Italian model and run by an admiral and intimate of the Caudillo, *was to direct the establishment of basic industries and supplement private investment.*
>
> (50, final paragraph, through the top of 51, first paragraph)

Natalie's writing cannot be judged as a deliberate attempt to claim unwarranted textual ownership because she makes an in-text reference to her source material, although this is ambivalent (it could be forward or backward referencing to points made) and imprecise (no year or page numbers are provided): "As Carr and Fusi argue . . ." Natalie has certainly copied certain phrases verbatim from Carr and Fusi (1981) with no clear attribution; however, she has not copied whole paragraphs or pages in a random or incoherent fashion. By rearranging the grammar, changing the order of certain propositions, and copying sentence fragments from across three pages of her source text, she has written a cohesive text that she has blended together to produce part of a paragraph of "her own" writing.

There are a number of questions that arise with respect to Natalie's text. Is such patchwriting (an example of a hybrid form of writing) acceptable academic writing practice for a novice student? On what basis should we make such a judgment? Considering the grade allocated to the assignment, the original grader judged the essay to be acceptable. According to the staff member with whom Natalie's writing was discussed, the Carr and Fusi (1981) text is very well known and would likely have been familiar to the grader, suggesting that that person would, therefore, have been aware of the textual similarities. The staff member also stated that he did not view Natalie's writing as highly problematic or indicative of deliberate deception; rather, he saw her text as showing a lack of attribution, thus more akin to the category of student as learner-writer, as opposed to an intellectually dishonest "Other."

Natalie's own account of her writing also needs to be considered. For her, the production of a comprehensively referenced text would have been too time consuming. Her priority was to submit the assignment on time. She also openly talked of her disdain for academic values and was aware that not only was her referencing incomplete, she had also copied. However, in addition, Natalie admitted that she found such essays very difficult to write in her first year and acknowledged that she used to procrastinate. She commented that by her third year, she had begun to find the writing of research-based essays much easier.

Reflexivity and the Politics of Writing in the Transcultural Contact Zone

While neither Frieda, Georgia, nor Natalie stood up to challenge the writing practices they were confronted with, they did show frustration and minor forms of resistance. Frieda felt that the constant insistence on referencing prevented her from expressing herself; Georgia struggled to come to terms with the version of language and knowledge that looked to her like the privatization of natural resources, rather than the use of shared commodities; Natalie quietly subverted writing practices with some clever patchwriting, producing texts that subject lecturers found acceptable. All three international students were surviving, perhaps also succeeding, in their academic environments, though each was struggling to find a way of developing a sense of authorial presence and control in her writing. What light do these studies shed on intertextuality in the transcultural contact zone?

Holton's (2000) account of homogenizing, polarizing, and hybridizing reactions to globalization provides a useful way of looking at this. Students who come to Australia for a Western education, for example, may believe that the cultural and economic capital that such an education will bestow on them will ensure employment and monetary success when they return to their countries of origin. Such students may be quite willing to accept the dictates of academic writing as laid out to them. They may believe that this will allow them to join that elite group of cross-national individuals who are able to exercise their newly acquired cultural capital to promote their own interests in the economic global marketplace, thus making them complicit in surrendering to the homogenizing and standardizing effects of learning English in which local or indigenous cultures are subsumed by the individual's "dreams of affluence (and) personal success" (Holton 2000, 142). Yet, even if this dream has some substance, this process only works to the extent that students can connect across cultural differences and see the point in such practices. More common, we would suggest, is that students see through such practices and learn how to get by in spite of homogenizing dictates on writing practices.

A polarizing position, by contrast, takes as a basic premise a deep cultural divide between different writing practices. From a student's point of view, it may lead to a fierce rejection of particular writing practices; from a teacher's point of view, it may lead to a view of cultural incommensurates. In such pedagogical encounters learners and educators may become polarized, resulting in the classroom becoming a site where apparent civilizations separate and clash. Notions of transcultural identities are vehemently rejected in favor of the assertion of mutually supporting cultural dichotomies. For example, "the East/Orient" in Western texts is often constructed as representing tradition and authoritarianism where the desires and promotion of the individual are secondary next to the collective welfare of the family and society. In contrast, "the West/Occident" represents progress and democracy in which the achievements of the individual are prized above the interests of the broader society (Kubota 2004). Each is reliant on this dichotomous existence (both physically and symbolically) of the Other to make sense of its own identity. While such a position may at least acknowledge difference, it does so in ways that renders identity fixed and one-dimensional. As Said (2001) has argued, any attempt to separate cultures "into water-tight compartments . . . does damage to their variety, their diversity, their sheer complexity of elements, their radical hybridity. The more insistent we are on the separation of cultures and civilisations, the more inaccurate we are about ourselves and others" (587).

The notion of hybridity, therefore, may offer us better grounds for an engagement with difference. A hybridization position attempts to partially address shortfalls in the two former positions in that it describes a dynamic process of cultural mixing and borrowing that, in some instances, may result in what Holton refers to as an indigenization of exogenous cultural factors (2000, 151). This sort of mixing and borrowing has long been the focus of cultural studies and may be seen in anything from the global spread of English to the local appropriation of rap and hip hop (see Pennycook 2007). Hybridization may cooccur with the forces of homogenization and polarization to create a transformational learning environment in which new cultural forms and practices can emerge. Being able to engage in pedagogically effective ways with such hybrid forms of text or knowledge production poses yet more challenges for educators working in the transcultural university classroom.

Lest hybridity become a simple notion of mixing, however, Bakhtin's concept of *dialogism* adds a useful dynamic element to the process. Firstly, it is precisely this "push-pull-mix" (Singh and Doherty 2004, 21) that Bakhtin conceptualizes as the "centripetal" (centralizing, homogenizing, and hierarchicizing) and "centrifugal" (decentralizing, denormatizing, and decrowning) forces that are constantly at play in all communicative interactions (1981, 425). By situating texts within historical, current, and possible future contexts, Bakhtin creates a dialogic framework for the construction of meanings across past, present, and future planes. He suggests that all individual contributions to textual creation come through the ways in which we *accent* and *articulate* the words and ideas of myriad others. We are all producers of "layers of language" (Recchio 1991) that intersect and inform or *interanimate* (Bakhtin 1981, 346) each other. It is precisely here at this point of intertextual engagement, we suggest, that Bakhtin's *dialogue* and battle for meaning occur, as teachers and students struggle to locate themselves in the constantly shifting transcultural contact zones that characterize today's global universities.

It is the immensely intricate linguistic and cultural push-me/pull-you context that educators of international students need to be aware of, understanding cultural difference in complex ways, student development along its unfolding pathways, writer identity as it emerges through struggle. We are arguing therefore at the very least for critical teacher reflexivity (see, for example, Lin 2004) if we are to gain a better understanding of the role played by different, competing, and sometimes resistant identities that constantly jostle for position in the global transcultural contact zone, as students struggle to establish ownership over and investment in the written academic texts they produce. As teachers we need to understand the impacts cultural differences, the politics of knowledge construction, and different writer identities have on the intertextual writing practices of international university students.

Notes

1. Data are drawn from a doctoral research project that looks at plagiarism, intertextuality, and pedagogy. Data include semistructured interviews with ten students and ten staff members, plus end-of-semester student assignments. Staff and students come from a range of matching disciplinary backgrounds including economics and commerce, media studies, modern and ancient history, political science, law, and linguistics. All names have been changed.

2. All student work is replicated exactly here, without editorial changes.

3. We use this term to suggest that the social and pedagogical practices of education are also deeply embedded in cultural formations.

4. Or, as is often the case in Hong Kong, a mixture of English and Cantonese; so-called English-medium schools have always largely been bilingual.

References

Angélil-Carter, S. 1997. "Second Language Acquisition of Spoken and Written English: Acquiring the Skeptron." *TESOL Quarterly* 31: 263–287.

Angélil-Carter, S. 2000. *Stolen language? Plagiarism in writing.* Essex, U.K.: Pearson Education.

Australian Bureau of Statistics (A.B.S.) Year Book, Australia 2007. Ethnic diversity in Australia. Retrieved February 26, 2007, from: www.abs.gov.au/AUSSTATS/ abs@.nsf/bb8db737e2af84b8ca2571780015701e/7056F80A147D09D3CA25723 600006532?opendocument.

Bakhtin, M. M. 1981. *The Dialogic Imagination.* Austin: University of Texas Press.

Bakhtin, M. M. 1984. *Problems of Dostoevsky's Poetics.* Minneapolis: University of Minnesota Press.

Bakhtin, M. M. 1986. "The Problem of the Text in Linguistics, Philology, and the Human Sciences: An Experiment in the Philosophical Analysis." In *M. M. Bakhtin: Speech Genres and Other Late Essays*, edited by C. Emerson and M. Holquist, 104–31. Austin: University of Texas Press.

Briggs, Robert. 2003. "Shameless! Reconceiving the Problem of Plagiarism." *Australian Universities Review* 46: 19–23.

Canagarajah, A. Suresh. 1997. "Safe Houses in the Contact Zone: Coping Strategies of African-American Students in the Academy." *College Composition and Communication* 48: 173–96.

Canagarajah, A. Suresh. 2002. *Critical Academic Writing and Multilingual Students.* Ann Arbor: University of Michigan Press.

Carr, R., and Fusi, J. 1981. *Spain: Dictatorship to Democracy.* London: Allen & Unwin.

Carroll, J., and Ryan, J. (Eds.). 2005. *Teaching International Students: Improved Learning for All.* New York: Routledge.

Chandrasoma, Ranamukalage, Celia Thompson, and Alastair Pennycook. 2004. "Beyond Plagiarism—Transgressive and Non-transgressive Intertextuality." *Journal of Language, Identity and Education* 3 (3): 171–93.

Clark, Romy, and Roz Ivanic. 1997. *The Politics of Writing.* London: Routledge.

Currie, Pat. 1998. "Staying Out of Trouble: Apparent Plagiarism and Academic Survival." *Journal of Second Language Writing* 7: 1–18.

Department of Education, Science, and Training (DEST). 2007. Higher Education Publications. Canberra, Australia: Commonwealth of Australia. Retrieved April 29, 2007, from: www.dest.gov.au/sectors/higher_education/publications_resources/ profiles/students_2006_first_half_year_selected_higher_education.htm#topics.

Hayes, N., and Introna, L. 2003. "Alienation and Plagiarism: Coping with Otherness in Our Assessment Practice." Centre for the Study of Technology and Organisation,

Lancaster University Management School, Lancaster University, U.K. Retrieved February 28, 2007, from: www.lms.lanc.ac.uk/publications/viewpdf/000239/.

Holton, Robert. 2000. "Globalization's Cultural Consequences." *The Annals of the American Academy* 570: 140–152.

Howard, Rebecca Moore. 1992. "A Plagiarism Pentimento." *Journal of Teaching Writing* 11: 233–245.

Howard, Rebecca Moore. 1995. "Plagiarisms, Authorships, and the Academic Death Penalty." *College English* 57: 788–806.

Howard, Rebecca Moore. 1999. "The New Abolitionism Comes to Plagiarism." In *Perspectives on Plagiarism and Intellectual Property in a Postmodern World*, edited by Lise Buranen and Alice Roy, 87–95. Albany: State University of New York Press.

Kristeva, Julia. 1986. In *The Kristeva Reader,* edited by T. Moi. Oxford, U.K.: Basil Blackwell.

Kristeva, Julia. 1996. In *Julia Kristeva Interviews*, edited by R. M. Guberman. New York: Columbia University Press.

Kubota, Ryuko. 2004. "Critical Multiculturalism and Second Language Education." In *Critical Pedagogies and Language Learning*, edited by B. Norton and K. Toohey, 30–52. Cambridge, U.K.: Cambridge University Press.

Lin, A. 2004. "Introducing a Critical Pedagogical Curriculum: A Feminist Reflexive Account." In *Critical Pedagogies and Language Learning*, edited by B. Norton and K. Toohey, 271–90. Cambridge, U.K.: Cambridge University Press.

Lin, A., W. Wang, N. Akamatsu, and M. Riazi. 2005. "International TESOL Professionals and Teaching English for Localised Communication." In *Reclaiming the Local in Language Policy and Practice*, edited by S. Canagarajah, 197–222. Mahwah, NJ: Lawrence Erlbaum.

Liu, Dilin. 2005. "Plagiarism in ESOL Students: Is Cultural Conditioning Truly the Major Culprit?" *ELT Journal* 59 (3): 234–41.

Luke, A. 1997. "The Material Effects of the Word: Apologies, 'Stolen Children' and Public Discourse." *Discourse: Studies in the Cultural Politics of Education* 18: 343–368.

Marshall, S., and M. Garry. 2006. "NESB and ESB Students' Attitudes and Perceptions of Plagiarism." *International Journal of Educational Integrity* 2 (1). Retrieved February 28, 2007, from: www.ojs.unisa.edu.au/journals/index.php/IJEI/article/view/25/17.

Pennycook, Alastair. 1996. "Borrowing Others' Words: Text, Ownership, Memory and Plagiarism." *TESOL Quarterly* 30: 201–230.

Pennycook, Alastair. 2001. *Critical Applied Linguistics: A Critical Introduction.* Mahwah, NJ: Lawrence Erlbaum.

Pennycook, Alastair. 2007. *Global Englishes and Transcultural Flows.* London: Routledge.

Phan Le Ha, X., and R. Viete. (2002). *The Growth of Voice: Negotiating Representations of Self in Research Writing.* Paper presented at the Knowledge and Discourse 2 Conference, June, University of Hong Kong, Hong Kong.

Price, Margaret. 2002. "Beyond 'Gotcha!': Situating Plagiarism in Policy and Pedagogy." *College Composition and Communication* 54: 88–114.

Recchio, Thomas. 1991. "A Bakhtinian Reading of Student Writing." *College Composition and Communication* 42: 446–454.

Said, Edward. 2001. *Reflections on Exile and Other Literary and Cultural Essays.* London: Granta Books.

Singh, Parlo, and Catherine Doherty. 2004. "Global Cultural Flows and Pedagogic Dilemmas: Teaching in the Global University Contact Zone." *TESOL Quarterly* 38 (1): 9–42.

Sowden, Colin. 2005. "Plagiarism and the Culture of Multilingual Students in Higher Education Abroad." *ELT Journal* 59 (3): 226–33.

Starfield, Sue. 2002. "'I'm a Second-Language English speaker': Negotiating Writer Identity and Authority in Sociology One." *Journal of Language, Identity, and Education* 1: 121–140.

Weedon, Chris. 1997. *Feminist Practice and Poststructuralist Theory* (2nd ed.). Malden, MA: Blackwell.

Welsh, Susan. 2001. "Resistance Theory and Illegitimate Reproduction." *College Composition and Communication* 52: 553–73.

9

We Never Wanted to Be Cops

*Plagiarism, Institutional Paranoia,
and Shared Responsibility*

Chris M. Anson
North Carolina State University

Increasingly, our higher-education institutions are interpreting student plagiarism through a lens of criminality, producing elaborate documents and procedures designed to punish offenders and legally safeguard themselves in the process. Students are assumed to know what plagiarism is and how to avoid it, thus relieving faculty of the responsibility to teach it. A "solution" to plagiarism that focuses primarily on policy, detection, and punishment does nothing to advance our presumed mission, which is education. Nor does it do anything to reform and enhance the way that writing is incorporated into classroom instruction across the curriculum. In the context of this blame-based and punitive orientation, alternative approaches have emerged that focus on analyzing the complex causes of both intentional and unintentional plagiarism (Wells 1993), defining what ought to count as plagiarism in the educational process (Howard 1999), and understanding the ways in which Net Generation students conceptualize text and text ownership as a result of the influences on their experience (Buranen and Roy 1999; Howard 2007). Instructionally, these richer treatments of plagiarism have inspired the development of useful educational strategies, such as talking with students about the nature of plagiarism, staging large research assignments, and more fully supporting the development of students' texts through multiple drafts. But although these strategies do much to replace the popular system of plagiarism reduction based on panopticon-like surveillance and threats of punishment, they are still often *driven by a desire to stop cheating*, not by deeper principles of and methods for education. So motivated, they divert attention from the goals of engagement, support, response, and intellectual scaffolding that are crucial for the development of students' advanced literacies.

Grounded in a goal-based instructional design model that supports the highest of three levels of thinking about teaching as schematized by John Biggs (2003), this chapter advocates an approach that deflates our concerns about student plagiarism and opens up possibilities for rethinking the nature of our assignments as tools for learning instead of static products designed purely for assessment. Using such a model, teachers can shape writing assignments and activities in creative, unique ways that engage students, give them ownership of their own work, and reduce our preoccupation with plagiarism through more principled and supportive pedagogy. At the institutional level, Biggs' construct helps us to imagine ways in which administrators, faculty, and students can share responsibility for achieving the goals of learning and teaching that define the real mission of higher education.

How We Think About Plagiarism

Digital technology has given students almost limitless access to information, texts, and other people's words and ideas. For most teachers, this technology is both a blessing and a curse. In the pursuit of learning, students have lightning-fast access to vast storehouses of information, increasingly rich and interconnected. Yet this information also comes to the computer virtually unscreened and unevaluated, making the Internet like a huge flea market where good finds are hidden among large quantities of junk. Worse, state-of-the-art search engines can find passages—or entire papers—that respond to many common writing assignments. Kimbel Library at Coastal Carolina University has long tracked and cataloged the Websites that store and sell (or give away) thousands of papers representing hundreds of different courses in dozens of fields. At this writing, the number of such sites exceeds 250 (Kimbel 2006). So enabled, students can earn decent grades not for their efforts at reading, researching, interpreting, writing, and revising, but for a few unscrupulous moments at a computer screen.

Our suspicion of plagiarism has increased in proportion to students' ready access to these sites, as well as to billions of other documents that can be snipped, spliced, modified, and pasted into their writing. At its most basic, our response is often defensive; we wonder how we can protect the walls of the academy from the plunderers of text, and we enjoin our administrations to impose ever-more severe punishments on offenders. This reaction partly explains the popularity of commercial plagiarism detection services, such as TurnItIn (http://turnitin.com) and EVE2 (Essay Verification Engine; www.canexus.com/). Across the academy, teachers pursue their suspicions of plagiarism with the energy and persistence of *Les Miserables*' Javert on the trail of Jean Valjean, sometimes spending hours or even days of their valuable time in the hunt.

Our preoccupation with plagiarism detection and its accompanying legalistic and punitive apparatus runs against many educational principles. It subtly begins to wear away at our collective personae as coaches, guides, and mentors, yielding a hardened attitude, detective-like and oppositional. Rows of naïve students take on the demeanor of cheats who blatantly disregard the rules of copyright, ownership, and individual authorship. Lacking the moral fiber of previous generations, students are to blame. The guardians of text, we demand honesty and integrity, and our students flout them. Our duty then requires us to search and seize, to discipline and punish, and we begin to develop a posture of mistrust and a disposition of control in our instruction.

A teacher's reflection about a case of plagiarism illustrates the feelings of frustration—even sometimes of assault—we experience when students deceive us:

> Last semester, two students plagiarized papers in my class. They stole about 15 hours of my time from my other students—if I had not had to track down their sources, print and save evidence, consult with the Honor Court President, worry about how to talk with the students, consult with other teachers, and follow through with the Honor Court, I'd have had other students' papers back to them much sooner, I'd have had time to hunt up a video I wanted to show, and I'd have had more hours for conferences with other students.
>
> These plagiarists also stole freedom of topic choice from my future students. For the first time in several years, I had allowed students considerable freedom to choose topics that really interested them. That opened the door for these two students to cheat. In the future, I'll go back to restricting topics much more, and I'll devise writing assignments that focus narrowly on particular texts in ways that published materials aren't likely to address. . . . Plagiarism not only wastes the students' and teachers' time, but it destroys trust. I'll be more suspicious of my future students because of the dishonesty of these two. (Ruggiero 2004)

Plagiarism's immediate effects on this teacher are understandable: frustration over the time needed for source sleuthing and for navigating the complicated institutional bureaucracy surrounding student conduct violations; anger over the subversion of her other responsibilities to the class. But more worrying is how her options for student learning appear to tighten as she vows to offer less freedom to explore ideas and the world of discourse; as she loses trust in students' integrity (and the positive classroom climate that trust engenders); and as she approaches the enterprise of education with a growing skepticism whose psychological effects may erode her excitement, her classroom attitude, and her desire to establish productive relationships with her students. This teacher's disclosure also suggests that she is allowing her revised construction of who her students are—potential or probable cheaters—to control her pedagogical decisions. She reverts to a more restrictive approach that she had abandoned, presumably because it was less instructionally effective than encouraging students to explore topics of their own interest; but it is the fear of plagiarism, not the realization of specific learning goals, that causes the change.

In some ways, this teacher's reversion to a less student-centered pedagogy can be productively interpreted through the theoretical construct of teaching and learning developed by John Biggs (2003). Biggs, an educational psychologist whose work has focused on learning theory, assessment, and pedagogy, is especially interested in the relationship between the activities teachers and students engage in and the relationship of those activities to students' success as learners. His book *Teaching for Quality Learning at University* (2003) proposes three levels of thinking about teaching that can affect not only individual class sessions and courses but entire curricula and institutions.

In Biggs' view, "Level 1" thinking about teaching focuses on what the student *is*. Students come to our campuses with predetermined sets of abilities, dispositions, work ethics, and talents (or lack thereof). Teaching is a process of providing new information to these disparate learners; "good" students learn it and perform well, while "bad" students fall by the wayside. The teacher's job is to sort out the good from the bad, using instructional methods (bell-curve grading, for example) explicitly designed for this purpose. Teaching is not concerned with disparities in ability because the student, no one else, is to blame for his or her own failing performance: "At Level 1, teaching is, as it were, held constant—it is transmitting information, usually by lecturing—so differences in learning are due to differences between students in ability, motivation, what sort of school they went to . . . and yes, their 'innate' approaches to learning" (21). Level 1 teaching emerges from a deficit model of education in which we focus not on what students need to succeed but on rewarding the good ones for what they already have and punishing the bad ones for what they lack—a perspective earlier described and critiqued by Mina Shaughnessy (1976) in the context of student writers at open-admissions universities and later by Frank Smith (1998), whose "official theory of learning and forgetting" assumes that students need to be threatened to be motivated to learn, that few students can learn well, and that when students fail it is always their own fault.

Representing a significant improvement, Level 2 thinking about teaching is "still based on transmission, but of concepts and understandings, not just of information . . . " (Biggs 2003, 3). Here, the emphasis shifts from what the *student is* to what the *teacher does*. "Good teachers" arm themselves with a wide assortment of teaching tricks, learn how to lecture with props, humor, and other interest-capturing devices, and place high value on teaching as performance. Learning, therefore, is understood in terms of "teacher presage factors" rather than "what sort of student one has to deal with" (23). Level 2 also reinforces a deficit model, according to Biggs, but with the blame for deficiencies now on the teacher: Success is based upon "what *I* the teacher am doing, not upon what *they* the students are learning" (23), a focus often reinforced by institutional teaching assessment practices (student opinions of teachers, for example, rather than measures of student development).

Teachers at Level 3 see learning as the confluence of what the teacher does, who the students are, and, most importantly, what the students *do* to learn. "Expert teaching includes mastery over a variety of teaching techniques, but unless learning takes place, they are irrelevant: the focus is on what the student does, on what learning is or is not going on" (Biggs 2003, 24). When teachers structure their pedagogy from this perspective, constantly gauging their students' progress against their objectives and supporting learning through active and constructivist strategies, students more often engage in "deep" rather than "surface" learning, a distinction Biggs bases on a taxonomy with simple memorization at the bottom and extended abstract understanding at the top (see Biggs 2003, 39–40). Although for Biggs Level 3 brings student activity and engagement clearly into view, what the teacher does cannot be ignored. As long as teachers coordinate class sessions, assign work to students, and monitor and assess their progress, they play a central role in "what the student *does*." For this reason, it is helpful to think about Level 3 from the perspective of shared responsibility, a socially determined relationship between teachers and students that has profound consequences for learning (and to which we will return later).

Biggs' theories of teaching and learning apply at general levels across a spectrum of educational contexts. However, they also offer us a useful scheme for understanding how we think about plagiarism. Teachers who assume that students are either honest and hardworking or duplicitous and unethical clearly view student behavior from Level 1. Plagiarism comes from student failures; our job is to reward those who don't cheat and punish those who do—much as we might reward those students who enter our classes already well prepared and punish (through failure) those who are deficient. Although cheating and academic performance might seem like apples and oranges, at Level 1 the practice of prejudgment applies to both: Teachers are often quick to point out that students who perform poorly do so by choice; it is who they *are* (lazy, uninspired, unprepared) that makes them poor learners, just as it is who they *are* (shiftless, sneaky, unscrupulous) that makes them plagiarists.

Level 2 thinking about plagiarism moves strongly away from a "blame the student" perspective. For one thing, teachers are actively considering what they can do to help, and that includes at least some sensitivity to the confusions, misapprehensions, bad prior knowledge, or poor ability to act on "told" information that many students bring into a college setting. All sorts of teacher-presented methods soon rush in, such as including in the syllabus large chunks of material on plagiarism and its consequences; handing out tip sheets on how not to plagiarize; giving mini lessons on source citation or—the staple of composition courses—how to quote, paraphrase, or summarize others' words; requiring students to visit a website on plagiarism; threatening or scaring them; or even trying to establish a feeling of mutual trust in the classroom that would make them feel guilty when plagiarizing. But none of this teacher-generated activity may go very far toward fixing the problem, any more than entertaining lectures or well-presented supplementary materials guarantee that all students learn what the teacher wants them to learn. In its teacher-centeredness, this approach still encourages the transmission of knowledge. Students can still willfully plagiarize. Some students who have "heard" the teacher may still not know how to distinguish plagiarism from writing their own words, may still cite sources incorrectly, or may still take the risk of passing off someone else's material as their own. The problem with Level 2 is that, in Bigg's words, "the focus should not be on the skill itself [e.g., a strategy for teaching about plagiarism] but on whether its deployment has the desired effect on student learning" (2003, 24).

In spite of its attempts to convey understanding, a Level 2 approach to plagiarism continues to frustrate teachers. Further cases of plagiarism either drive them back to the assumptions at Level 1 or subvert their best efforts to help students learn the subject matter of their disciplines. Aware of the risks (or having experienced them), teachers often resort to more and more dramatic devices to reinforce what they provide. As illustrated in a line from a syllabus for a political science course ("If you plagiarize even a single sentence from another person, *you will fail this course*"), these tactics often border on desperation.

When we consider what *students do* relative to our learning goals and objectives—that is, how their own active learning processes build new knowledge on top of old—our focus shifts toward activities that support the learning of good writing practices and a heightened understanding of issues of copyright and intellectual property. From a Level 3 perspective, a teacher might set up activities in the classroom in which students wrestle with challenging passages and learn how to incorporate them into their own texts, or paraphrase them so as not to quote them directly but still cite their source. Or students could be given a series of vignettes illustrating nuanced uses of text and then, in small groups, negotiate judgments about whether they represent plagiarism. (For some additional strategies, see *Defining* 2002.) All this focus on what students do goes a long way toward solving the problem of *nescience:* cases in which students blamelessly mess up because they don't have the skills and abilities, or prior experience, or (for some) the cultural knowledge about Americans' passion for ownership of intellectual property, to get it right when they come to our campuses. If this nescience characterizes even a portion of our students, then such an orientation toward learning will already do much to create an environment in which students work carefully and knowledgably with text.

But although such a learner-focused approach might help to educate students about plagiarism, it still doesn't *cause* them not to claim ownership of text they didn't write. Behaving responsibly with text is not a predictable outcome of literacy education. Furthermore, many teachers in discipline-based courses across the curriculum don't have time or expertise to manage long classroom sessions on source work, citation practices, and the like. This is because the overt learning goal of such student-centered work is to teach students how to use and cite others' words. In the context of writing across the curriculum, teachers may have other, more immediate goals, such as helping students to learn the complex properties of momentum and velocity in physics, or wrestle with multiple accounts of a conflict in Latin American history, or practice seeing cultural behavior from an anthropological perspective. In their information-heavy courses, driven by curricular coverage, how can they assign lots of writing and also show students how to work responsibly with text?

The answer to this question comes from an instructional design model that helps us to consider the relationship among our learning goals, the nature of our assignments, and support for students' learning. This model helps us to understand how other manifestations of Level 3 teaching provide a new approach to the problem of plagiarism and largely remove it from our daily concerns in our classrooms, including the problem of whether anything we do as *teachers* can guarantee that students won't turn in other people's texts as their own.

Goal-Directed Writing and the Adjustment of Educational Focus

In the context of writing, a fully developed version of Level 3 teaching is illustrated in Figure 1. Here, everything begins and ends with clearly articulated learning goals tied to the objectives and outcomes of a course. If students need to learn how to analyze culture from an anthropological perspective, then assignments are carefully designed to help them acquire that ability. Although Figure 1 focuses on the use of writing assignments, it is important to realize that many other activities and processes might as effectively accomplish a specific learning goal as writing (in-class group problem solving, micropresentations, observations, reflective discussions, visits to websites, and the like).

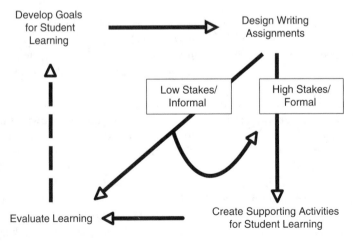

Figure 9–1 Instructional Design Model

As shown in the options for assignment design, writing assignments can be relatively informal, focusing mostly on the concepts, ideas, readings, data, or other information in a course instead of the formal characteristics of the writing; or they can be longer, more formal, and more extended, with higher stakes for the nature and quality of the text. The longer and more formal the assignment, and the higher its stakes, the greater the teacher's responsibility to support its development through, for example, the practice of certain intellectual and analytical skills and processes and through work on multiple drafts. Evaluation of low-stakes writing assignments typically considers students' progress meeting the learning goals and is therefore formative. Evaluation of higher-stakes assignments considers the product as output: an example of what the student is capable of *doing* with sufficient support. In both cases, evaluation is tied explicitly to learning goals, making the process of reaching judgments much faster and clearer.

A model of writing instruction based on learning goals pushes us away from "stock" assignments, which are often designed to test instead of teach. When we focus on what the student *does* in completing the assignment and meeting certain learning goals, countless possibilities open up for unique, engaging writing activities. When assignments have clearly expressed instructional purposes and an interesting design, topic, or set of processes, students who might have turned in plagiarized work will be both unable and unwilling to do so. But the motivation for creating such assignments comes from a focus on student learning, not from a desire to keep plagiarism at bay or safeguard the teacher from the additional burdens of hunting down the source of suspicious work.

The following "stock" assignment looks as if it's designed to test how well students have read the first act of *King Lear*, though we can't be sure because it contains no explicit learning goal or objective:

> After reading up through Act 1, Scene 3 in *King Lear*, describe what has happened so far in the plot, noting especially Cordelia's situation.

A Google search for papers on *King Lear* yields 1,030,000 entries with perhaps hundreds that might fulfill this short assignment. Here are excerpts from a summary of *Lear* at bookrags.com—not a student paper mill but a site designed for research and learning (with a distinctive Cliffs Notes–like orientation). For an unsuspecting instructor, this material might easily fulfill the assignment's requirements:

> The plot opens at King Lear's retirement. Lear has decided to give up the throne and divide his kingdom among his daughters. Before allotting the portions of the kingdom, Lear asks each of his daughters to profess her love for him in the best way she knows how. Doing so will guarantee each girl her portion of the entitlement. While Goneril and Regan delve into expressions of adoration for their father, Cordelia remains speechless, saying that words cannot express her love. Lear becomes enraged by what he considers his favorite daughter's lack of attachment and affection. With that, Lear cuts Cordelia off,

> deciding she will receive none of the entitlement. Her share is divided
> between the other two girls, who receive almost the entirety of the royal court.
> The only thing Lear keeps for himself is a retinue of 100 knights who will take
> him back and forth between the two girls for visits. (bookrags.com 2007)

A literature teacher who receives this text will either reward the erring student
with a favorable assessment or set off on a hunt for the source and then spend
valuable time consulting, accusing, and punishing. But it takes almost no
time—just a little imagination and a focus on the kind of teaching and learning
that characterizes Biggs' third level—to frame a modest learning goal and then
to craft an assignment sensitive to what students must *do* and how those
actions might best accomplish the goal.

> The purpose of this short assignment is to help you (1) review what has hap-
> pened up to the end of Act I, Scene 3 of *King Lear* by sending you back into
> the play, and (2) think more fully about Cordelia's perspective. As we will
> see, letters play an important role in *King Lear*. Imagine that you are Cordelia
> at this point in the play. Write a one- to two-page letter to Lear explaining
> how you feel. (Shakespearean language optional.)

A search for letters from Cordelia to Lear yields nothing on the Internet except
essays about a letter Cordelia sends to Kent in Act II (and consulting this material would only enrich students' response to the assignment). A student who
wants to use someone else's commentary on *King Lear* would probably have
to devote so much time to twisting such a text to "fit" the letter genre and the
constraints of the task that he would be putting more cognitive and composing
effort into "cheating" than is required to write the letter from scratch.
Furthermore, this assignment can be varied from class to class without losing
any of its uniqueness and interest level and still accomplish the same goals of
careful reading, review, and analysis.

> The purpose of this short assignment [etc.]. Imagine that the world of *King
> Lear* includes just one piece of contemporary technology: an Instant
> Messenger system. Write an IM chat between Lear and Cordelia in which
> you make it clear what these two characters' positions are by the end of Act
> II, Scene 3 of the play. (Shakespearean language optional.)

Technology-savvy instructors could also set up an imaginary blog that characters
would write to, expressing their positions. Or the world of *Lear* could have
Facebook or MySpace accounts, and characters could "friend" each other to
share their thoughts. Teachers who want to preserve the authenticity of the play's
historical context could imagine a series of notes "couriered" by a page,
passenger pigeon, or other method. Other characters—Regan and Goneril, for
example—could be added to the exchanges, or different groups of students
could be assigned to represent any of the characters in a kind of role-play dialogue.

This kind of rhetorical and genre manipulation based on clearly defined learning goals can be employed in any course in any discipline. In the crop science program at North Carolina State University, for example, faculty design innovative, low-stakes assignments to support specific learning goals. In a required course in plant genetics, students are asked to find a metaphor for DNA replication, transcription, and translation that third graders would understand, and then do a five-minute presentation (using props) as if they were addressing a third grade science class. Tapping into third graders' knowledge, the groups invent fascinating representations that have included a *Charlotte's Web* model, a pizza model, and a candy model. The teacher of this course, Dr. Susana Milla-Lewis, claims that in spite of the small percentage of the final grade devoted to this project and the informal nature of the assessment, students willingly and enthusiastically pour their energy into preparing it, learning about the processes of DNA more successfully than with any other strategy she has used. In another, earlier assignment designed to inspire students about the field of crop science, Milla-Lewis has her students scour the Web for recent developments and discoveries related to topics covered in the class. Students do a three- to five-minute oral "news update" and turn in an informal report on their discovery. In one of dozens of intriguing examples, a student learned about a genetically modified weed (Thale Cress) that can be seeded from the air over areas with buried land mines. As it grows, the weed turns red when it is exposed to the traces of nitrogen dioxide emitted by the land mines, which can then be safely located and detonated. The student's discovery not only inspired her and her classmates about their chosen profession but also furthered their understanding of plant genetics. These goals were facilitated by the very medium that so worries teachers concerned about plagiarism. The low stakes of the assignment, its reportorial genre, and its inclusion of a brief class presentation make plagiarism a moot point; the focus is on what students must *do* in order to learn principles of genetics and become interested in their chosen profession.

The brief *King Lear* and plant genetics assignments are meant to be done quickly between class sessions. Because such low-stakes assignments individually contribute only a little to students' overall course performance, they reduce what scholars argue is one the motivations for students to turn in work that is not their own: fear of failure (Michaels and Miethe 1989; Calabrese and Cochran 1990; Schab 1991; Errey 2002). A focus on writing as "input" (what is practiced, experienced, and gained—that is, what the student *does*) instead of "output" (what is measured or tested as an index of accumulated knowledge or skill) encourages us to give more frequent, low-stakes assignments that help students to practice or engage in the intellectual processes tied to our learning goals. The results of such assignments can tell us much about where students are in reaching those goals. They are, then, just as valuable to our own continuing pedagogy as they are to students' continuing struggles to master the knowledge, skills, and strategies that are at the heart of our curricula. They also give us excellent opportunities to activate and energize our class sessions and to further reduce the desire to find an existing text that fits the requirements of the assignment. Among the limitless possibilities for low-stakes assignments across the curriculum are the following easily adapted or particularized examples:

- Vignettes, scenarios, and minicases
- Short papers based on "provided data" (students must use the data to make an argument or reach a conclusion)
- Imagined letters, dialogues, or other correspondences between authors, scholars, theorists, or characters, or with the student (contexts can be varied; in one linguistics assignment, students create a transcript of a talk show involving a host and two guests—Noam Chomsky and B. F. Skinner—debating the nature of language acquisition)
- Double-entry notebooks in which students draw a vertical line down a page and record passages, ideas, data, or other material on one side of the page, then analyze and reflect on this material on the other (see, for example, Berthoff 1978)
- Brief descriptions connecting material from a course to current news events in the media
- Explanations of concepts to varied audiences ("describe to a kid brother or sister why water stays in a pail when you swing it around your head")
- Interpretations of course material from the perspective of assigned "lenses" (environmental, political, gender-based, economic, cultural, physical, and the like)
- Electronic dialogue journals in which students alternate between solo entries and dialogic responses to or discussions of those entries (see Anson and Beach 1995)

Raising the Stakes and Supporting Development

If writing is used primarily to help students work with subject matter, practice various intellectual processes, or extend their learning, then it is possible and even desirable to use only low-stakes writing. Quickly assessed or responded to, this type of writing can be assigned regularly throughout a course without placing additional burdens on the teacher. Because such assignments are not teaching a specific academic form, they can involve hybrid genres, they can draw on class discussions and even specific comments by other students (which can increase attention, attendance, and participation), and they can be highly creative and original.

However, in many courses, especially within the major, teachers may want students to practice some of the discipline-based writing common in the field. This writing tends to be more formal, more audience focused, and more constrained by formats, structures, and styles. Such "canonical" texts can be found elsewhere because they are what professionals produce, and that opens possibilities for students to represent others' work as their own.

It is beyond the scope of this chapter to describe the many ways that courses across the curriculum can most effectively help students to improve their formal writing. Of relevance here, however, is the way that the component of *support* in Figure 1 reinforces Level 3 thinking about teaching by encouraging us to make longer and more formal assignments *teach* students through engagement in the processes required to complete them. Instead of simply expecting students to do what is required to write a paper—that long, lonely, confusing, and often last-minute struggle to meet the demands of an assignment that is never fully brought into a course—teachers who use assignments as teaching tools engage students in practicing the skills and processes tied to the assignment's learning goals. They *maximize* the learning potential in formal assignments.

Consider the following example. A teacher of landscape design assigns a high-stakes project (25 percent of the grade) that requires students to locate and study a landscaped or unlandscaped space, analyze its present design (if any), and propose a plan for (re)landscaping, based on the principles being studied in the course. Students write the final paper as if it were a *pro bono* assessment for the owner of the space. Left to their own devices, students would produce papers of varying quality, some missing or not fulfilling important expectations of analysis, structure, and so forth. The teacher would then take on the burden of telling the students where they went wrong, assuming an after-the-fact, trial-and-error approach that is pedagogically ineffective. Instead, the teacher supporting the development of this assignment provides the class with a three-dimensional virtual space that they examine at computer terminals, taking careful notes. They then work in groups to analyze the design of the space and present their analysis to the class, referring to principles from the course. This focus on what students *do,* even before they begin their own analysis, realizes Level 3 teaching by helping them to acquire the very learning goals embedded in the assignment. So prepared, they can then begin at a more advanced place as they choose and analyze their landscaped area. Further support includes breaking the project down into manageable parts that are shared and discussed in class, and conducting peer-response sessions in which students take their rough drafts through at least one substantive revision. These instructionally principled methods help to *interweave* writing assignments into "course coverage." Furthermore, the sequencing of the project into smaller assignments, together with the original nature of the task itself (focusing on something local), makes it both difficult and unnecessary for students to find an existing text to turn in as their own.

Creating unique formal assignments tied explicitly to learning goals, weaving those assignments into the fabric of the course content, supporting their development by attending to what students do as they work, and collecting the artifacts of students' in-process work—all these and other student-centered, constructivist activities draw students into the activity of learning, diminishing our obsession with plagiarism and our paranoia of its possibility.

Implications for Institutional Policy

Although Biggs' levels of thinking about teaching are best applied in the classroom, they can be extended to institutional ideologies of education. Instead of imagining the teacher and his or her construct of students as learners, we now imagine the institution as an administrative entity, crafting policies, managing its operations, and supporting the development of all its members. In this sense, it is instructive to consider the ways in which plagiarism is "framed" on college and university campuses (Adler-Kassner, Anson, and Howard 2008). How far have we collectively developed in our approaches to plagiarism?

From the institutional perspective, Level 1 thinking about plagiarism focuses on what members of its community *are;* it assumes that students either are or are not ethical or either do or do not conform to the rules of conduct, regardless of whether they bring to campus sufficient understandings of the nuances of source use, citation, and attribution to perform according to standards. (These assumptions also apply to other members of the community, including faculty, staff, research assistants, post-doctoral students, and graduate students.) Because almost all the onus of responsibility falls to the individual, the institution develops increasingly elaborate processes of accusing, convicting, and punishing those who are "inherently" malfeasant. Teachers who believe students have committed acts of plagiarism are encouraged to contact offices of student conduct that employ full-time personnel such as "directors of judicial affairs." With the help of staff members and, at some institutions, the provision of "executive orders," they set into motion a carefully orchestrated and scripted series of "hearings" usually involving "plagiarism juries" consisting of faculty, students, and administrators, with an appointed chair—the equivalent of a jury foreperson. Student conduct and disciplinary codes, often rendered in legalese and organized by alphanumeric sections (3.a.1, 3.a.2, and so on), define the nature and severity of the "crime." At some public universities, conduct codes are authorized and defined by state-level rules (such as California's Title 5 Code of Regulations, Section 41301, which lists infractions of the code of conduct for which students may be sanctioned; another section gives the chancellor of the California State University authority to create disciplinary processes and procedures for all the campuses in the system). The formal processes set in motion by an accusation require multiple forms for the request of hearings, appeals, and the like. If found guilty, students receive punishments that include probation, sanctions, suspension, or expulsion, and they can even be branded for their crime through permanent "scarlet letter" grades or footnotes on transcripts. This focus on what students *are* and how to rid our institutions of miscreants is reified in the language used to characterize plagiarism, as even a quick Web search for the coterminous words *plagiarism* and *crime* soon reveals.

Of course, many colleges and universities achieve Level 2 thinking about plagiarism by focusing on the institution-as-educator. Like its parallel in classroom teachers and their interest in the transmission of understanding, institutional thinking about plagiarism at Level 2 places the burden for reform on various instructional programs designed to educate the community about ethical uses of text. Here the metaphors shift away from the "crime," "sin," or, as one site puts it, the "highway robbery" of plagiarism to viewing plagiarism as an "epidemic," "disease," or "virus" in need of "immunization." As medic or caregiver, the institution feels obliged to offer workshops and seminars, learning modules, and elaborate Websites to cure the community and sanitize the campus. This burden often falls to the staff of the campus library, but composition programs, divisions of undergraduate studies, and instructional technology units may also be involved. From a Level 2 perspective, institutions that don't successfully eradicate the plague of plagiarism have not provided enough information, from enough directions, and are therefore derelict or deficient in their responsibilities. Yet, as at the classroom level, focusing resources in this way may also result in failure.

Biggs' scheme offers us a new way to think about what institutions can do to lessen the incidence of textual misappropriation and simultaneously reduce their preoccupation with plagiarism. A Level 3 institutional approach focuses not on institutionally provided information about plagiarism but on what faculty and instructional staff *do* in their courses, those educational spaces where students produce most of their work. Conferences on plagiarism are rife with examples of elaborate honor code systems, detection processes, self-directed Web modules for students, and the like. But almost never is the problem of plagiarism discussed in the context of campuswide programs of faculty development based on more insightful matching of educational goals, student support, and methods of assessing learning outcomes. It is assumed that teachers will continue to incorporate writing into their courses in such traditional and highly suspect ways as the "assign-and-collect" method (for example, when students receive a term paper assignment at the start of a course and must turn it in during the last week—opening the door wide to plagiarism, encouraging procrastination, and losing a valuable opportunity, through *support*, for the assignment to help the students accomplish the learning goals in the course).

Imagine an institutionwide goal: "All instructors will use writing in ways that support students' learning through creative, unique, student-centered approaches to assignment design, classroom processes, and authentic forms of

assessment." Such a goal would best be achieved by encouraging greater awareness of the relationship between what faculty do as teachers and what students
do as learners. Institutional policy, and financial support for it, would then shift
away from blaming the student, the teacher, or the institution and refocus on the
shared responsibilities of our institutions and its members (e.g., through further
education and development of faculty and a stronger focus on student learning).
Many current approaches, such as faculty learning communities, semester-long
seminars, workshops, individual consultations, and programs in the development of teaching portfolios, could be used profitably to help faculty find ways to
create assignments that engage students fully and are woven into instruction in
ways that maximize their instructional potential. What is a disabling paranoia
about plagiarism can thus be converted into a new, exciting reform of tired
educational practice.

Coda: Should We Ever Be Cops?

I have argued in this chapter that attention to the relationship between specific
learning goals and artfully designed, engaging, goal-directed assignments will
do much to lessen our apprehension about plagiarism and restore our role as
educators. But some will be uneasy with the proposition that teachers should
be only mentors and guides, eschewing the regulatory and disciplinary orientations that have historically characterized and stereotyped the professional educator. Don't we have an obligation to attend to the moral characters of our
students? Are we just conduits of knowledge, or should we educate students
more broadly—in all their intellectual, personal, and ethical complexity?

The answer to this question draws us into gray areas. Students become
who they are from countless experiences that include the admonitions and
encouragement of mentors, the multidirectional influences of peers, and the
(mis)behavior of role models in the public eye. A number of scholars claim
that higher education has an obligation to attend to students' moral and ethical
development as well as their base of knowledge and skills (see Kohlberg 1981;
Kibler et al. 1988; Colby et al. 2000), and many teachers are inspired to think
that they contribute to the education of the "whole person," not small areas of
information storage in students' brains.

But finally, plagiarism is not a clearly definable construct, and as such it
does not fall neatly into an ethical duality. Practices that constitute plagiarism in
one context are perfectly acceptable in another. One person's appropriation of
someone else's text is considered a violation of intellectual property (an author
who, without permission or attribution, publishes something that garners
income for another author) while another's represents the useful dissemination
of important information (the owner of a Web-based recipe archive who, with
no attribution, cuts-and-pastes into his site a document on safe food handling
from an FDA Website; see Adler-Kassner, Anson, and Howard 2008). Because

plagiarism "involves social relationships, attitudes, and values as much as it involves texts and rules of citation" (Valentine 2006, 90), it cannot be rendered as an ethical or moral "binary." Teaching students that complex, negotiated, and situated uses of text can be divided into "right and wrong" or "ethical and unethical" misrepresents the way that language works and equates discursive practice with moral behavior. The effect of an ethical discourse on plagiarism, writes Valentine, that "situates students within a binary of honest or dishonest creates several interrelated problems: the work of regulating plagiarism is also the work of regulating students' identity for professors and administrators, the categorical labels associated with plagiarism are inaccurate, the ability to nego-tiate plagiarism as a practice and performance is compromised, and some kinds of work are not acknowledged or considered valid" (90).

In classroom instruction, we are fundamentally entrusted to educate students in our subject areas, perhaps inspiring them to continue exploring domains of knowledge that define our own professional lives. If we can say that our students were fully engaged in our courses—that they participated, through writing and other activities, in the creation and mediation of knowl-edge there—we've done good service. More important, strategies that align learning goals with what students do, and that tap into our most creative, engaging, learner-centered ideas, are driven not by the goal of subverting pla-giarism but by *good teaching practices*; they are driven not by the procedures in a police manual but by principles, theories, research, and practice in higher education. Nothing in what we do in our courses will guarantee that students won't cheat, steal, or commit deliberate acts of malfeasance against others elsewhere and in the future. But those moral and ethical possibilities are beside the point. In the few short months that students spend with us, if we can focus on the quality of their learning and the extent to which they are engaged in the work of our courses, we will have fostered a community of involvement and shared responsibility that, by tacit example, shows the rewards of participatory integrity. And if those temporal rewards seep into the developing core of our students' ethic, so much the better.

Authors Note

Several lines in the introduction to this chapter appeared in my essay "Student Plagiarism: Are Teachers Part of the Solution or Part of the Problem?" *Essays on Teaching Excellence*, Vol. 15 (1). Nederland, CO: Professional & Organizational Development Network in Higher Education, 2003–2004.

References

Adler-Kassner, Linda, Chris M. Anson, and Rebecca Moore Howard. 2008. "Framing Plagiarism." In *Originality, Imitation, and Plagiarism: Teaching Writing in the*

Digital Age, edited by Martha Vicinus and Caroline Eisner. Ann Arbor: University of Michigan Press.

Anson, Chris M., and Richard Beach. 1995. *Journals in the Classroom: Writing to Learn.* Norwood, MA: Christopher-Gordon.

Berthoff, Ann E. 1978. *Forming/Thinking Writing: The Composing Imagination.* Rochelle Park, NJ: Hayden.

Biggs, John. 2003. *Teaching for Quality Learning at University* (2nd ed.). Philadelphia: Society for Research into Higher Education and Open University Press.

Bookrags.com. 2007. "King Lear Book Notes Summary." Retrieved on January 4, 2007, from www.bookrags.com/notes/kl/SUM.html.

Buranen, Lise, and Alice Myers Roy, eds. 1999. *Perspectives on Plagiarism and Intellectual Property in a Postmodern World.* Albany: State University of New York Press.

Calabrese, Raymond L., and John T. Cochran. 1990. "The Relationship of Alienation to Cheating Among a Sample of American Adolescents." *Journal of Research and Development in Education* 23: 65–72.

Colby, Anne, Thomas Ehrlich, Elizabeth Beaumont, Jennifer Rosner, and Jason Stephens. 2000. "Higher Education and the Development of Civic Responsibility." In *Civic Responsibility and Higher Education,* edited by Thomas Ehrlich. Phoenix, AZ: The American Council on Education and The Oryx Press.

Defining and Avoiding Plagiarism: The WPA Statement on Best Practices. 2002. West Lafayette, IN: Council of Writing Program Administrators. Retrieved on December 10, 2006, from www.wpacouncil.org/node/9.

Errey, Lynn. 2002. "Plagiarism: Something Fishy? . . . Or Just a Fish Out of Water?" *Teaching Forum* 50 (Autumn): 17–18. Retrieved on November 30, 2006, from www.brookes.ac.uk/virtual/NewTF/50/T50errey.pdf.

Howard, Rebecca Moore. 1999. *Standing in the Shadow of Giants: Plagiarists, Authors, Collaborators.* Stamford, CT: Ablex.

Howard, Rebecca Moore. 2007. "Understanding 'Internet Plagiarism.'" *Computers and Composition* 24: 3–15.

Kohlberg, Lawrence. 1981. *Essays on Moral Development—Volume I: The Philosophy of Moral Development.* San Francisco: Harper & Row.

Kibler, William L., Elizabeth Nuss, Brent G. Paterson, and Gary Pavela. 1988. *Academic Integrity and Student Development: Legal Issues and Policy Perspectives.* Asheville, NC: College Administration Publications.

Kimbel Library. 2006. "Cheating 101: Internet Term Papers." Conway, SC: Coastal Carolina University. Retrieved on December 12, 2006, from www.coastal.edu/library/presentations/mills2.html.

Michaels, James W., and Terance D. Miethe. 1989. "Applying Theories of Deviance to Academic Cheating." *Social Science Quarterly* 70: 870–885.

Ruggiero, Cheryl. (2004). "Plagiarism and Honor." Blacksburg: Virginia Polytechnic Institute and State University, Department of English, Integrated Learning Environments. Retrieved on January 7, 2004 from www.english.vt.edu/~IDLE/plagiarism1.html <http://www.english.vt.edu/~IDLE/plagiarism1.html>

Schab, Fred. 1991. "Schooling Without Learning: Thirty Years of Cheating in High School." *Adolescence* 26: 839–847.

Shaughnessy, Mina P. 1976. "Diving In: An Introduction to Basic Writing." *College Composition and Communication* 27: 234–239.

Smith, Frank. 1998. *The Book of Learning and Forgetting.* New York: Teachers College Press.

Valentine, Kathryn. 2006. "Plagiarism as Literacy Practice: Recognizing and Rethinking Ethical Binaries." *College Composition and Communication* 58 (1): 89–109.

Wells, Dorothy. 1993. "An Account of the Complex Causes of Unintentional Plagiarism in College Writing." *WPA: Writing Program Administration* 16 (3): 59–71.

10

Beyond Plagiarism

Kathleen Blake Yancey
Florida State University

Researching isn't an easy task, even when you choose the question, you bring methodological expertise to it, you have the luxury of time to pursue it, and you have an audience in the wings already interested in hearing about it. Too often, of course, this context doesn't remotely resemble the one in which students write. And then we're surprised when students don't "get it." Instead, they ask,

> What's the point? Is it to learn about the processes of researching, or is it to produce a text? And OK, tell me what it is that you want: how many pages, how many quotes, and where should I put them? What kind of citation format do you want, and why is it that my teacher in biology wants a completely different format?

Moreover—and ironically—with the electronic resources currently available (not to mention those in the wind), researching *is* more difficult. In terms of how we research, which has to do with how we know, we are in the midst of a paradigm shift that we can see in our own practices but whose general outcome is still obscured. On the one hand, we insist on documentation and citation such that students believe form is the key factor, an emphasis that fits all too well with other dimensions of our teaching of writing, as George Hillocks (2005) argues. Such an approach also frequently leads to error avoidance on the part of students: If only I can find an authority to agree with me, insert him or her into my own opinion, and cite it correctly! If only I can show that I'm not dishonest! On the other hand and at the same time, in what is now a postmodern "remix culture" where various materials are combined for one text and then divided up and recombined for another, and where copying without permission is an everyday occurrence—on your cassette player, your VHS, your DVD—plagiarism seems both oxymoronic and anachronistic. In such a culture, isn't the point to create a richly resourced multivocal text, and if all the voices are identified by citation, what's the point? And on a third hand, let's not forget public intellectuals and scholars like Pulitzer Prize–winning Doris Kearns Goodwin, whose plagiarism at the end of the day seems to get a pass. In such a world, it's not surprising that students would plagiarize—unintentionally, intentionally, and *both* intentionally and unintentionally; it's surprising that there *isn't* more of it.

Is there another way to approach the "problem" of plagiarism? In the language of medicine, plagiarism is a symptom, not a cause. Might it be more productive, more useful, and more accurate to begin not with manifestation, but with deeper issues—with the *idea* of research, with the practices and assumptions of research? That is the way I tend to start a very specific class, one focused on research-making per se, the graduate course in research methods in rhetoric and composition. And even here, on reflection, I think I don't begin with the idea of research, or even with the various ways it is made. Rather, I jump right in, beginning with methods historical and theoretical, then moving to qualitative empirical methods, and then moving again, to quantitative empirical methods. Sometimes treated separately, sometimes woven throughout are ethics of research and "new" methods of researching located in digital environments as well as the myriad ways that knowledge is vetted and distributed (including items like peer review and the hierarchy of publication venues) and the ways that distribution itself contributes to knowledge's being understood and commodified and valued.

But as full as it may be, this notion of research, which I take to be standard, leaves out a lot. It makes no mention of the social practices of research: how scholars routinely talk to one another, how writers seek out response to their work, in person and online. It makes no mention of material practices and how they might vary given the focus of a project or its scale, the fact that we need a fundamentally different organization for a large project than we might for a small one. It makes no mention of intellectual networks: the fact that scholars working on the same problems and questions, sometimes in the same discipline and sometimes in different fields, know each other's work and often collaborate, implicitly as well as explicitly. It makes no mention of common metaphors like "joining the conversation" or entering the Burkean parlor, which metaphors in their domestic reference suggest, at least implicitly, that research will be an informal if not intimate practice, regulated by a kind of familial civility if not affection, the implication that we are all engaged in the research together. As important, the parlor metaphor suggests a class distinction related to the intellectual capital of those with the "right" to converse, which capital and which right students (and less successful scholars) seek to acquire, although such a parlor does not necessarily admit all these aspirants. My course description of research, in sum, seems arhetorical when all research, perhaps especially research in both rhetoric and composition, is by definition rhetorical, always about the how and the what and the for whom and the why. And in sum, it ignores the *idea* of research.

I want to return to the notion of research as conversational practice because, in some ways, it is an accurate description, especially when understood as occurring in multiple sites—a metaphorical space, a large disciplinary space, a smaller subdisciplinary space, a material space, and increasingly—especially in the twenty-first century—an electronic space.[1] Materially and conceptually, as Becky Howard (1999) has suggested, the conversation is invented with bits of text from others that we borrow and cite, that we bring together with our words and, increasingly, our images into a new text, one that is collagelike in its intertextuality and that later may become part of someone else's research collage, too. If it's so that research can be characterized this way—as a collagelike, intertextual, ongoing conversation—it's worth asking what the practices are that impede our work and what the practices are that assist it. On one level, such practices include the ways that we construct research as an activity as well as how we identify ourselves as scholars. As important, on another level, such practices are the stuff of composition classrooms, where bits and "patches" (Howard 1999) of borrowed text alternate between being the material of intellectual work—that is, a practice we reward—and evidence of plagiarism—a practice we penalize and abhor.

Space may be a concept, then, that can help both undergraduate and graduate students understand the various research practices informing the field as well as the assumptions underlying them. To pursue this claim, I examine four models of research, thinking of them as case studies, considering how each one assumes a kind of research space as a way of framing the research and considering as well what knowledge making is supported and what discouraged. More specifically, these approaches include the following:

- A first and basic research practice, perhaps the most common, is what we might call "fill-in-the-blank" spatial approach. Articulated by John Swales (1990), the idea is to clear the research space of old work so that we have a place for the new.

- A second practice is to use a scholar as an icon, situating the work relative to his or hers as a means of claiming space. While early college writers tend to use icons exclusively as a way of authorizing their own views, scholars are more inclined to use them as a means of both support and critique. We might call this practice research-by-way-of-iconic-space.

- A third practice is to divide the "research space" among camps, in the case of composition, for example, between expressivists and rhetoricians. We might call this practice research as placement-within-dichotomous-space.

- A fourth practice, research within contextual space, requires the researcher to identify the possible contexts within which the research might appear and use that multiciplicity as a means of exigence and interpretation both.

It's worth noting, as will become obvious, that this chapter works within model one and model four simultaneously: that is, I'm attempting to move beyond model one, which (as we will see, and as Olivia Frey [1990] notes, tends to position scholars as antagonists or opponents), although I want to acknowledge earlier work, in part because to do so is appropriate but also in part to locate a space where I might make a contribution. In other words, working in model four offers a means for honoring what came before, by thinking with and through that earlier material to make our own contribution—in the knowledge that another generation of scholars will do likewise with that contribution. Such is the life of research.

And although using such an approach with students is unlikely to "solve" the "problem" of plagiarism, it will invite students to think differently about the research environments in which plagiarism-qua-symptom can occur.

When I began graduate school, I enrolled in the required research course intended to show me how knowledge in literature is created. There, I also was introduced to a now-canonical way of researching, the method John Swales (1990) later captured in his well-known CARS schema: *Create A Research Space*. Briefly, the model lays out a three-part structured space, providing the outline for research based on a kind of need. First the author "claims territory" by "claiming centrality," showing that the research area is important; second, the author makes a generalization setting up a quick review of previous research; third, the author demonstrates through the combination of the first claim and the quick literature review that additional work is needed. In Swales' (1990) term, a niche is thus created that the author can fill. The niche can involve one of the following research goals—sharing findings that contradict earlier research findings; identifying a gap in what we know that the author can fill; raising a question that has an impact on earlier research; or sharing findings that continue (and typically, expand or amplify) a tradition. In this view of writing research, then, the first principal move is to locate space that hasn't already been occupied: the researcher, much like a soccer player, is well advised to find and go to (open) space.

In some ways, this model of research making is enormously valuable. Researchers working in quantitative research methods typically work inside the "continuing the tradition" mode, for example, because the epistemological paradigm constructs knowledge as the function and outcome of ongoing, accretive activity. Understanding that this is the way that research is organized provides a place to begin for even the nascent scientist. And even qualitative research studies can find such an approach efficacious. In working with ESL graduate students in science, for instance, Jenny Bourne (2002) observed several difficulties with the drafts of their theses. Faculty responses to the drafts focused on syntactic dissonances, infelicitous lexical choices, and usage errors, but these problems didn't seem to account for the difficulties Bourne was observing, and over the course of the next year, she analyzed twenty-six thesis introductions to try to give a name to the problems she saw. Using John Swales' CARS approach, Bourne was able to show that the problems with the introductions were not syntactic or lexical but rather rhetorical. Their central problem, in her analysis, was an inability to clear space to create a niche they could fill. In this case, then,

Bourne showed that CARS provided a spatial way in for the graduate students, and she showed it by means of her own CARS approach.

Still, this method, like all methods, brings with it certain disadvantages. I can clearly remember writing my dissertation, which articulated a model of composing process, and hoping that Linda Flower and John Hayes (1981) and Sondra Perl (1980)—who were developing models of composing concurrent with and better known than mine—would not develop and publish a definitive model before mine was completed. Were they to do so, I wondered, what contribution would "my" model have to make? In this view of research activity, the space of research opportunity can seem very small. As important, as Olivia Frey (1990) has argued, in practice the CARS model has tended to invite an agonistic approach located in contradiction and refutation. Her plea, of course, is that we find another way to approach research, one that allows us to honor (rather than disavow) what has come before. I'm very sympathetic to her plea. At the same time I'm aware that sometimes there is a prior claim that you want to talk back, to if not correct, and that it can be difficult to do so without being specific, that is, without referring to a specific study or a specific researcher's approach or model. Being specific, in other words, seems fundamental to the CARS schema. More theoretically, I'm left with a set of questions about how one creates a niche and how that is part of the intertextuality that we think of as the material of research. Does intertextuality mean building on each other's work? Does intertextuality include refuting others' work? Given work that has come before, how can I *both* honor it and clear it away?

A second approach is to use iconic space as a site for research. In other words, the site occupied by an icon is usually sufficiently large that others may seek to occupy part of the space as well, linking their work to that of the icon's. Moreover, this space can be used both to forward the agenda of the icon and to speak against the icon's position.

In identifying iconic space, I'm indebted to Shane Borrowman, who in his coauthored article in *Writing with Peter* (White and Borrowman 1999) discusses how he wrote inside of Peter Elbow's iconic shadow when he authored the article "The Trinity of Portfolio Placement: Validity, Reliability, and Curricular Reform" (Borrowman 1999). Given that the article focused on portfolios and given Elbow's connection to them, this linkage makes sense. But what's remarkable is how Borrowman explains the use of the iconic space and his motive for it. He begins by noting that Elbow

> had become a locus for an approach to writing instruction and writing assessment, an icon of sorts, almost indispensable to our discussions of pedagogy. When we point and click on the "Elbow" icon, just what do we get? (49)

In Borrowman's case, he was using the Elbow icon as a figurehead, reducing him to a stick figure icon rather than a researcher with nuanced, complex, even changing views:

> I was using "Elbow" instead of engaging Elbow. Instead of addressing his theories about writing assessment in all of their rich complexity, I relegated them to the status of a weak partner in the binary of my argument. I made Elbow into a straw man.

What's interesting is Borrowman's retrospective admission of his use of Elbow, his laying out of that use for us to see. The article was published early in Borrowman's career, and we might expect that scholars early in their development would be more inclined than more experienced scholars to rely on an icon; we see this particularly, of course, in the situation of graduate students working with the intellectual materials of their mentors. But icons can trigger negative response as well, and a quick review of some of the more contentious issues in rhetoric and composition proves that more mature scholars use iconic space, too. In fact, an icon can exert considerable influence even after death.

One figure in composition studies with such iconic status is Maxine Hairston, whose detractors and supporters find in her a place to argue as much as to research, with the argument often taking a personal turn and sometimes an agitated tenor. We see some of each in a recent listserv exchange between Bill Thelin (2007) and Irv Peckham (2007). Invoking Hairston as icon, Thelin begins by outlining his concerns:

> Not only do I see severe hypocrisy in her words, a disguised political agenda, and a willingness to distort the facts to serve her purposes, she has [no] respect for her students. Further, she has an either-or rhetoric. Despite that Ira Shor is quoted elsewhere in the same issue, Hairston makes no mention of his Freirean-based problem-posing method, which, as she wishes, puts student interests at the forefront of the classroom. (np)

In Thelin's view, then, Hairston's approach is not apolitical but explicitly political, and she misunderstands (and worse, misrepresents) the work of another icon, Paulo Freire, as interpreted by Ira Shor. But as important to Thelin is a fundamental confusion surrounding the politics of teaching and of composition more generally:

> Too many people construct a false dichotomy because of the chasm she tried to create between understanding the politics of our teaching and teaching composition. She did such damage and I hate seeing her lionized. I hope I have exposed your hero or at least shown you that I am not creating a straw person.

Several points here are worth noting. First, both Borrowman (1999), who regrets his use of Elbow as iconic strawman, and Thelin (2007), who underscores the fact that he is not using Hairston as straw[wo]man, are both wary of the straw man fallacy that can accompany the icon approach. It is to be avoided. Second, the iconic approach, as in the case of Hairston, who is a "hero" requiring "exposure," lives on precisely because the icon crystallizes a disciplinary fault line that carries on long after the icon's mortal existence, and in Thelin's view, the effect of this has been to create a false dichotomy.

But it may be that over time, an icon is viewed less ideologically, and interestingly, as Irv Peckham (2007) explains, the icon also becomes a tool to be used by others more generally.

> I think Hairston has been used as a strawperson or a wedge issue by people who want to use the writing classroom to urge students toward sociopolitical positioning with which most of us would probably align ourselves. It's always useful to go back to her original statement that caused such an uproar. . . . The outcry (I remember a session with John Schilb in particular at the 4cs) repositioning Hairston as imagining that writing instruction could be class neutral has been one of the more enduring myths by activist teachers (let me use that phrase for want of a better one right now).

Again, the strawman is linked to iconic status, which in turn can be linked to a myth that takes on a life of its own, generating a continuing set of repudiations. The correction that Peckham (2007) offers makes for a more nuanced argument and for a reduction in iconic status, thus permitting much less space:

> She was quite clear that she was arguing about degrees of activism, not an on/off choice. Her dominant concern in that article was that reading and arguing about politics in the classroom would displace what we had learned about effective writing instruction, e.g., that we would shortchange process strategies so that we would have more time to engage students in the reading and arguments. She was of course contextualizing that concern within previous discussions about writing teachers (graduate students and lit people) using the first-year classroom as a place to have students read & write about literature. I think the history of the 90s and certainly if one looks at many of the theoretical articles in our major journals might suggest that her concern was not entirely unfounded. There is a certain irony in a pedagogy that began as a student-centered movement (from Dewey through Freire) evolved into one that regularly concerns itself with student resistance.

Peckham's approach, citing Hairston's "degrees of activism" as well as her concern about a displacement of attention to process and a return to precomposition days, characterizes the icon as a scholar more human than figure, one committed to maintaining hard-won research-based pedagogical applications.

The icon, like the figure in history, offers one way of interpreting the world—for good or for ill. It can be convenient and useful to link one's work to that of a respected figure, especially if a researcher is carrying forward earlier research. At the same time, it's a good question as to what we gain, but more particularly what we lose, by focusing on an icon rather than on space that may be more difficult to make our own.

A third use of space for research identifies space and then divides it between camps, seeing one camp as laudatory and a second and perhaps even a third in opposition. This space, then, is a combination of both model one and model two. Like model one, it uses the opposing camp as means of identifying available space, and like model two, it has an icon, only it's collective rather than single figure. In Kenneth Burke's terms, this approach relies on an opposition-camp-as-scapegoat to create a good cop/bad cop of research at the same time that it fosters a kind of unity with the reader.

In the early days of rhetoric and composition, the most common opposi-tional camp was "current-traditional" rhetoric, which was soon superseded by process pedagogy and then postprocess pedagogy. In each case, the camp relies on another camp to define it and highlight its claims, as Paul Matsuda (2003) explains:

> The so-called process movement arose in the 1970s, contributing significantly to the development of composition studies as a respectable profession. In recent years, the process movement has come under critical scrutiny as the term post-process has gained currency, representing intellectual currents that began to emerge in the late 1980s and the early 1990s. Although neither process nor post-process is monolithic, the dichotomy between "process" and "post-process" seems to have led to an oversimplification of diverse and sometimes conflicting theoretical perspectives and pedagogical practices. (np)

Interestingly, this analysis of the "oversimplification" caused by the dichotomiz-ing parallels Peckham's (2007) observations about characterizations of Hairston. As interesting, Matsuda notes that both process and postprocess rely on an over-simplification of the current-traditional that came before—"By examining the construction of current-traditional rhetoric by process theorists and of process by post-process theorists, this paper explains how intellectual movements often cre-ate [an] Other in order to gain legitimacy" (np). The "Other," then, sets up the dichotomous space, and the default for rhetoric and composition is current-traditional. Moreover, current-traditional is now sufficiently villainized that no case against it need be made. Carl Whithaus (2001), for example, borrows from Huot (1996) in adapting and extending it to set up his argument for new methods in writing assessment—"The discontent among composition specialists with current-traditional methods of writing assessment, and a more general discontent with standardized educational testing, has begun to be felt" (np)—and more recently, Richard Fulkerson (2005) acknowledged that current-traditionalists "you'll always have with us," again as backdrop only. Dividing a field of interest into camps, then, is not uncommon; some of the camps become stereotyped and assume a kind of truism for a field. One might go even further and suggest that a field gains definition to the extent that it has such camps.

During the last twenty years, however, another means of dichotomizing space has been developed, one that is principally ideological. In part, the ideo-logical plays such an influential role in rhetoric and composition because the stakes are so high: Fundamentally, what we research and what we claim affects real human beings, our students, which students have always held the heart of the field. At the same time, I'm not the first to observe that more recently the political seems to be playing a larger role in the field, though it's fair to say that this emphasis has been in play for at least fifteen years. For an example of this, we can turn the clock back to the 1991 publication of the award-winning edited collection *Contending with Words* (Harkin and Schilb, 1991). In this volume, as Sosnoski (1991) notes, "Harkin criticizes the Linda Flower and John Hayes model; Jarratt, the expressivist model; Vitanza, the idea of a textbook" (212), while "Ann E. Berthoff, Louise Weatherbee Phelps, and David Bartholomae are singled out for commentary in these pages because their work is regarded as insufficiently responsive to cultural contexts" (Sosnoski 1991, 193). Bartholomae in particular functions as a repeated icon: "Bartholomae sins because his vision of community, however well intentioned, just doesn't jibe with our experience as teachers" (194). The complaints are personal; icons abound. But ultimately, the icons go collective: "The villain in this volume seems to be the 'expressive pedagogy' of Peter Elbow, Donald Murray, and others" (208). And the largest camp is connected not to research per se, but to the ends of both teaching and research: "It remains to be seen whether or not freshman composition [sic] can be radicalized in the service of social justice. Some of us seem willing to try" (194). The ends here aren't research ends, but pedagogical ends defined by a Platonic ideal more worthy than knowledge: goodness. Such a division of space into camps that aren't parallel—with one concerned with writing issues but with a default interest in social justice, and with the other concerned with social justice but with a default interest in writing—tends to reduce productive research, in large part because of the absence of common terms and of the assumptions that always define a research agenda.

In some ways, the three earlier models of research rely on a closed system of space. It has to be cleared; it's already inhabited by icons and camps in such a way as to consume the space of opportunity. It's not, then, the capacious, ever-expanding space of Bakhtin, but rather space exhausted. By way of contrast, research as an exercise of multicontextual space assumes an interlayering, an overlayering whose remix, whose intertextuality is the incubator for ideas, for knowledge.

The implications for such an approach are many. Seen pragmatically, it's quite simple: The researcher discovers or invents a claim, researches that claim, sees what others have said, and writes inclusively. Of course, if the others have articulated the full line of research, there won't be very much to add, it's true, unless the researcher can find another angle, can approach it from another context, can interpret through another lens. Or: Multicontextual is located in and values the *another*.

In still another way, this spatial approach, given its commitment to multiplicity and thus to the impossibility of knowing everything, makes the most sense given that it's impossible to trace down all the influences and texts we compose in and with. Although not an academic writer, Bob Woodward (2006), in his latest volume, *State of Denial,* includes a prefatory note that researchers might consider adopting:

> I am certain that I have used material that sources told me about or informa-
> tion reflected in records that has appeared earlier in some form in another
> publication or news account or book. I have not done the archeology to see
> who should be given credit for first reporting on various episodes or issues,
> but the endnotes give specific citations for material that was used. (424–25)

I recommend this not to encourage sloppy citation practices or deliberate over-
sights. I'm thinking here more of the Amish, who include in each quilt a mistake to remind them of the essential humanity of the enterprise, no matter how
beautiful the quilt. By analogy, in observing the impossibility of crediting
everyone due, we tip our hats to those we unintentionally slighted, while
reminding *ourselves* of the rhetorical stance research demands.

Understanding research as the exercise of multicontextual space also suggests that researchers look beyond divisions toward a common end or outcome. Joe Harris (2004), whose interest in revision has been seen as at odds
with social justice, articulates a rhetorical stance located in seeking alternative
explanations for real differences:

> Our approaches to teaching don't conflict so much as branch away from
> each other. We need to find ways of talking about such divergences that
> don't lock us into fixed antagonisms—and especially that resist valorizing
> some teachers for "empowering" students while others as serving the
> "dominant ideology." (557)

In this case, then, Harris invokes "branching" as a metaphor, putting contrast-
ing ideas not in conflict with each other but in connection, thus allowing each
argument its own space and its space of connection.

These strategies are likely to become ever more necessary given the
advent of the Internet, of blogging, of the remixing of images, words, and texts
that is becoming common practice. As Kevin Kelly (2006) explains, "The
Search Changes Everything," including what and how we know:

> Copies of isolated books, bound between inert covers, soon won't mean
> much. Copies of their texts, however, will gain in meaning as they mulitiply
> by the millions and are flung around the world, indexed and copied again.
> What counts are the ways in which these common copies of a creative work
> can be linked, manipulated, annotated, tagged, highlighted, bookmarked,
> translated, enlivened by other media and sown together into the universal
> library. (71)

As Utopian as this forecast may sound, the intertextuality that Kelly speaks of is
already upon us; it is the intertextuality of the Burkean parlor electrified. Given
that intertextuality, created and rearranged and created again by means of *index*
and *links* and *tags,* the space of a closed system will be claustrophobic; the power
of an icon will shrink; camps will proliferate; and the persuasive rhetoric will be
of the open hand. In such a "net/worked" spatial model, *knowledge is ongoing,*

one bit connected to other bits in a process that is never finally completed, even in a prepostmodern world and certainly in the world of the twenty-first century.

These four models of text-based scholarship raise questions—about the need for excellence in reviewing; about the ethics of scholarship; about the relationship of form and content; about the materiality and thus the integrity of the central concept of intertextuality; and about how we create the ongoing conversation that in turn creates us. Collectively engaging these questions might even lead to pragmatic guidelines for text-based scholarly work. Toward that end, I'd like to close with some pragmatic suggestions and questions:

- What role does reviewing play in constructing space? Reviews are definitional in the academy; we count on them for publications and for job appointments, for tenure and promotion and for award nominations. In the case of making knowledge, however, reviews are uniquely critical, not only because they vet ideas, methods, and conclusions, but also because they establish the relationship of material and methods to the value of any given project to the field at large. Accordingly, I offer these three recommendations: generally (1) reviewers should encourage a capacious view of research space from authors; and specifically (2) reviewers should encourage less authorial reliance on icons; and (3) reviewers should encourage researchers to deconstruct camps, to write beyond the camps.

- Scholarship itself has an implied ethics, but perhaps implied isn't enough; it needs to be the ethics of an open but a *shared* space. Implied to me is that we do give credit—always. That seems obvious, and yet, what does "give credit" mean in terms of specifics? In theory, like the *Oxford English Dictionary,* we could trace everything back to Plato, but in most cases, that's not the point, nor is it helpful. Is being helpful the basic principle we seek to honor? Is it also to represent and give credit fairly—even generously? Philosophers, I'm told, operate on a principle of charity: they are obliged to represent as generously as possible the position of an other. It reminds me of Rogerian argument, popular at one time in composition studies: The author writes the argument of the opposition as a member of the opposition, the hope being not so much that the writer will argue better, but that he or she will understand. What effect on argument and tenor might this exert?

- And I can't close without suggesting that the reviewers are only one player in a large research space; another very important player is the graduate faculty member who teaches methods classes. What role can she or he play? Might the discipline organize parallel or common efforts focused on best practices in such a course? Might researchers representing a wide variety of methodologies—Deborah Brandt (2001) and Ellen Barton (2000), for example—reflect on how they teach such courses? Might practiced teachers point to successful readings or assignments? In short, how might we create a space fostering a more capacious research space?

How we conduct research, it has been argued, is important because it constructs the discipline. That's true. But how we construct the space in which the research is conducted constructs each of us and shapes who we will be to each other and thus, ultimately, who we will be toward our students. Creating a capacious space, one for the free flow and creation of intertextuality, benefits us all.

Note

1. Although it's not the purpose of this chapter, a major change in research methodology that will change what and how we know is the power of Web-interfaced databases to help us call up articles and other research reports in many and diverse ways.

References

Barton, Ellen. 2000. "More Methodological Matters: Against Negative Argumentation." *College Composition and Communication* 51 (3): 399–416.

Bourne, Jenny Goforth. 2002. *A CARS Analysis of Thesis Introductions in Entymology.* Unpublished MA thesis, Clemson University.

Borrowman, Shane. 1999. "The Trinity of Portfolio Placement: Validity, Reliability, and Curriculum Reform." *WPA: Writing Program Administration* 23 (1/2): 7–28.

Brandt, Deborah. 2001. *Literacy in American Lives.* Cambridge, U.K.: Cambridge University Press.

Flower, Linda, and John Hayes. 1981. "A Cognitive Process Theory of Writing." *College Composition and Communication* 32 (3): 365–87.

Frey, Olivia. 1990. "Beyond Literary Darwinism: Women's Voices and Critical Discourse." *College English* 52: 507–26.

Fulkerson, Richard. 2005. "Composition at the Turn of the Twenty-First Century." *College Composition and Communication* 56 (4): 654–87.

Harkin, Patricia, and John Schilb, eds. 1991. *Contending with Words: Composition and Rhetoric in a Postmodern Age.* New York: Modern Language Association.

Harris, Joseph. 2004. "Joseph Harris Responds." *College English* 66 (5): 556–58.

Hillocks, George. 2005. "At Last: The Focus on Form vs. Content in Teaching Writing." *Research in the Teaching of English* 40 (2): 238–48.

Howard, Rebecca. 1999. *Standing in the Shadow of Giants: Plagiarists, Authors, Collaborators.* Norwood, NJ: Ablex Publishing.

Huot, Brian. 1996. "Toward a New Theory of Writing Assessment." *College Composition and Communication* 47(4): 549–566.

Kelly, Kevin. 2006. "Scan This Book." *New York Times Magazine* (May 14). www.kk.org/writings/scan_this_book.php.

Matsuda, P. K. 2003. "Process and Post-Process: A Discursive History." *Journal of Second Language Writing* 12 (1): 65–83.

Peckham, Irving. 2007. October 7. "Teaching Composition: Rhetorical Analysis of Scientific Research Report." http://mailman.eppg.com/pipermail/teaching_composition/2006-October/002623.html.

Perl, Sondra. 1980. "Understanding Composing." *College Composition and Communication* 31: 363–69.

Sosnoski, James. 1991. "Postmodern Teachers in Their Postmodern Classrooms: Socrates Begone!" In *Contending with Words: Composition and Rhetoric in a Postmodern Age,* edited by Patricia Harkin and John Schilb. New York: Modern Language-Association.

Swales, John. 1990. *Genre Analysis: English in Academic and Research Settings.* Cambridge, U.K. Cambridge University Press.

Thelin, Bill. 2007, October 7. "Teaching Composition: Irv, Hairston, and Citation." http://mailman.eppg.com/pipermail/teaching_composition/2006-October/ 002626. html

White, Edward, and Shane Borrowman. 2001. "Elbow as Icon." In *Writing with Elbow*, edited by Pat Belanoff, Marcia Dixon, Sheryl Fontaine, and Charles Moran. Logan: Utah State University Press.

Whithaus, Carl. 2001. "Evaluating Student-Created Hypertexts: What Do We Do With These Things?" *Kairos* 6 (2). http://english.ttu.edu/kairos/6.2/coverweb/hypertext/whithaus/Whithaus-Evaluating.pdf

Woodward, Robert. 2006. *State of Denial.* New York: Simon & Schuster.

Afterword

Plagiarism, Difference, and Power

Bruce Horner
University of Louisville

> I quote Marx without saying so. . . . When a physicist writes a work
> of physics, does he feel it necessary to quote Newton and Einstein?
> —Michel Foucault, *Power/Knowledge*

This collection argues that plagiarism must be "pluralized" in how it is
defined and how it is addressed pedagogically and publicly. Among the collection's many observations and insights about plagiarism that lead to this
argument are the following: (1) what constitutes plagiarism varies across disciplines and cultures; (2) definitions of plagiarism (and its obverse of "appropriate" citation practice) are not only various but ideological; and (3) at least
some forms of plagiarism (e.g., "patchwriting") may represent writers'
progress in developing mastery of a particular kind of academic writing. Thus,
monolithic understandings of and approaches to plagiarism will not do. And
not only that—various contributors argue that there is a politics to how plagiarism is defined and to the levying of charges of plagiarism, shaping what
does and doesn't get identified as plagiarism and with what consequences.

In making these arguments, this collection participates in a larger movement in composition, applied linguistics, and literacy studies that has challenged monolithic understandings of and approaches to languages, writing
standards, and literacy and has brought forward the politics of such understandings. In fact, versions of each of the claims regarding plagiarism listed
above have also been made about languages, writing standards, and literacy
(see, for example, Street 1984, Lees 1989, Kachru 1990, Widdowson 1994,
Gal and Irvine 1995, Lea and Street 1998). Such participation is not surprising
given the entanglement of matters of plagiarism with matters of error, literacy,
and standards. Plagiarism can be understood as a species of error, or as a
deviant form of literacy, or a construct within a particular notion of literacy;
and at least some forms of plagiarism can be accounted for in terms of
"error"—that is, confusion about or failure to comply with certain conventions
commonly accepted within particular social contexts for notating textual
borrowings.

171

But just as challenges to monolithic undestandings of error and literacy do not always lead to addressing the politics of these, so challenges to monolithic views of plagiarism do not automatically lead to addressing the politics of its identification. As the history of colonialism demonstrates, recognition of differences does not in itself lead inexorably to addressing those differences in terms of power relations. I use this afterword to caution against several moves by which the political character of plagiarism may be elided despite recognition of its plural character, drawing on parallel moves by which the politics of error and language difference generally have been elided in composition and literacy scholarship.

I'll begin by reducing the observations about the "plural" character of plagiarism cited above and equivalent observations about "error" to the issue of difference: Plagiarism, like "error," is defined differently by different groups, takes different forms, carries different significance for different readers. Two responses to such differences—what I term the developmentalist and the archipelago responses to error and plagiarism—elide the politics of differences by isolating them in time or space as either temporary or separate. The developmentalist response to differences treats them as signaling stages in writers' development, the assumption being that as writers develop further, they will abandon the practices identified as different. Teacher/scholars involved in error studies, for example, have argued that patterns of error in students' writing constitute an "interlanguage" representing the writers' attempts to approximate conventional writing, following idiosyncratic interpretations of the rules for such writing (see Kroll and Schafer 1978: Bartholomae 1980). Pedagogies based on this view of error assume that students will gradually master correct writing by more closely approximating the rules for its production. The equivalent pedagogy addressing plagiarism would involve working with students to identify and adjust their idiosyncratic rules for referencing other texts—for example, their engagement in "patchwriting"—to enable them to master conventional practices for doing so.

Without questioning the utility of such views and pedagogies based on them, I think it's worth noting that such an approach leaves unchallenged the notion of a fixed set of conventions constituting academic writing that students are expected ultimately to accept as well as "master" as they "develop." Defining difference in terms of a developmental stage elides its possible political significance—for example, the possibility that writers are identifying with and engaged in notational practices some view as "plagiarism" or in "error" to produce meanings and effects not associated with conventionally "correct" writing.

What I term the "archipelago response" understands differences between accepted and unaccepted writing practices to represent differences in literacies and languages, a.k.a. discourses. In this view, practices that might be understood to constitute plagiarism in one kind of discourse, for example, are understood to represent playfulness, say, or a form of honoring another, in other discourses.

Those adopting this approach call on teachers both to recognize and respect different cultural practices in textual borrowing in addressing plagiarism. This approach parallels arguments that "errors" in students' writing represent the expression of students' home or other literacies (e.g., text-messaging), or clashes between these and privileged (e.g., academic) forms of literacy (Gee 1989). Pedagogies based on this understanding tend to emphasize both the need to respect the various forms of literacy students bring with them and the need to provide direct instruction in the conventions ostensibly constituting the privileged versions (see, for example, Delpit 1988).

But while this approach honors students' particular practices as something other than a set of mistakes to be corrected or violations to be punished, it treats particular literacy practices as operating in spaces isolated from, rather than in contact with and informing and changing, one another, and it leaves largely unchallenged the hierarchical relations between the various literacies. What emerges instead is an image of an archipelago of isolated, different practices. Pedagogies adopting this approach aim simply for substituting, rather than eliminating, nonprivileged practices with those privileged—a strategy that reinforces, by understating, the role of power relations in determining what may or may not constitute practices "appropriate" to a given situation and according to what and whose interests a particular practice is deemed "appropriate" (cf. Fairclough 1992). The possibility of promoting interaction among different practices in ways that change them all is not considered, nor is the possibility of challenging the privileging of some over others. More troubling, writers' agency in engaging any one practice is slighted in the image of writers caught up in the particular practices of their "home" or "culture." The historicity of particular practices—their vulnerability to challenge and change and blurring—and thus the politics of engaging in particular ways are thereby at risk of being effaced.

The developmentalist and archipelago approaches to understanding plagiarism also elide two other senses in which plagiarism can be understood as political. First, both leave unquestioned the existence of a plagiarism crisis. This begs the question of what else might prompt claims of such a crisis. Second, and relatedly, both collude in eliding readers' labor in producing recognition of plagiarism by accepting its "textualization." Plagiarism, like error, is located in the text and on the page rather than being understood as a perception resulting as much from specific reading practices as from writing. Of course, the current climate of hostility, paranoia, and self-righteous moral outrage surrounding any suggestion of plagiarism makes eliding the politics of plagiarism tempting as a means of toning down the clamor. But here the history of public debates on literacy and "error" (as one ostensible manifestation of "illiteracy") is instructive. Literacy scholars have shown that official claims about a literacy "crisis" usually signal not a decline in the literacy required for adult survival in a particular society but rather a perceived threat to the dominance of a particular group. Claims during the late nineteenth century and again in the 1960s that the United States faced a literacy crisis and the likely demise of higher education, for example, coincided with pressures from populations previously excluded from higher education for access to it (Trimbur 1991: Horner and Lu 1999).

For example, students enrolling in the City University of New York in the late 1960s under its highly publicized open admissions program were attacked as "illiterates" and "barbarians" who threatened universities' "academic integrity." For the most part, those defending the rights of open admissions students against the public smearing to which they were being subjected elided the politics of these charges, strategically arguing instead that differences in the students' writing, a.k.a. their errors, represented either (1) evidence of their efforts and development as writers, or (2) evidence of a different culture whose ways merited respect as appropriate to spheres outside the academy, and in any event (3) no threat at all to existing academic values and practices. The students aimed simply to acquire, not subvert or change, them. The subsequent, rapid, and full retrenchment of CUNY's open admissions program does not encourage hope in the effectivity of such a strategy.

The public uproar about a plagiarism crisis, and responses to such uproar, do not exactly parallel debates about literacy crises, but they can be understood as arising from comparable tensions and taking comparable directions. First, insofar as differences in referencing practices are associated with low-status immigrant groups, claims of a plagiarism crisis displace anxieties about those groups onto anxieties about language, in alignment with the displaced anxieties of English Only advocates. Second, the emergence of claims that the United States and the world are facing a plagiarism crisis speaks to the tensions over intellectual property produced by the increasing dominance of what is called an "information" or "knowledge" economy. Those invested in such an economy must incessantly finesse the problematics inherent to the commodification of knowledge to capitalize (literally) from such commodification. Put simply, the more frequently people are confronted with the contradictions inherent in treating knowledge, a social achievement, as private property, the more strident ideological assertions occluding those contradictions must be. Put less simply, there are contradictory interests involved in the operation of such economies. On the one hand, knowledge is and must be shared—for example, distributed among workers in a corporation—for it to be used. Indeed, even the notion of "sharing" or "distribution" fails to capture the ways in which what is known is dependent for its existence on being continually reworked by its knowers in the process of learning, teaching, and using it. On the other hand, for capitalization to occur, the concrete labor of knowing must be occluded through the commodification of knowledge: Knowledge must be treated as a thing to be owned rather than in need of continual reworking.

One means of doing so is to reify knowledge in texts—to "textualize" knowledge by claiming that it inheres in a specific form and sequence of notations. This textualization occludes the full social materiality of textual production—the physical and social conditions of time, training, equipment, support, and so on that contribute to textual production—beyond the labor of the individual "author." Standard definitions of plagiarism are based on just such a textualization of knowledge. Those definitions treat knowledge as inhering in the textual forms. More specifically, they occlude the labor of *readers* as they engage in particular literacy (reading) practices yielding (or not) recognition of those formulations themselves, which are, after all, abstractions from material artifacts rather than objective manifestations, forms being the product of perception rather than attributes inherent to markings.

Conversely, any acknowledgment of such labor leads to recognition of plagiarism, like error, as a peculiar, and highly politicized, kind of social achievement: the product of the labor of not only writers but readers, who engage for particular purposes in particular reading practices that lead to the perception of a particular set of notations as instances of plagiarism. Joseph Williams' (1981) study of the "phenomenology" of error is instructive here. Williams points to both the necessity of readers' labor and the politics of that labor in the recognition of error by observing that "if we [teachers] could read . . . [error-ridden] student essays unreflexively, if we could make the ordinary kind of *contract* with those texts that we make with other kinds of texts, then we could find many fewer errors" (159, emphasis added). We may say similarly that the instances of plagiarism some readers now find in student (and other) texts are the product of the kind of contract they make with those texts. Hence the new "crisis" in plagiarism is symptomatic of the kinds of contracts at least some readers have decided to make with some writings, in pursuit of particular interests.

Contracts, of course, involve at least two parties. Particular practices by writers call on readers to adopt particular contracts with the writing. In the epigraph to this afterword, for example, Foucault engages in a negotiation with the interviewer (and those the interviewer represents) with what is required, at least of Foucault himself, in the way of acknowledging his intellectual predecessors. And he is negotiating competing ideological positions on the necessity, and even utility, of such "explicit" acknowledgments—citing, tellingly, the practices of physicists in support of his own.

Writers and readers continually engage in just such negotiations with one another over the acceptability and specific uses and values of particular conventions for referencing others. The fact that students' referencing practices differ from what particular readers may expect or demand can be understood not simply as evidence of their attempts to approximate such demands, or the interference of past training or overfamiliarity with new technologies of textual production, or their confusion about why and how to reference in particular ways, or even their yielding to a tempting solution to their lack of time and energy, but as engagements in just such negotiations with readers over what different people find necessary, useful, or acceptable in who, what, and how much to cite, as well as why and how to do so. Recognizing their participation in such negotiation is what it can mean to take students' writing seriously.

I am arguing that plagiarism is "political" in at least three intersecting ways. First, the recognition of a particular writing as plagiarism (and the recognition of a particular text as not plagiarism) is not a matter of disinterested, objective examination of texts but the result of concrete reading practices exercised as part of a contract a reader decides to make with a text, usually as a result of, and to maintain, particular relations of power obtaining between the reader and the writer. As several contributors note, readers commonly accept as legitimate in the writing of their peers and superiors practices they condemn as plagiarism in the writing of those they view as their subordinates. Second, plagiarism can become a weapon in the battles of conventional politics, in the sense of partisan conflict, as evidenced in debates on the writings of public figures like Ward Churchill, discussed in this volume. Third, claims about a plagiarism "crisis" instance a move in the politics of knowledge commodification, a practice, as suggested in Michele Eodice's chapter, in which academics have a contradictory relationship as, on the one hand, educators responsible for the social production of knowledge and, on the other hand, as claimants to ownership of intellectual property (in the form of c.v. lines, if not patents).

Efforts like this collection to "pluralize" plagiarism forward the important work of contesting such politics at all levels by demonstrating the ideological character of both concepts and charges of plagiarism. If what constitutes plagiarism varies across history and between as well as within cultures, and even within the experience of individual readers, then binary approaches to plagiarism, like binary approaches to "error" in writing, are not just inaccurate but misleading. There is a politics to this misrepresentation of plagiarism that is worth exploring, as Amy Robillard has her students explore in the course she describes in her chapter. There is also an inherent politics to reference practices in writing involving identity and purpose that students and teachers can not only acknowledge but address explicitly in their writing courses. Having acknowledged the plurality of different referencing practices, we need not only to teach students the different practices of particular disciplinary communities but to challenge these practices, as T. Kenny Fountain and Lauren Fitzgerald ultimately suggest, or to help students do what Celia Thompson and Alastair Pennycook claim that at least some students often already do: "see through such practices and learn how to get by in spite of homogenizing dictates on writing practices" (135).

The political, as well as plural, character of plagiarism does not mean that charges of plagiarism are never warranted or that plagiarism somehow doesn't exist, any more than the lack of biological basis for racialism means that racism has no reality (see Appiah 1990, 277). That notions of plagiarism are "socially constructed" simply means that their sociality must be addressed as social—that is, as historical—subject to contestation and change. For particular notions of plagiarism are not simply social constructs; they (re)construct the social; hence the political potential of the work of teaching and scholarship on plagiarism like that described and represented in this collection. If plagiarism is always already also political as well as plural, the question teachers and students face is not whether to politicize what should be taken as, instead, a private ethical issue of ownership and abstract labor, but what politics operate in how plagiarism is understood and addressed in teaching, learning, reading, and writing. That work begins with acknowledging the plural character of plagiarism.

References

Appiah, Kwame. 1990. "Race." In *Critical Terms for Literary Study*, 2nd ed., edited by Frank Lentricchia and Thomas McLaughlin, 274–87. Chicago: University of Chicago Press.

Bartholomae, David. 1980. "The Study of Error." *College Composition and Communication* 31: 253–69.

Delpit, Lisa. 1988. "The Silenced Dialogue: Power and Pedagogy in Educating Other People's Children." *Harvard Educational Review* 58: 280–98.

Fairclough, Norman. 1992. "The Appropriacy of Appropriateness." In *Critical Language Awareness*, edited by Norman Fairclough, 31–56. London: Longman.

Foucault, Michel. 1980. *Power/Knowledge: Selected Interviews and Other Writings, 1972–1977*, edited and translated by Colin Gordon. New York: Pantheon.

Gal, Susan, and Judith T. Irvine. 1995. "The Boundaries of Languages and Disciplines: How Ideologies Construct Difference." *Social Research* 62: 967–1001.

Gee, James Paul. 1989. "Literacy, Discourse, and Linguistics: Introduction" and "What Is Literacy?" *Journal of Education* 171 (1): 5–25.

Horner, Bruce, and Min-Zhan Lu. 1999. *Representing the "Other": Basic Writers and the Teaching of Basic Writing*. Urbana, IL: National Council of Teachers of English.

Kachru, Braj. 1990. *The Alchemy of English: The Spread, Functions, and Models of Non-Native Englishes*. Urbana: University of Illinois Press.

Kroll, Barry M., and John C. Schafer. 1978. "Error Analysis and the Teaching of Composition." *College Composition and Communication* 29: 242–48.

Lea, Mary, and Brian Street. 1998. "Student Writing in Higher Education: An Academic Literacies Approach." *Studies in Higher Education* 23: 157–72.

Lees, Elaine O. 1989. "'The Exceptable Way of the Society': Stanley Fish's Theory of Reading and the Task of the Teacher of Editing." In *Reclaiming Pedagogy: The Rhetoric of the Classroom*, edited by Patricia Donahue and Ellen Quandahl, 144–63. Carbondale: Southern Illinois University Press.

Street, Brian. 1984. *Literacy in Theory and Practice*. Cambridge, U.K.: Cambridge University Press.

Trimbur, John. 1991. "Literacy and the Discourse of Crisis." In *The Politics of Writing Instruction, Postsecondary*, edited by Richard Bullock and John Trimbur, 277–95. Portsmouth, NH: Heinemann Boynton/Cook.

Widdowson, H. G. 1994. "The Ownership of English." *TESOL Quarterly* 28: 377–89.

Williams, Joseph. 1981. "The Phenomenology of Error." *College Composition and Communication* 32: 152–68.

Contributors

Chris M. Anson is University Distinguished Professor of English and Director of the Campus Writing and Speaking Program at North Carolina State University, where he helps faculty in nine colleges to use writing and speaking in the service of students' learning and improved communication. A scholar of writing, language, and literacy, he has written or edited fourteen books and has published over 80 articles and book chapters. He has spoken widely across the United States and in eighteen foreign countries.

Tracy Hamler Carrick teaches writing wherever writers gather: in classrooms, writing centers, community centers, coffee houses, park benches. She is Assistant Professor of English and Director of the Farnham Writers Center at Colby College. She writes with and about writers to explore the dynamic ways that people compose together both to deepen individual writing skills and to imagine social and institutional change. Her work has been published in professional journals like *Community Literacy Journal* and *Language and Learning Across the Disciplines* as well as in several edited collections.

Kami Day is associate professor of English at Johnson County Community College. Her research interests center on collaboration, and her scholarship includes work on collaborative writing, learning communities, and plagiarism. She, with her coauthor Michele Eodice, published *(First Person)²: A Study of Co-Authoring in the Academy* in 2001, and she has published several journal articles and two chapters for edited collections.

Michele Eodice is the director of the writing center at the University of Oklahoma, where she also leads a campuswide writing initiative for writing in the disciplines. Michele currently serves as president of the International Writing Centers Association and the associate editor of *Writing Center Journal*. She coauthored *(First Person)²: A Study of Co-Authoring in the Academy* with Kami Day in 2001 and recently published, with four other authors, *The Everyday Writing Center: A Community of Practice*.

Lauren Fitzgerald is Associate Professor of English at Yeshiva University where she is Director of the Yeshiva College Writing Center and previously directed the YC Composition Program. Her work on teaching writing and administering writing programs at religiously affiliated institutions has appeared or is forthcoming in *WPA: Writing Program Administration* (with Elizabeth Vander Lei) and the edited collections *Negotiating Religious Faith in the Composition Classroom* and *Judaic Perspectives in Rhetoric and Composition Studies*.

A former Assistant Director of the Yeshiva College Writing Center and a former WAC Director at Bilkent University in Ankara, Turkey, **T. Kenny Fountain** is finishing up his Ph.D. at the University of Minnesota. Along with plagiarism and academic discourse, his research interests include the rhetoric of medicine, visual rhetoric, and gender/sexuality studies. His work has also appeared in the *Journal of Technical Writing and Communication*.

Bruce Horner is Endowed Chair in Rhetoric and Composition at the University of Louisville, where he teaches courses in composition, composition theory and pedagogy, and literacy studies. His books include *Writing Conventions* (Longman, 2008) and *Representing the "Other": Basic Writers and the Teaching of Basic Writing* (NCTE, 1999), both coauthored with Min-Zhan Lu, and *Terms of Work for Composition: A Materialist Critique* (SUNY, 2000), winner of the W. Ross Winterowd Award for the Most Outstanding Book in Composition Theory.

Rebecca Moore Howard earned her Ph.D. in English at West Virginia University and is now Associate Professor of Writing and Rhetoric at Syracuse University. With Tracy Hamler Carrick, she is coeditor of *Authorship in Composition Studies* (Wadsworth, 2006). Earlier books are *Coming of Age: the Advanced Writing Curriculum* (2000); *Standing in the Shadow of Giants: Plagiarists, Authors, Collaborators* (1999); and *The Bedford Guide to Teaching Writing in the Disciplines* (1995).

Sandra Jamieson is Professor of English and Director of Composition at Drew University. Her publications include *The Bedford Guide to Writing in the Disciplines: An Instructor's Desk Reference* (with Rebecca Moore Howard), and *Coming of Age: The Advanced Writing Curriculum* (with Linda Shamoon, Rebecca Moore Howard, and Bob Schwegler). She has also published articles on the vertical writing curriculum, writing across the curriculum, the role of textbooks in composition, and multicultural education.

Alastair Pennycook is concerned with how we understand language in relation to globalization, colonial history, identity, popular culture, and pedagogy. He has been involved in English language teaching for many years and worked as an English teacher in England, Germany, Japan, China, Canada, and Hong Kong. Publications include *The Cultural Politics of English as an International Language* (Longman, 1994), *English and the Discourses of Colonialism* (Routledge, 1998), *Critical Applied Linguistics: A Critical Introduction* (Lawrence Erlbaum, 2001), and *Global Englishes and Transcultural Flows* (Routledge, 2007). Alastair is Professor of Language in Education at the University of Technology Sydney.

Amy E. Robillard is Assistant Professor of English at Illinois State University, where she teaches courses in both the undergraduate and graduate English Studies programs. Her most recent work has appeared in *College English* and *JAC*.

Celia Thompson, Ph.D., is a lecturer in the School of Languages and Linguistics at the University of Melbourne. Celia studied French, German, and Russian before lecturing in English as a Second Language and Communication. She completed her undergraduate studies in French language and European literature at the University of Warwick in the U.K. She has also studied German in Munich and Bremen and Russian language and culture in St Petersburg. Celia undertook Postgraduate Certificates in Teaching and Counseling and an R.S.A. Diploma in TEFLA before completing her MA studies in Applied

Linguistics at the University of Melbourne, Australia. The title of Celia's PhD thesis is "Plagiarism or Intertextuality? A Study of the Politics of Knowledge, Identity, and Textual Ownership in Undergraduate Writing," which she completed in 2006, under the guidance of Alastair Pennycook at the University of Technology, Sydney. Celia has published in the areas of critical pedagogies, plagiarism, and intertextuality.

Kathleen Blake Yancey is Kellogg W. Hunt Professor of English at Florida State University, where she also directs the graduate program in Rhetoric and Composition Studies. Past President of the Council of Writing Program Administrators and Past Chair of the Conference on College Composition and Communication, she is President of the National Council of Teachers of English. She is the author, editor or coeditor of ten books and more than 60 chapters and refereed articles; her books include *Portfolios in the Writing Classroom* (1992), *Assessing Writing Across the Curriculum* (1997), *Electronic Portfolios* (2001), *Teaching Literature as Reflective Practice* (2004), and *Delivering College Composition* (2006). Her current projects include the monograph based on her CCCC Chair's Address, *Composition in a New Key: A Theory and Practice of Composition in the 21st Century.*